IMAGES
of America

CAPE MAY COUNTY

I0806258

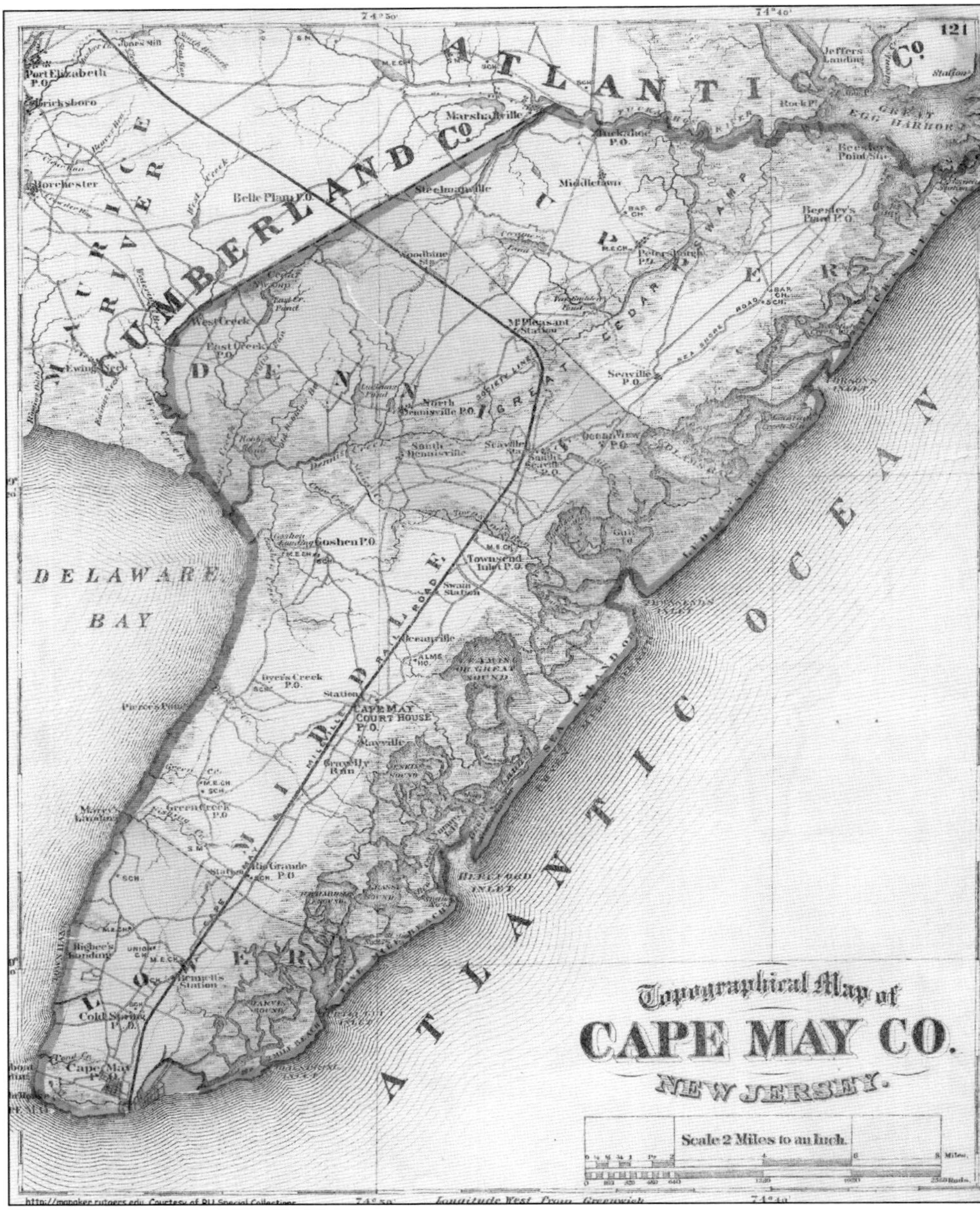

The 1872 Beers *Atlas of Cape May County* shows the county's four townships—Upper, Middle, Dennis, and Lower—in addition to Cape May City at the southern tip. The barrier island resorts had yet to be founded and are identified by their original names of Ludlam's Beach, Seven Mile Beach, and so on. The dark line running through the center represents the Cape May & Millville Railroad line, established in 1863. (Rutgers University Special Collections.)

On the Cover: Sewell's Point, located three miles northeast of Cape May City and seen here in 1902, was named for Civil War veteran and railroad director Gen. William Sewell, who created a recreational site there for vacationers in the 1860s. Tourists arrived by boat or by trolley, and overnight guests stayed in a two-story hotel with broad verandas. Today, the site is part of US Coast Guard Training Center Cape May. (Cape May County Historical and Genealogical Society.)

IMAGES
of America

CAPE MAY COUNTY

Joseph E. Salvatore, MD, and
Joan E. Berkey

ARCADIA
PUBLISHING

Copyright © 2017 by Joseph E. Salvatore, MD, and Joan E. Berkey
ISBN 978-1-4671-2443-0

Published by Arcadia Publishing
Charleston, South Carolina

Printed in the United States of America

Library of Congress Control Number: 2016953984

For all general information, please contact Arcadia Publishing:
Telephone 843-853-2070
Fax 843-853-0044
E-mail sales@arcadiapublishing.com
For customer service and orders:
Toll-Free 1-888-313-2665

Visit us on the Internet at www.arcadiapublishing.com

To the county's 35 founding families—among them, Leaming, Spicer, Hand, Stites, Corson, Cresse, Eldredge, Hughes, Shaw, Gandy, Foster, Ludlam, Townsend, Stillwell, and Whilldin.

Contents

ACKNOWLEDGMENTS

The authors wish to thank the Cape May County Historical and Genealogical Society, the Historical Preservation Society of Upper Township, the Wildwood Historical Society, Avalon History Center, H. Gerald MacDonald, Philippa Campbell, George Brewer, Clay Sutton, Marie Iaconangelo, Chris Brown, Donna Matalucci, and the Stone Harbor Museum. All of these people and organizations contributed knowledge, resources, and support for this book. We also thank our acquisition editor, Henry Clougherty, who expertly guided us through the publishing process. Unless otherwise noted, images in this book appear courtesy of the Naval Air Station Wildwood Aviation Museum (NASW), the Cape May County Historical and Genealogical Society (CMCHGS), H. Gerald MacDonald (HGM), the Library of Congress (LOC), the Wildwood Historical Society (WHS), the Historical Preservation Society of Upper Township (HPSUT), Stone Harbor Museum (SHM), and the Avalon History Center (AHC).

INTRODUCTION

Cape May County, located on a peninsula in southeastern New Jersey, is bordered by the Atlantic Ocean on the east and the Delaware Bay on the west. The county is named for Cornelis Jacobsen Mey (later spelled May), a Dutch captain who sailed around its shores between 1616 and 1624 in search of new trading routes for the Dutch East India Company. Beginning in the 1680s, English-speaking farmers, whalers, and their families permanently settled in the county, migrating from northern New Jersey, Long Island, and New England. Some set up profitable whaling companies, while most raised crops and cattle on large tracts of land they called plantations. Several brought African American slaves with them. For many centuries before their arrival, the area was home to the Lenni Lenape tribe of Native Americans.

In the 1680s, Dr. Daniel Coxe, a London physician who never came to the New World, bought most of the land comprising present-day Cape May County and founded a town called New England Town, in Lower Township along the Delaware Bay. Coxe also established a whale fishery, saltworks, and winery, but all, including the town, never flourished.

Coxe sold his Cape May properties in 1692, the same year the county's boundaries were formally drawn. Modest changes were made along the northern and northwestern boundaries and by 1710, the present-day bounds had been established. In 1723, the county was divided into three precincts, or townships, unimaginatively named Lower, Middle, and Upper for their placement within. These three divisions lasted until 1826, when Dennis Township was created from the lower half of Upper Township. Today, the county has those four townships and sixteen cities or boroughs; the county seat of Cape May Court House was established in 1764.

By 1700, about 350 people lived on the Cape May peninsula, but a devastating plague in 1714 killed more than 40 of them in a four-month period. The first reliable census, taken in 1726, showed 654 residents, the smallest population among the state's nine counties. Religion appears to have played only a small part in attracting new families as no church was formally established on the Jersey Cape in the 17th century. Quakers settled in Upper Township, where they met in houses until building their first meetinghouse in 1727. Baptists settled in the center of the county, near present-day Cape May Court House, completing their first meetinghouse in 1719. That same year, Presbyterians erected their first church, rebuilt in 1828 and known as "Old Brick," in Lower Township.

In 1697, the courts authorized a road from Cape May to Burlington, the provincial capital in Burlington County, but it was not completed until 10 years later. In 1706, most of the north-south road that is present-day US Route 9 was established, running from the Great Egg Harbor Bay south to Cold Spring in Lower Township. With the completion of other roads, the county had a basic overland transportation network within its borders by 1710. Travel by ship, however, was still the most expedient way to reach such cities as Philadelphia, Wilmington, and New York.

One of the county's greatest natural resources was its large stands of oak and cedar trees, which were harvested to make ship masts, barrels, shingles, boards, and other goods. Most of these products were shipped by boat to Philadelphia and other ports along the Eastern Seaboard. So valuable was this trade that most of the county's largest trees were cut down by the mid-1700s. Although whaling never became a dominant industry, it supplemented income from the farming and timber enterprises until the American Revolution.

The only Revolutionary War battle conducted in Cape May County involved two British warships chasing the American brig *Nancy*. Loaded with war supplies for the government in Philadelphia, she took refuge in an inlet near the present-day resort of Wildwood Crest where she was quickly off-loaded before being blown up by the British. British ships patrolling the ocean and the Delaware Bay and River were a constant presence throughout the war, and British soldiers raided several county farmsteads in search of water and food.

Most of Cape May County's historic mainland villages trace their beginnings to the early 1800s. Centered on an industry—like a sawmill, a shipyard, or a landing where goods were imported and exported—these villages were populated primarily by tradesmen like sawyers, boatbuilders, blacksmiths, and lumbermen, as well as shopkeepers, ship captains, and inn or tavern keepers.

Shipbuilding began in the opening decades of the 19th century, flourishing on creeks with easy access to both open water and timber resources. The earliest documented post–Revolutionary War shipyard appears to have been that established by 1812 on the north side of Dennis Creek in Dennis Township. In the 1830s, a second shipyard was built on the south side of the creek. The industry supported villages on both sides of the creek, known today as Dennisville and South Dennis. Other major shipyards were located on Cape Island Creek in Cape May City, on Goshen Creek in Middle Township, on Cedar Swamp Creek near Petersburg in Upper Township, and on the Tuckahoe River in Tuckahoe, also in Upper Township. In all, over 200 ships were built in Cape May County until the industry collapsed in the early 1900s as rail travel revolutionized the transportation of goods.

Despite the railroad's negative impact on the shipbuilding industry toward the end of the 19th century, the introduction of train service in 1863 between Philadelphia and Cape Island, now Cape May City, provided the latter with a much-needed economic boon. By the 1760s, Cape Island's sandy beaches and salt air had become a popular place where "a number resort for Health, and bathing in the Water." Thus began the oldest seaside resort in the country. Before 1863, travelers had three ways to get there: overland by private carriage, a two-day stage ride from Camden, or passage on a boat from Philadelphia that took most of the day. With the new rail line, tourists took a ferry from Philadelphia to Camden, boarded a train there, and arrived in Cape Island several hours later. By the time Cape Island incorporated as Cape May City in 1869, the resort had more than 22 hotels and was booming despite competition from nearby Atlantic City, which was founded in 1854.

The railroad also benefited the rest of the county. Mainland communities in Woodbine, South Seaville, and Rio Grande sprang up at newly established station stops, bringing more newcomers into the county between 1865 and 1870 than during any previous decade. Farmers, clammers, and oystermen now had a faster way to get their products to broader markets. New industries of glassmaking, fertilizer production, and sugarcane processing were also introduced, some more successful than others.

Establishment of rail service also fostered—directly and indirectly—the founding of other seaside resorts on the county's barrier islands. These resorts included Ocean City on Peck's Beach, Strathmere and Sea Isle City on Ludlam's Beach, Avalon and Stone Harbor on Seven Mile Beach, and the Wildwoods on Five Mile Beach and Two Mile Beach. Prior to development in the late 1800s, these largely uninhabited beaches were used to forage livestock and, since 1848, were home to several lifesaving stations built to aid ships that wrecked along the Atlantic coastline.

Ocean City was founded in 1879 as a planned religious resort with restrictions against travel and ocean bathing on Sunday, immorality, and liquor. In 1882, Charles K. Landis established the resort of Sea Isle City just south of Ocean City, which he envisioned as a "sanitary and art city by the sea" with canals, Italian-style piazzas, and fountains. The "Wildwoods," a term that collectively refers to North Wildwood (originally Anglesea), Wildwood (originally Holly Beach), and Wildwood Crest, were adjoining seaside resorts founded in the 1870s and 1880s and also served by trains. Avalon and Stone Harbor, located on Seven Mile Beach, were the last to be developed in the late 1880s, supported by railroad spurs bringing not only tourists but also building materials needed for the inns and summer cottages in which they stayed. In 1894, a second railroad line servicing the county established new stops in Dennisville and South Dennis. Between Cape May Court House and Cape May City, their tracks ran parallel to each other, which often led to races between competing trains to see which one could get to Cape May first.

Although not on a barrier island, Sea Grove (now Cape May Point) was founded in 1875 by the Presbyterians as a religious summer community. Located at the southwestern tip of the Cape May peninsula, the resort banned liquor and amusements, while attracting such notables as Philadelphia department store owner John Wanamaker, US senator William Sewell, and Pres. Benjamin Harrison.

In Cape May City, a devastating fire in the heart of town in 1878 led to a rebuilding of hotels and cottages boasting broad porches and eaves lavished with gingerbread trim. Today, most of Cape May City is a National Historic Landmark in recognition of its well-preserved collection of these Victorian-era buildings.

As the county entered the 20th century, the era of prosperity that preceded it began to fail. Several real estate development schemes on both the mainland and the barrier islands failed, and shortages of coal, railroad cars, and building materials during World War I brought further delays. But after the war, construction began anew, bringing a new wave of shore-bound visitors eager to build their own summer cottages near the ocean.

With the same impact as the arrival of train service six decades earlier, automobiles had a profound effect on the county's economy and landscape in the early 20th century. Henry Ford, Louis Chevrolet, and others raced their machines along the Cape May beach as overflow crowds watched this exciting new form of entertainment. Tourists who now arrived by car instead of train needed paved roads on which to travel and a place to park at their destinations. Seaside resorts began touting paved streets in their advertisements, while builders offered one-car detached garages as part of their construction packages. Major roadways and bridges were improved, and the Benjamin Franklin Bridge, which connects Philadelphia with Camden, opened in 1926, accelerating the influx of visitors to Cape May County.

With less passenger traffic, however, the two rail lines merged during the Great Depression in 1933. Cape May City entered a slow decline as visitors found the roads leading to it inadequate and the city's carriage-friendly streets too narrow for car travel. Several of the larger hotels were torn down and replaced with smaller ones offering parking lots. Road improvements on the mainland brought new amenities, like gas stations and diners, which catered to the car-driving public.

During World War II, U-boats patrolled dangerously close to the Cape May County coastline, attracted by the large shipments of war goods traveling the Delaware River. A lookout tower that was part of a harbor defense system was built in 1942 on Sunset Boulevard. Today, it is operated as a museum, offering those guests willing to climb its six floors a breathtaking view of the Delaware Bay. In 1943, construction began on US Naval Air Station Wildwood, located at what is today the Cape May County Airport in Lower Township. The air station trained thousands of US Navy airmen who flew some of the war's most lethal bombers; only a handful of the station's original buildings remain. Located a few miles to the southeast was US Naval Air Station Cape May, now home to the US Coast Guard Training Center; during World War II, it hosted a US Navy experimental flight squadron and housed two dirigibles.

After the war, construction in 1954 of the four-lane Garden State Parkway, which originates in northern New Jersey, accelerated both seasonal travel and the growth of the county's permanent population. Recognizing the need to counter increased development with measures to protect the county's fragile natural environment, open-space programs were instituted that protected the Jersey Cape's dwindling farmlands, established bird sanctuaries, and created wildlife preserves and refuges. The area has since become a world-class destination for birders, fishermen, and naturalists.

Toward the end of the 20th century, the concept of using the county's rich history as another way to attract tourists blossomed. The Mid-Atlantic Center for the Arts and Humanities (MAC) in Cape May City was founded in 1970 to promote preservation of the city's rich collection of Victorian-era buildings. MAC restored the 1879 Emlen Physick Estate, the 1859 Cape May Lighthouse, and the 1942 World War II Lookout Tower and now has a year-round calendar of tours and special events geared toward cultural and heritage tourism.

Historic Cold Spring Village, an open-air living history museum in Lower Township, was founded in 1973. Composed of 29 historic buildings moved from other parts of the county to save them, the village portrays Early American life in Cape May County. Naval Air Station Wildwood Aviation Museum began in 1995 and is housed in a former World War II hangar that serves as the backdrop for various military history exhibits. Other historic sites were restored and opened to the public, including the Cape May County Historical and Genealogical Society's c. 1704 Cresse-Holmes House, the c. 1815 Gandy Farmstead and the c. 1830 Friendship School managed by the Historical Preservation Society of Upper Township, the Hereford Inlet Lighthouse, and many others.

Today, tourism is the county's largest industry, attracting more than 12.5 million visitors a year.

One

Early Years

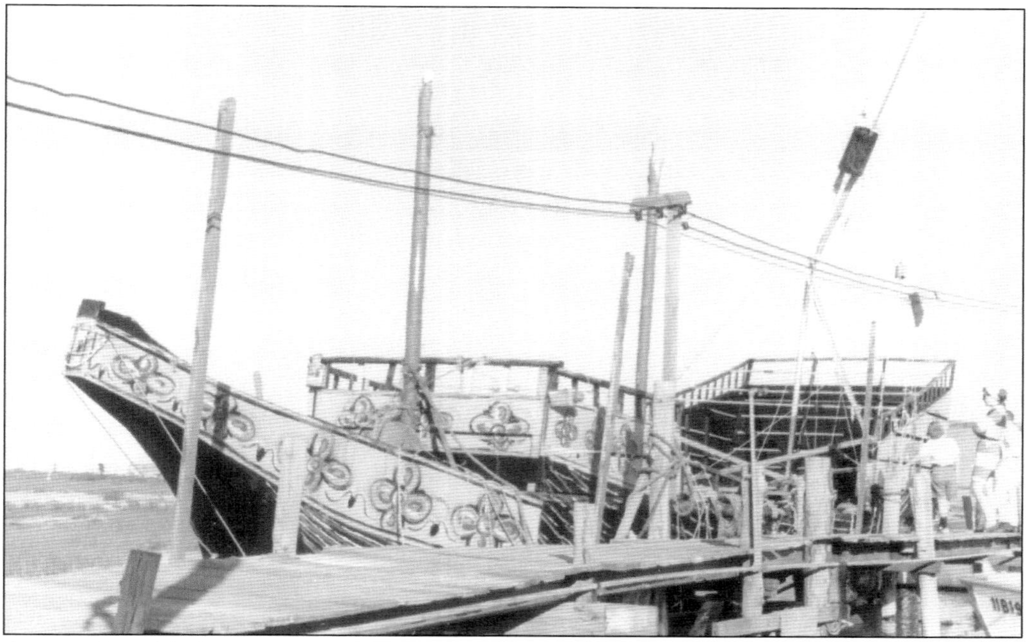

As part of the 350th anniversary celebration of Henry Hudson's voyage from Amsterdam to North America in 1609, a replica of his 63-foot-long Dutch ship *Half Moon* was anchored off of Cape May for the summer of 1959. Hudson's explorations took him along the coast of New Jersey, where one of his officers noted their discovery of a "great bay and rivers." (CMCHGS.)

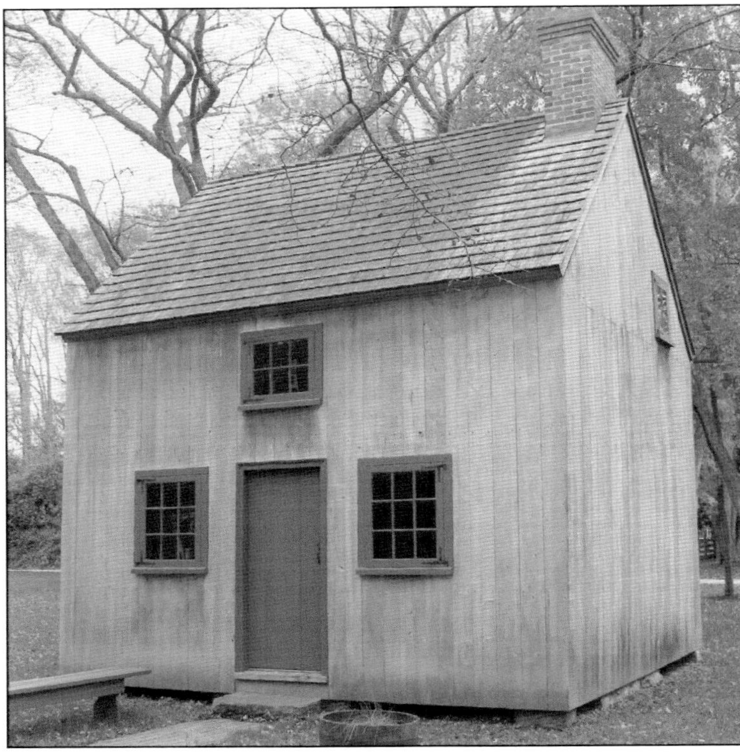

Moved to Historic Cold Spring Village and restored in 2006, this small cottage is thought to be part of Coxe Hall, a manor house built in 1691 by Col. Daniel Coxe, a London physician. Coxe never came to the New World, but he established a town in Cape May County and sold farmsteads to English-speaking settlers. Coxe Hall was the site of religious services, court sessions, and town meetings. (Joan Berkey.)

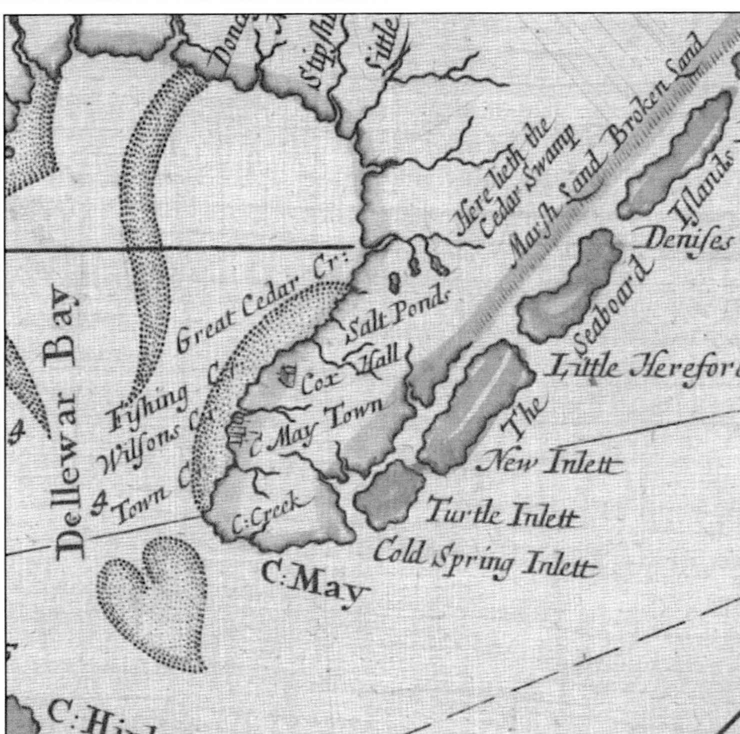

This is a detail from a larger map of New Jersey drawn in 1706 by Londoner John Thornton. This section shows the Cape May peninsula, its barrier islands, major creeks, and significant physical landmarks such as the cedar swamp, marshland, and salt ponds. The buildings in "C[ape] May Town" were overrun by the waters of the Delaware Bay by the mid-1700s. (LOC.)

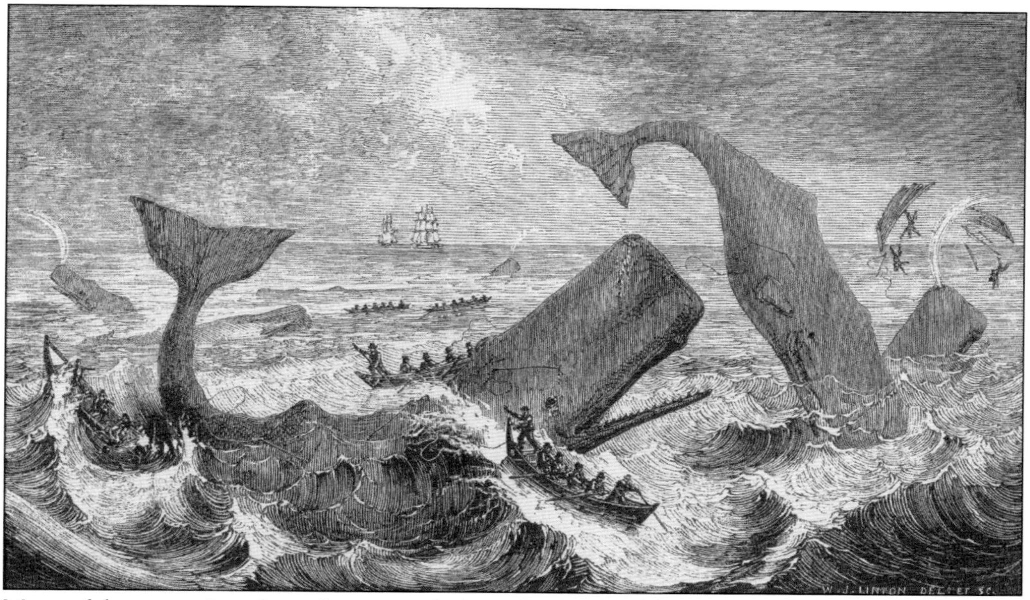

Many of the county's early settlers were whalers who migrated from Long Island and New England in the late 1600s and early 1700s. Whales were plentiful in the Atlantic Ocean and Delaware Bay and sought for their blubber and spermaceti, which were processed to create whale oil. Cape May farmers went "a-whaling" in the winter months. This 1839 etching depicts the often-dangerous nature of the hunt. (New York Public Library.)

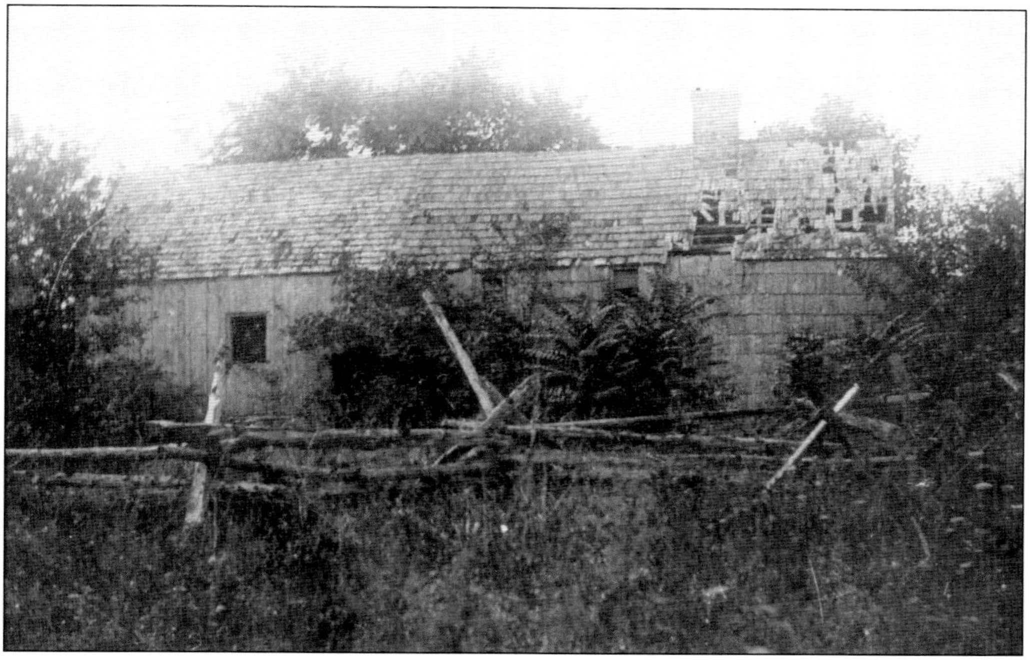

In near ruins when photographed about 1900, the Goldin House in Beesley's Point was probably built in the late 1600s by William Goldin, an Irishman who immigrated around 1691. The house shows many characteristics of early construction, including a large brick chimney and walls covered with both wood shingles and vertical planks. It no longer stands. (CMCHGS.)

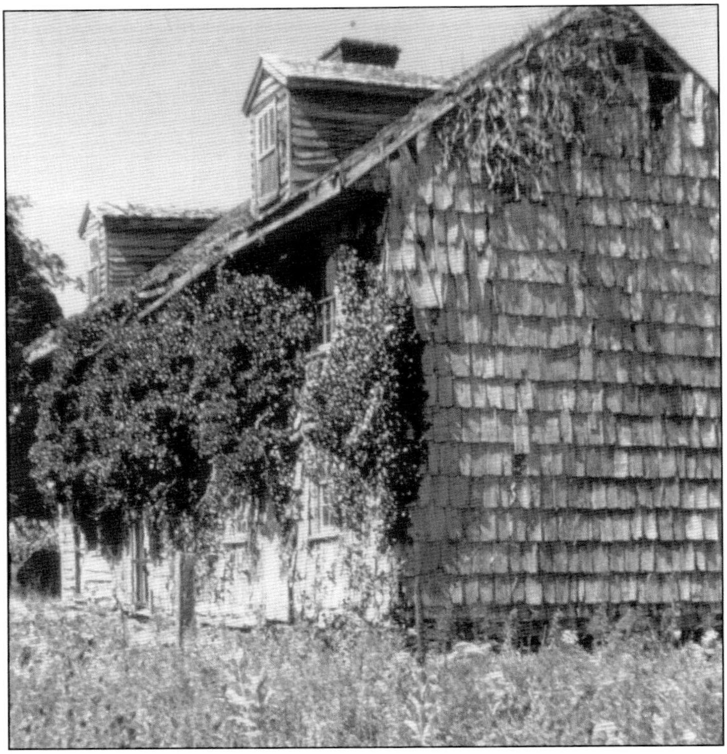

The Reeves-Iszard-Godfrey House, built before 1700, was moved across a frozen cornfield and up the Garden State Parkway to save it from demolition in the 1960s. It was lovingly restored and is the county's best preserved example of New England–influenced, post-medieval heavy timber frame construction. Its interior features a summer beam, board walls, and carved post heads, all characteristics of 17th-century Massachusetts houses. (CMCHGS.)

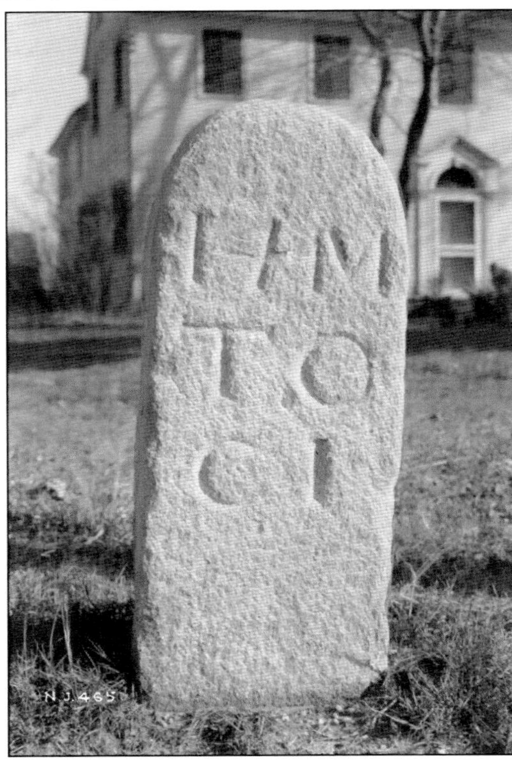

The road from northern Cape May County south to Cape Island, as the city of Cape May was known until 1869, was laid out in 1706. At various times, it was called the Queen's Road, the King's Road, or Old Cape Road. Stone markers like this one were placed every mile along the path, announcing how far the traveler had yet to go before reaching "CI," or Cape Island. (LOC.)

Two

Shipbuilding and Other Industries

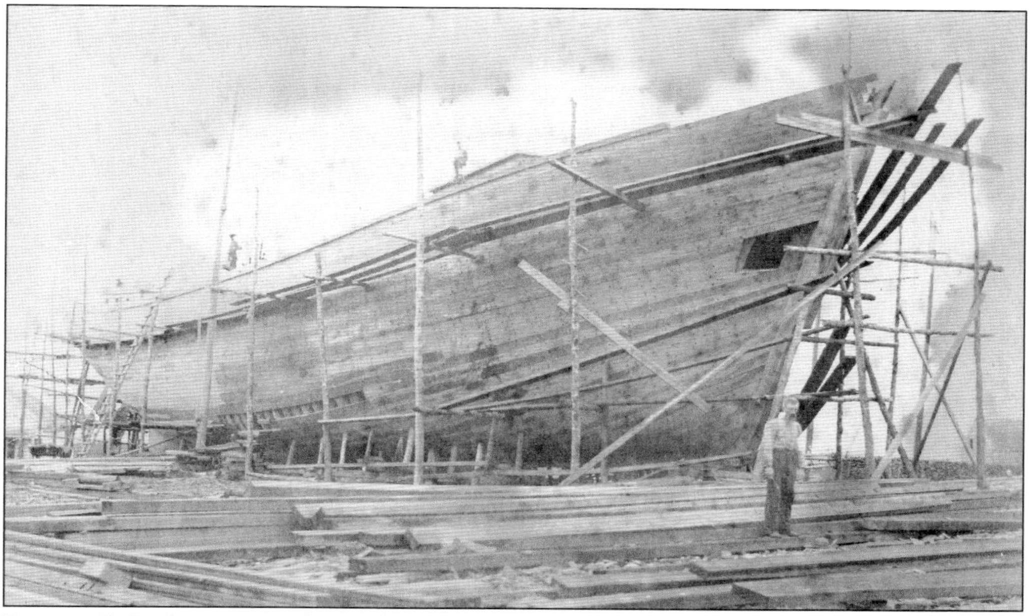

Dennisville had two active shipyards in the 1800s, one on each side of Dennis Creek. Seen here is the *Gertrude Abbott*, a three-masted schooner built there in 1882. In November 1888, laden with 823 tons of coal, she ran aground in Boston Harbor during a gale. Her eight-man crew was saved by the heroic efforts of local lifesavers, and the schooner was remarkably only modestly damaged. (CMCHGS.)

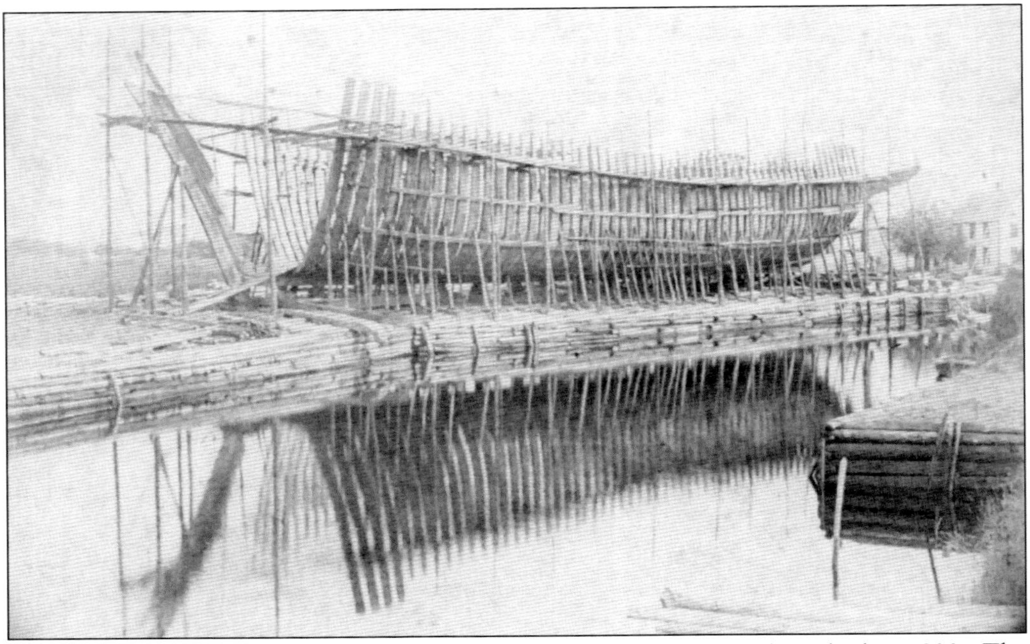

This unidentified schooner was built on the north side of Dennis Creek in the late 1800s. The first step was to steam white oak ribs and then bend them to create the ship's hull. Scaffolding and braces held the frame in position, allowing workers to complete the construction. This view shows how narrow the creek was and explains why the ships were launched sideways. (CMCHGS.)

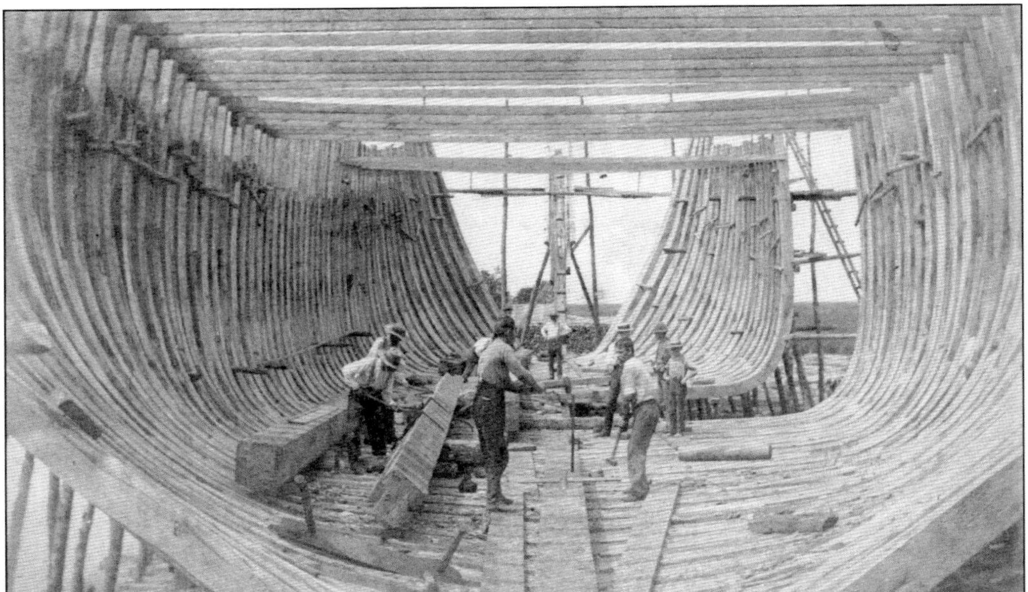

The interior spaces of each ship required as much attention to detail as the exterior. Seen here in the Goshen boatyard, workers using a variety of hand tools lay planks on the lowermost deck of this unidentified vessel. Most of these schooners were built for the coastal trade, carrying coal, ready-made goods, or wood products along the Eastern Seaboard. (CMCHGS.)

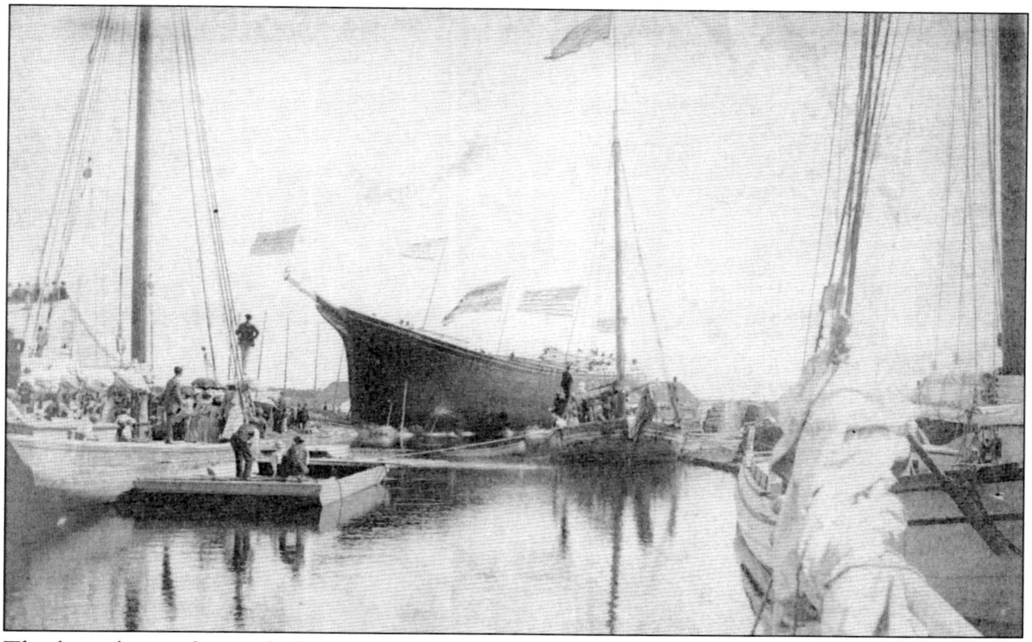

The launching of a newly built schooner was always a cause for celebration. Seen here about 1890, men, women, and children watch from rooftops, the shoreline, and other boats as this unidentified vessel slides sideways into Dennis Creek. From 1812 through 1891, approximately 69 vessels were built here. The earliest was the *Hannah and Amelia*, a 104-ton schooner used to ship goods between New York and Charleston. (CMCHGS.)

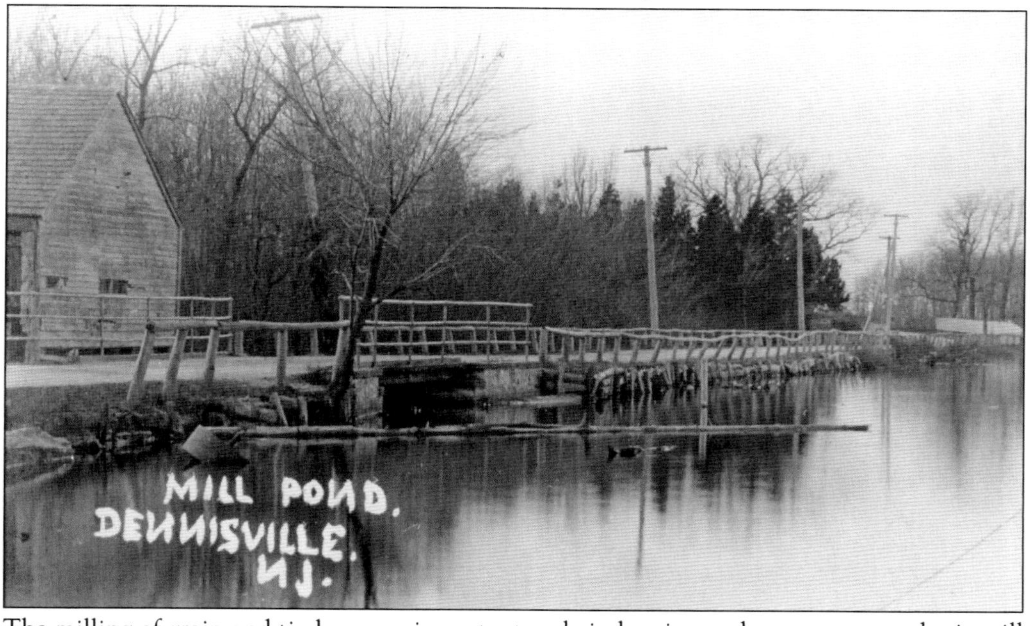

The milling of grain and timber were important early industries, and a water-powered gristmill was operating as early as 1694 in Lower Township. This c. 1900 photograph shows Johnson's sawmill in Dennisville. A tide mill, it was established in 1749 and operated until about 1905. It was destroyed by a storm several years later. (CMCHGS.)

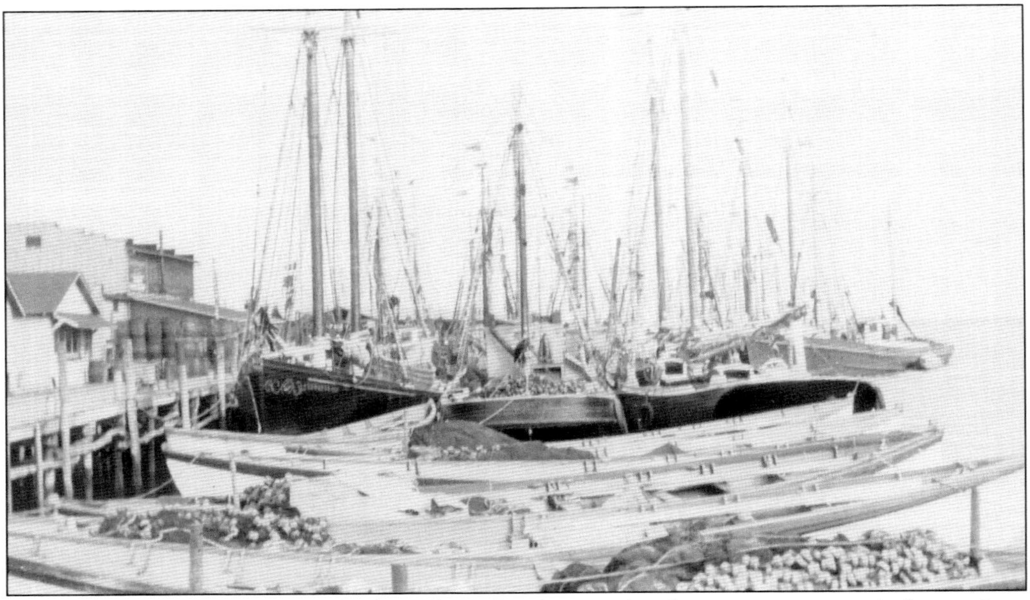

The harvesting and sale of seafood caught in local waters has been an important industry since the county was founded in the late 1600s. This photograph, taken in March 1932, shows a fleet of mackerel boats tied to the dock in Cold Spring Inlet, now part of the Cape May Canal. Today, the port of Cape May is the second largest fishing port on the East Coast. (CMCHGS.)

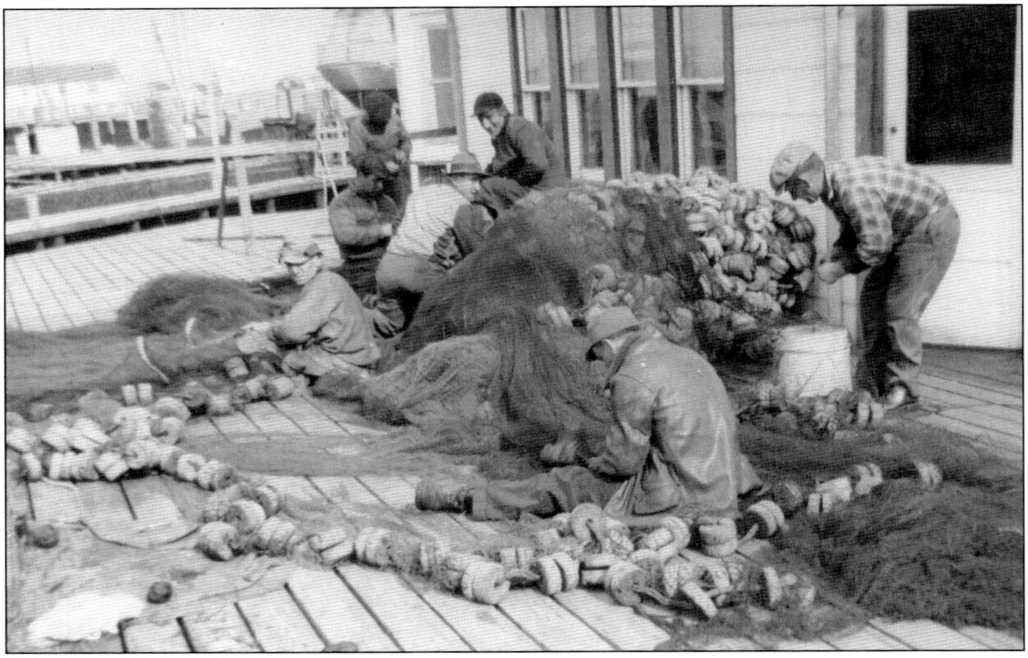

Seen here on the docks of Wildwood in the mid-20th century, local fishermen mend the gill nets used to commercially harvest a large variety of fish off the Cape May coast. Typical catches included scallops, mackerel, clams, bunker, and black sea bass. Ports in Cape May and Wildwood continue to serve commercial fishing, deemed the most hazardous occupation in the United States. (CMCHGS.)

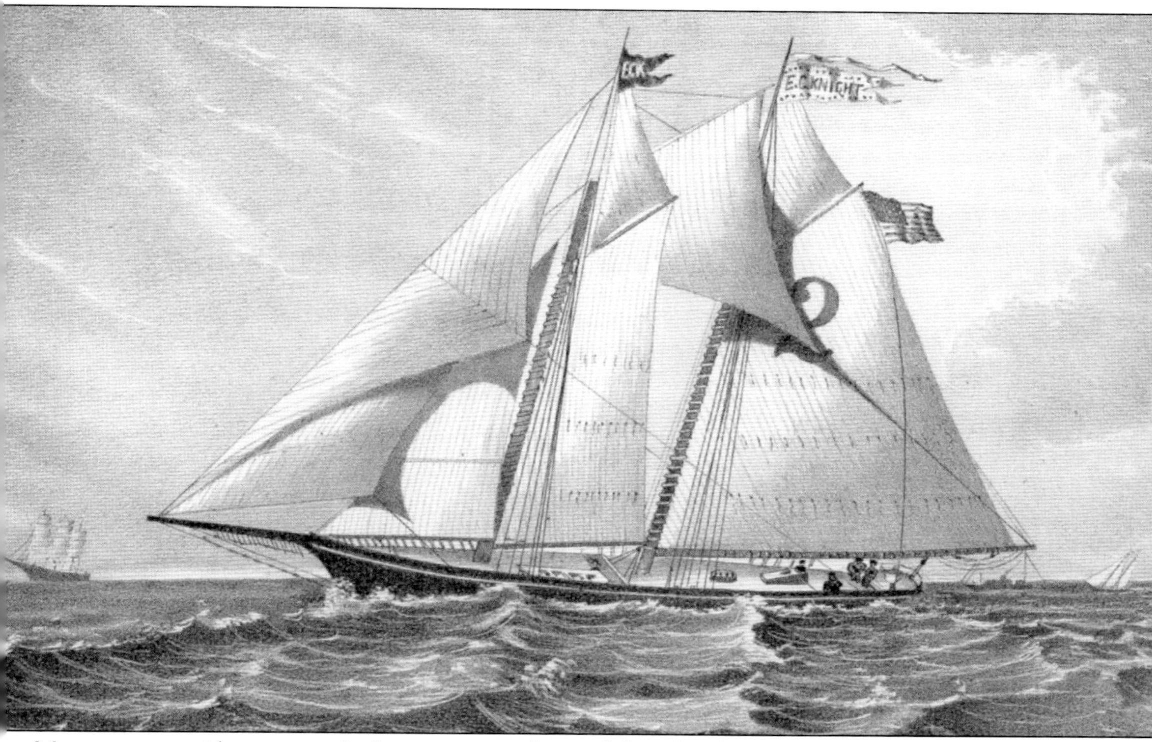

Many county residents were pilot boat captains who used their detailed knowledge of local waterways to help cargo-laden ships navigate past the dangerous sandbars and shoals in the Delaware Bay and River. Pilot boat captains, sailing on a sleek boat like the *E.C. Knight*, seen here about 1878, met ships at the mouth of the Delaware River, boarded them using a ladder hung overboard, then safely guided them to such upriver ports as Philadelphia, New Castle, Camden, and Wilmington for a fee. The process was repeated coming back down the river. Typically, the first pilot to reach the incoming or outgoing ship was hired for the job, leading to intense competition. The 94-foot-long *E.C. Knight* was reputedly the fastest, capable of beating other competing pilot boats in the race to greet cargo ships. She is named after the Philadelphia sugar refiner who financed its construction. Thirty-six pilots worked on her at various times, including eight Eldredges, seven Hugheses, and five Bennetts, all from Cape May County. (NASW.)

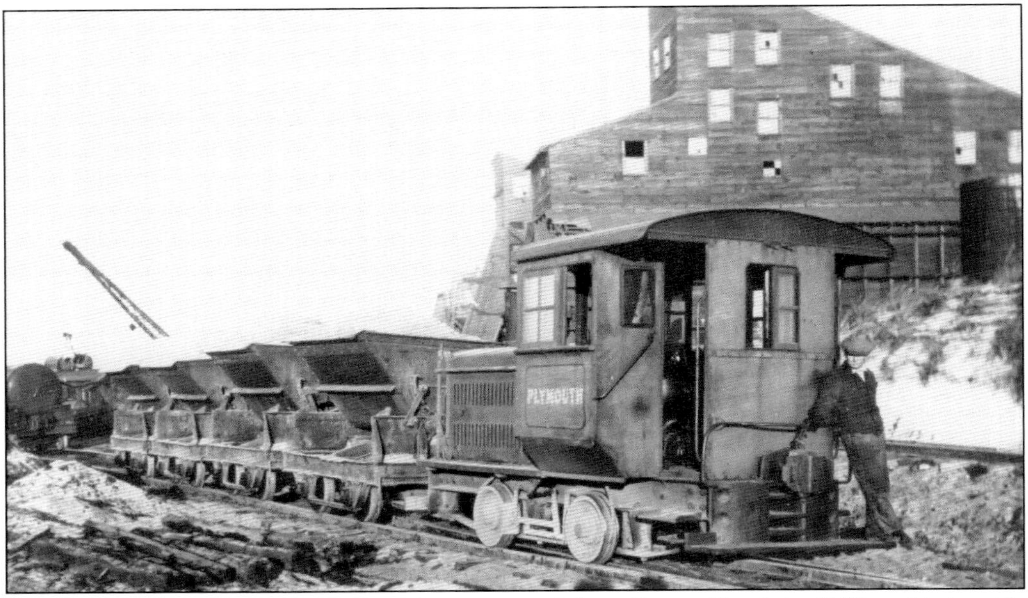

The Cape May Sand Company started mining sand from Sunset Beach in 1905 at this bayside facility located north of Cape May Point. Because of the sand's high quartz composition, much was transported by rail to several glass factories in Millville, about 30 miles to the north. Some was also reportedly shipped to construct the Panama Canal. The plant ceased operation in the 1920s or 1930s. (CMCHGS.)

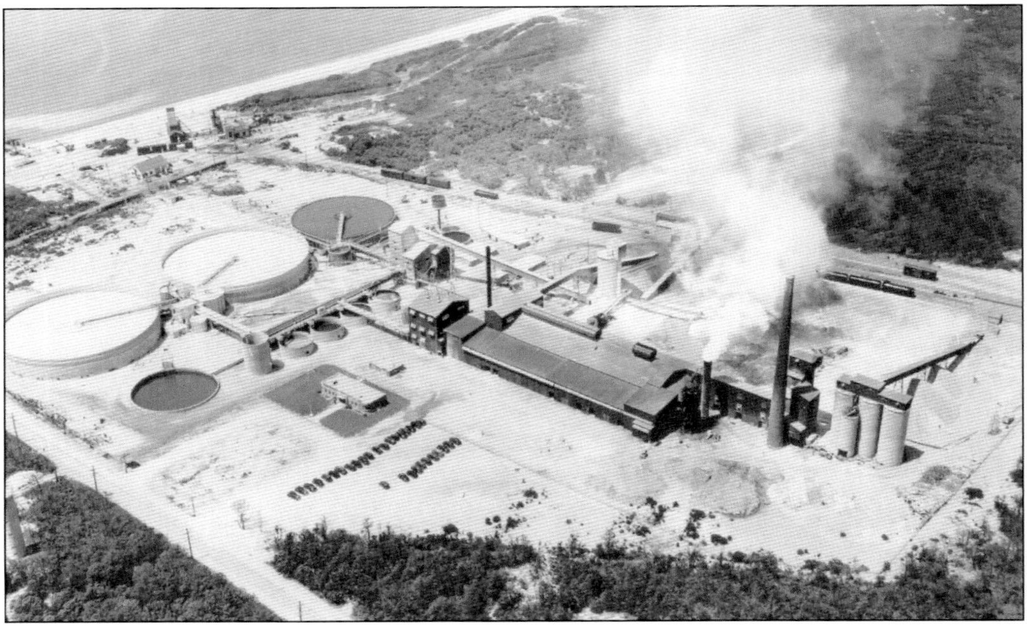

The Harbison-Walker Magnesite Plant, seen here about 1943, opened in 1942 adjacent to the sand plant, utilizing the same railroad branch. It processed clarified seawater from the Delaware Bay with limestone to create magnesite. The compound was then refined to produce refractory bricks, which were used to line steel factory furnaces producing goods for the US steel industry. The plant closed in 1983 and was demolished. (HGM.)

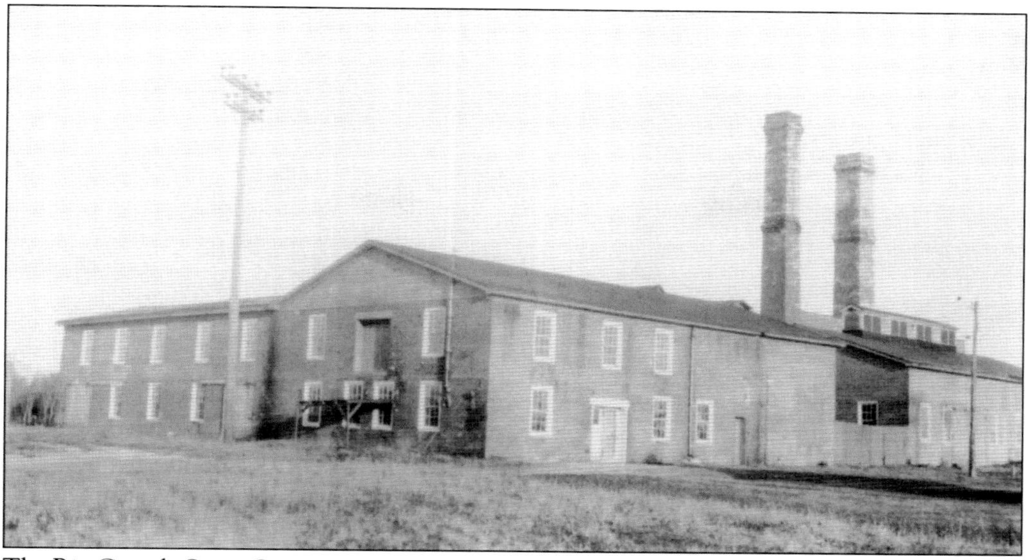

The Rio Grande Sugar Company was incorporated in 1881 for the manufacture and sale of sugar made from locally grown beets, sorghum, and other sources. A state subsidy on sugar made the venture profitable for a few years, but ultimately cost outweighed profit and the venture closed. The building, which no longer stands, became a cannery in 1889 and later a slaughterhouse. (CMCHGS.)

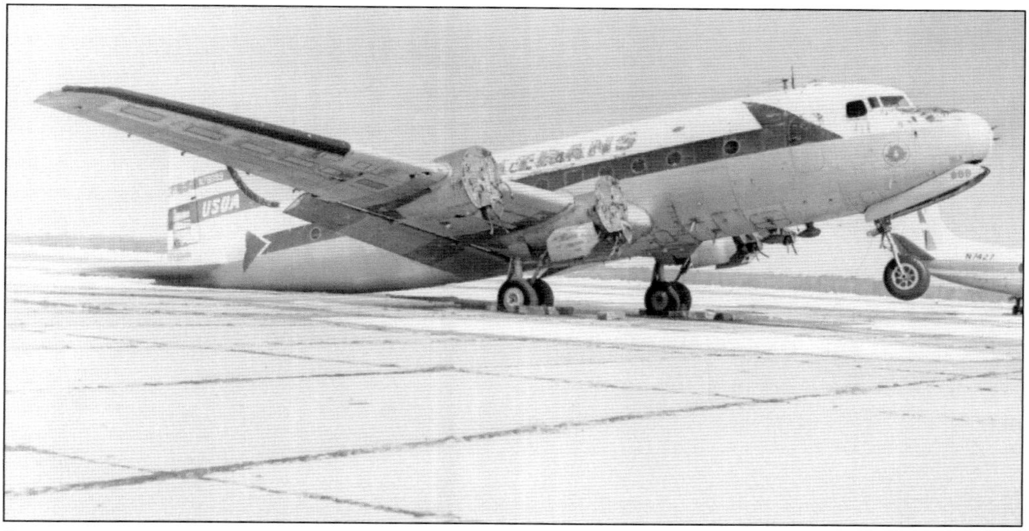

From 1949 to 1964, Dr. Ralph Cox operated US Overseas Airlines from Hangar No. 1 at the former US Naval Air Station Wildwood, now Cape May Airport outside of Rio Grande. At one time, the airline was the largest employer in the county. Cox bought surplus airplanes from other airlines, refurbished them, and put them back into service. His planes flew cargo and passengers on various routes around the world. (CMCHGS.)

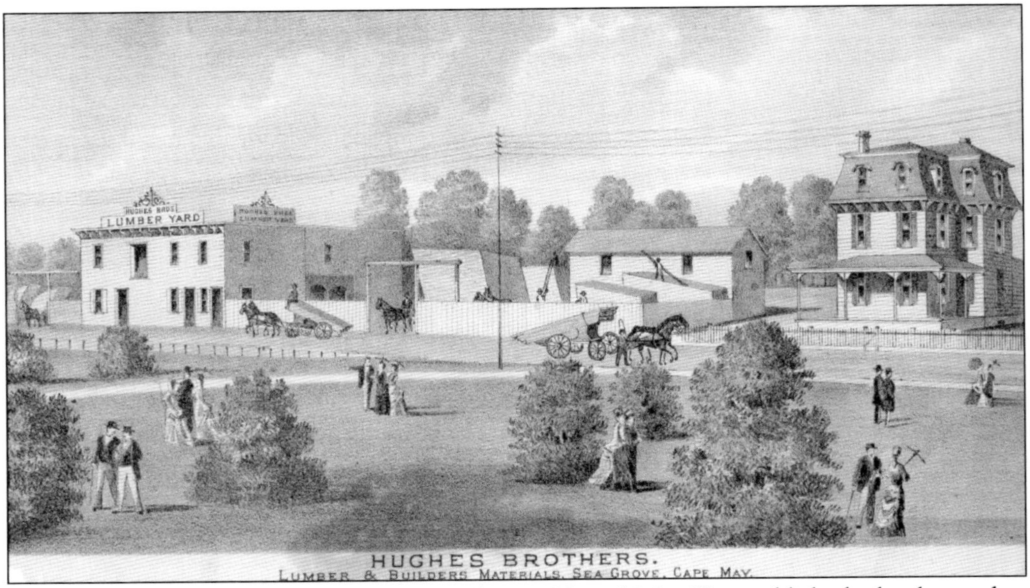

The Hughes brothers, possibly carpenters Thomas H. and John H., established a lumberyard to serve the construction industry in the newly established resort of Sea Grove, now Cape May Point. The community was founded as a religious retreat in 1875 at the southern tip of the county overlooking the Delaware Bay. The lumberyard was located on the north side of present-day Sunset Boulevard; it no longer stands. (CMCHGS.)

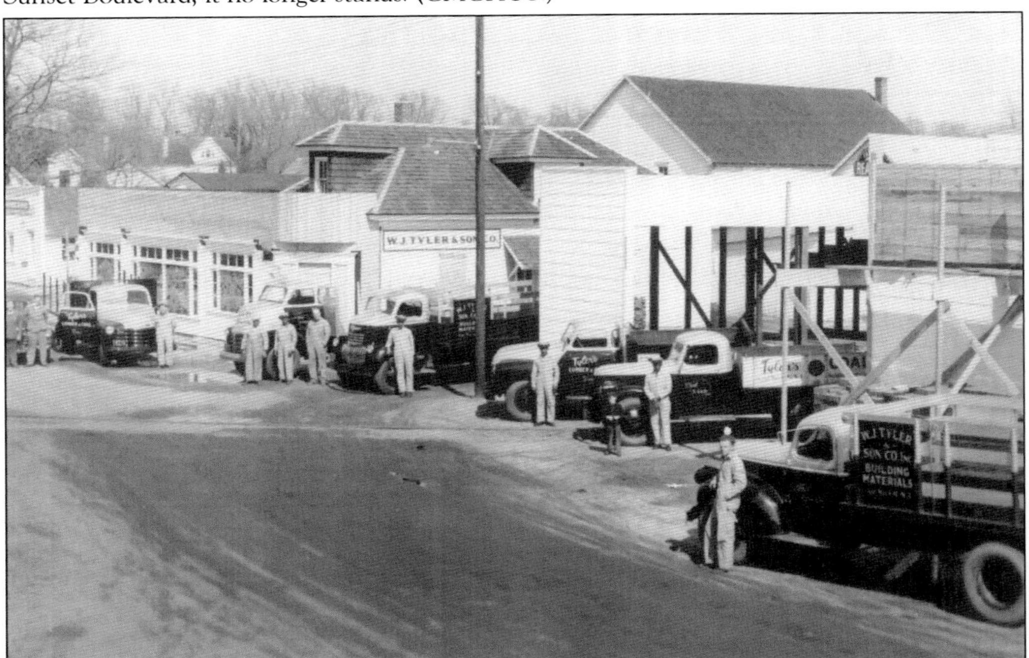

William J. Tyler established a lumber and coal yard in Cape May Court House in the early 1900s; his son, Boyd, later joined him. The business, seen here about 1940, was located on the east side of the railroad tracks, north of Mechanic Street. The site is still used for building supplies, but most of the original buildings have been demolished. (CMCHGS.)

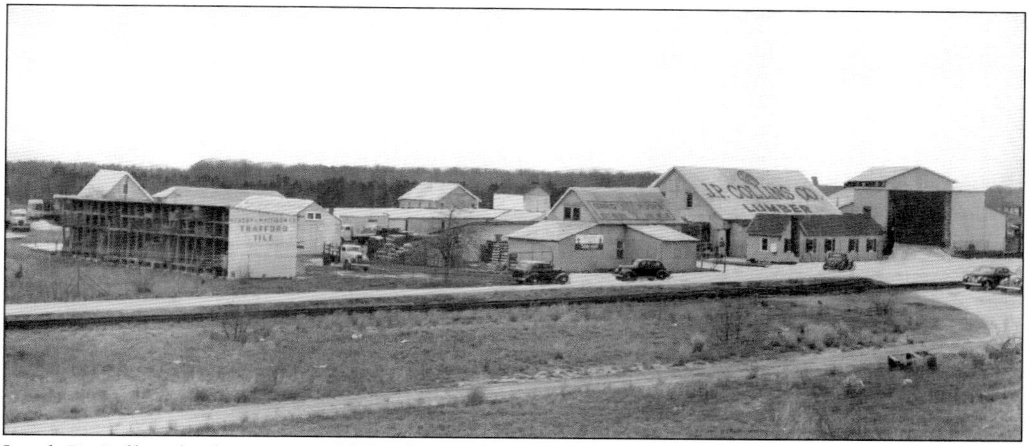

Jacob P. Collins built a successful lumberyard in South Seaville along the west side of the West Jersey & Seashore Railroad tracks in the late 1800s. Seen here about 1930, the yard featured about a dozen structures, most of which still stand, used to store a variety of building materials that were brought in by rail. The business closed in the early 21st century. (CMCHGS.)

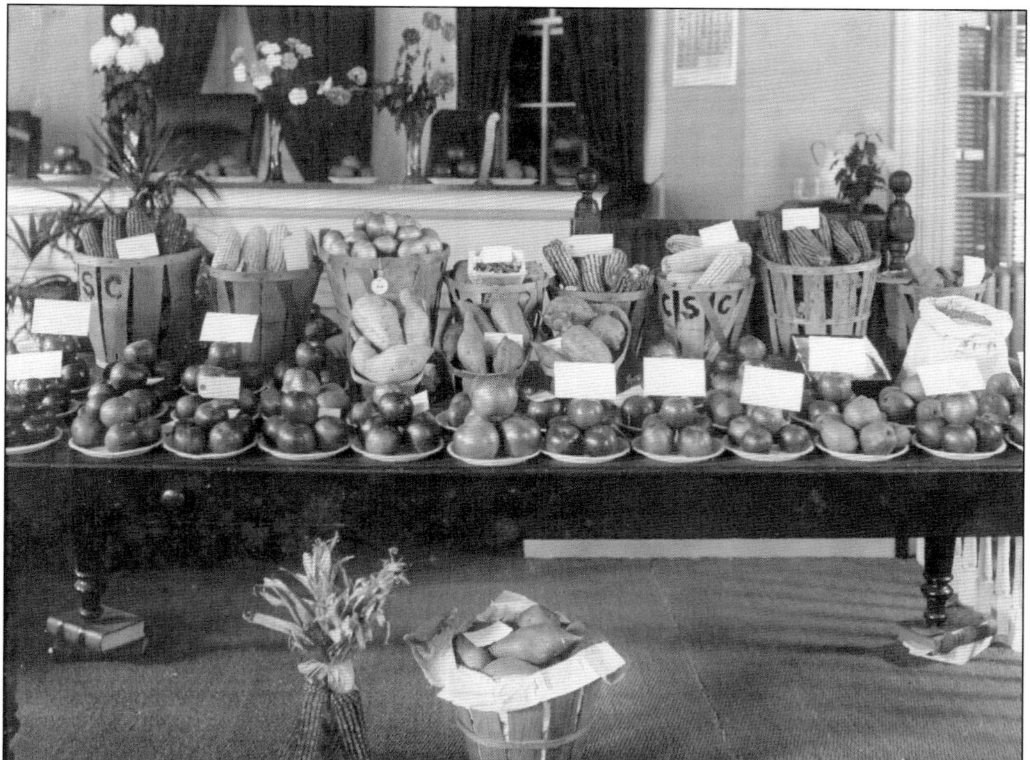

The Cape May County Agricultural Society, founded in 1847, sponsored public school agricultural contests in the early 1900s. In the fall of 1915, students displayed their best apples, sweet potatoes, and dried corn in the county courthouse courtroom. Since the late 1600s, the raising of crops (like corn and wheat) and livestock played an important part in the county's economy. (CMCHGS.)

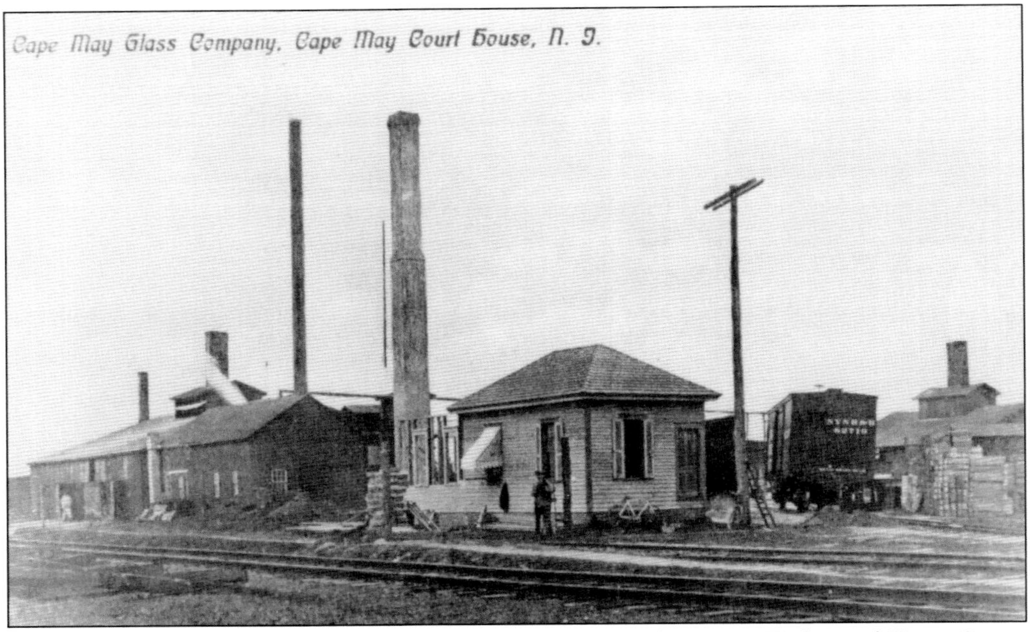

First called the Taylor and Stites Company for its two founders, L.G. Taylor and Harry Stites, the Cape May Glass Company began operation in November 1901. Located on the west side of the railroad tracks at the southern edge of Cape May Court House, the company manufactured bottles used for medicine, cologne, foods, soda, liquor, and beer. Apprentices, some as young as eight, worked a minimum of five years before becoming glassblowers. Glassblowing required great lung power, skill, and physical stamina. The ovens ran 24 hours a day maintaining temperatures between 2.400 and 2.700 degrees, and employees worked in shifts day and night. Due to the heat, the factory was closed in July and August. Sometime between 1930 and 1950, the factory burned to the ground and was never rebuilt. (Above, CMCHGS; below, LOC.)

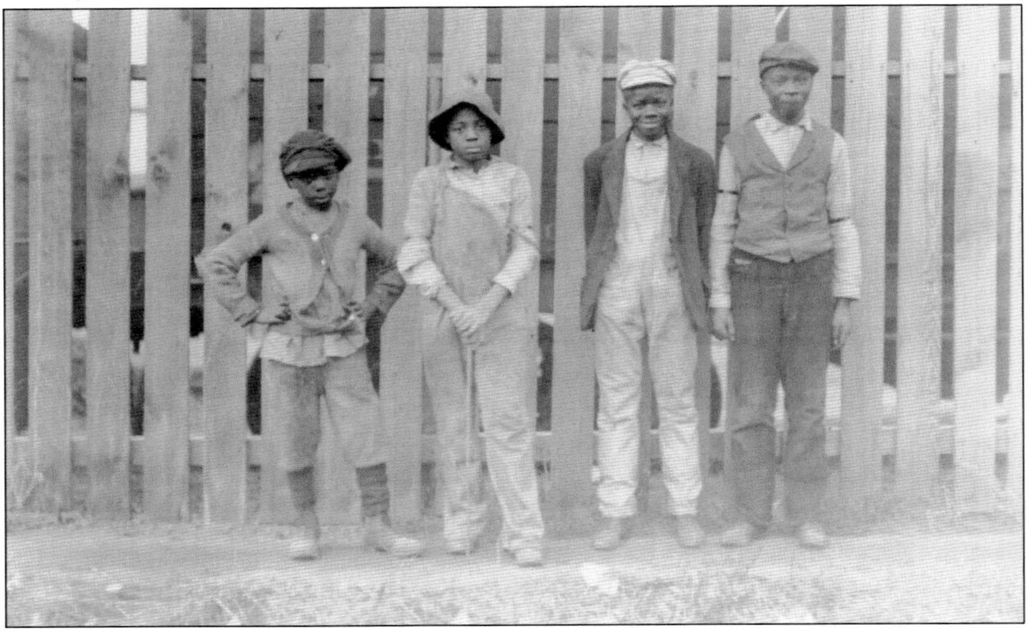

Three

MAINLAND VILLAGES AND COMMUNITIES

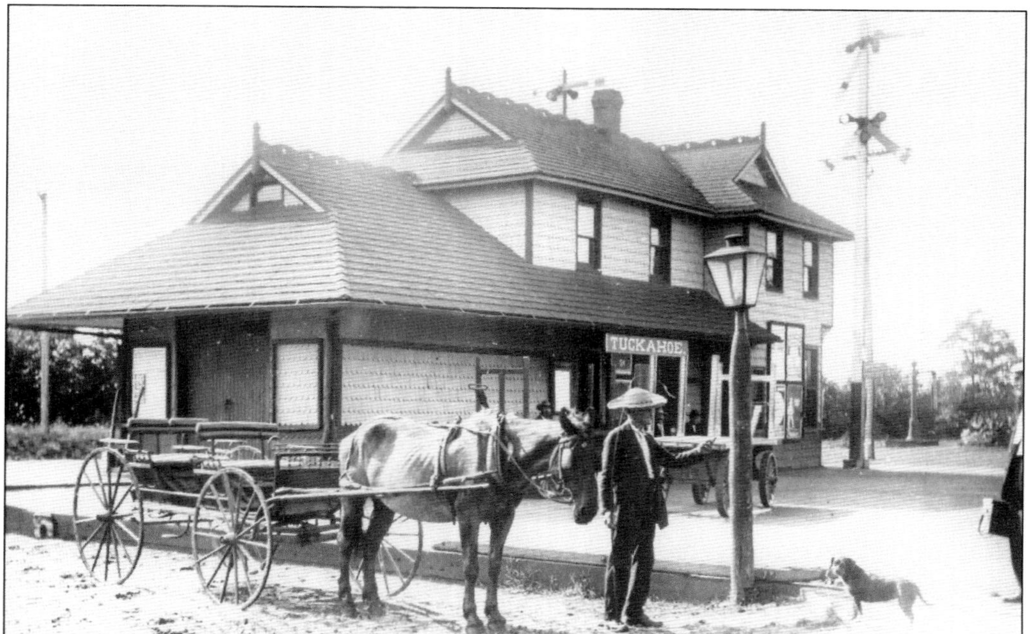

Tuckahoe, located in the northwest corner of Upper Township, received train service in 1893 when the Atlantic City Railroad, a subsidiary of the Reading Railroad, extended a line on its Camden to Atlantic City route. As the main junction from which trains from Philadelphia fanned out to Cape May's seashore communities, the village became an important railroad hub. The station, seen here about 1900, still stands. (HGM.)

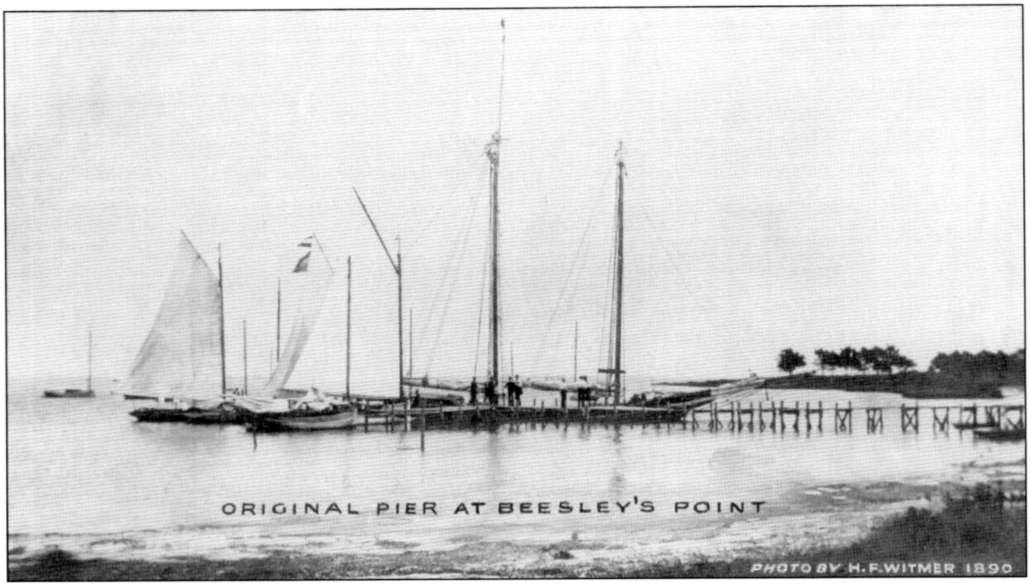

Beesley's Point, named for a Thomas Beesley who lived here in the early 1800s, is located on the south shore of the Great Egg Harbor Bay in Upper Township. This 1890 photograph shows the original pier, which was probably located not far from the Garden State Parkway Bridge. Yacht races, regattas, and sailing matches were held here in the summer, and boats could be hired for fishing, sailing, and swimming excursions. (CMCHGS.)

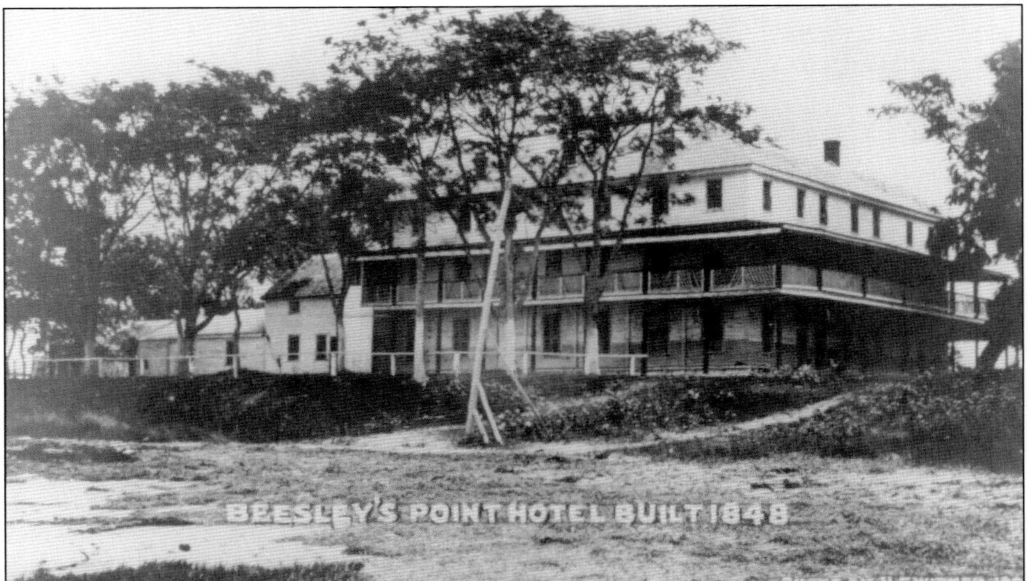

The Beesley's Point Hotel, seen here in 1890, was built in 1848 by Richard Stites on the east side of present-day US Route 9. It was in continuous operation until the 1930s. During World War I, it was a local Red Cross headquarters. The building was partially destroyed by fire in 1960 and was rebuilt, now serving as the Tuckahoe Inn. (CMCHGS.)

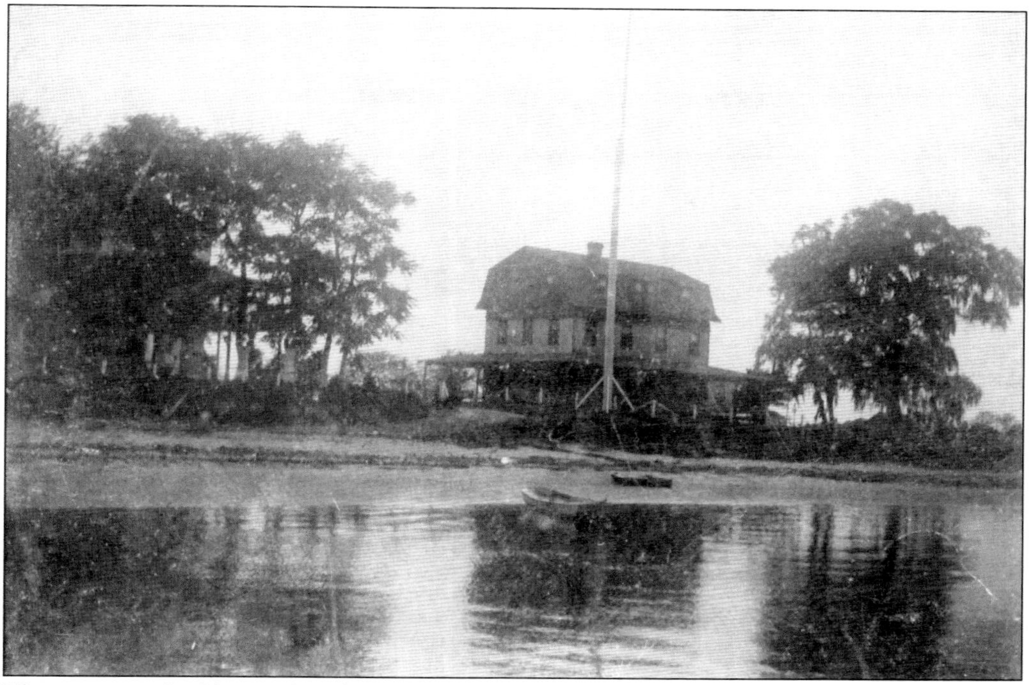

This two-story building in Beesley's Point overlooks the Great Egg Harbor Bay. The oldest part served as an inn in the mid-1700s when owned by Nicholas Stillwell. His wife, Rebecca, is locally famous for thwarting an attempted landing by British soldiers here in 1777. Highly altered over the years, the building housed travelers until after the Civil War; it later served as a fishing club and a training school. (HPSUT.)

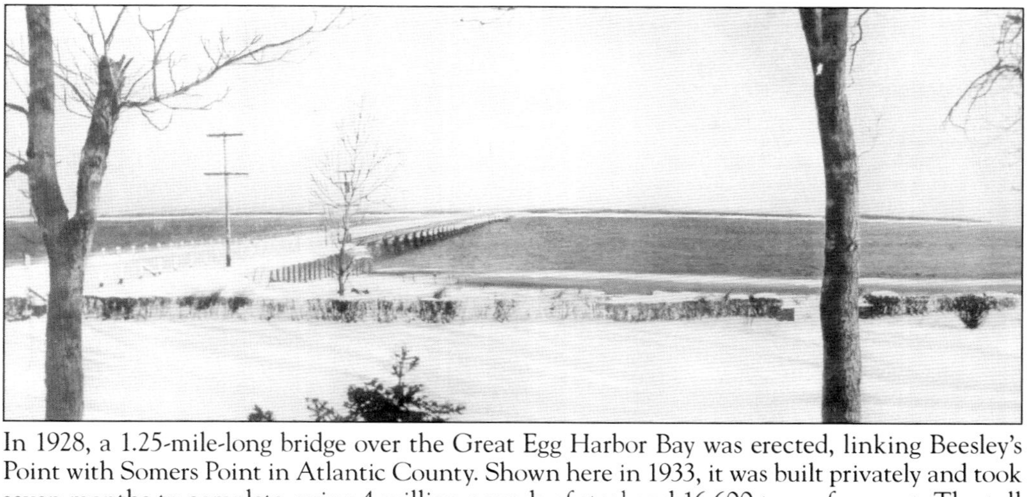

In 1928, a 1.25-mile-long bridge over the Great Egg Harbor Bay was erected, linking Beesley's Point with Somers Point in Atlantic County. Shown here in 1933, it was built privately and took seven months to complete, using 4 million pounds of steel and 16,600 tons of cement. The toll to cross was 25¢. (HPSUT.)

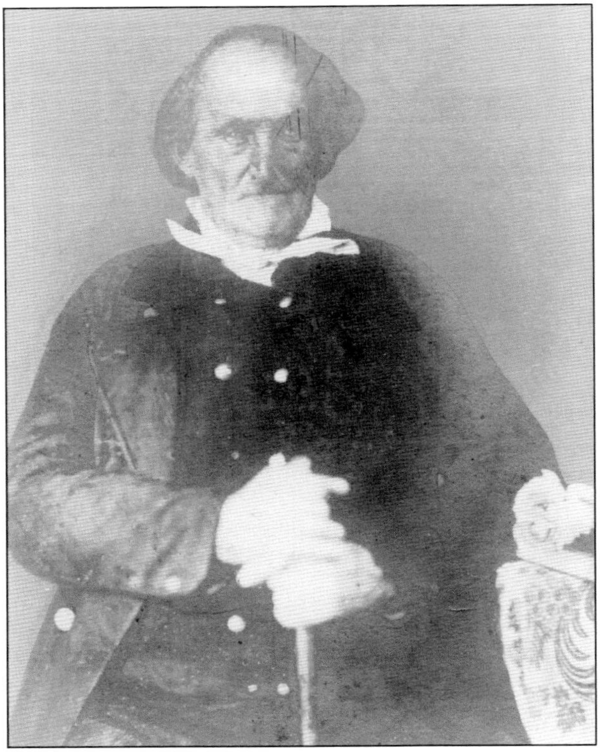

Rem Goldin, shown at left, posed for this portrait shortly before his death in 1860. An Upper Township resident, he lived not far from his great-grandfather William's plantation near Beesley's Point. William Goldin immigrated to Cape May County from Ireland in the early 1690s. He was a justice of the court and occupied other prominent positions in the newly founded county. William Goldin's house, seen below, no longer stands, but its small windows, large chimney, vertical board siding, and wood shingles in the gable suggest he built it soon after his arrival. The house was later used as a barn and eventually demolished. (Both, HPSUT.)

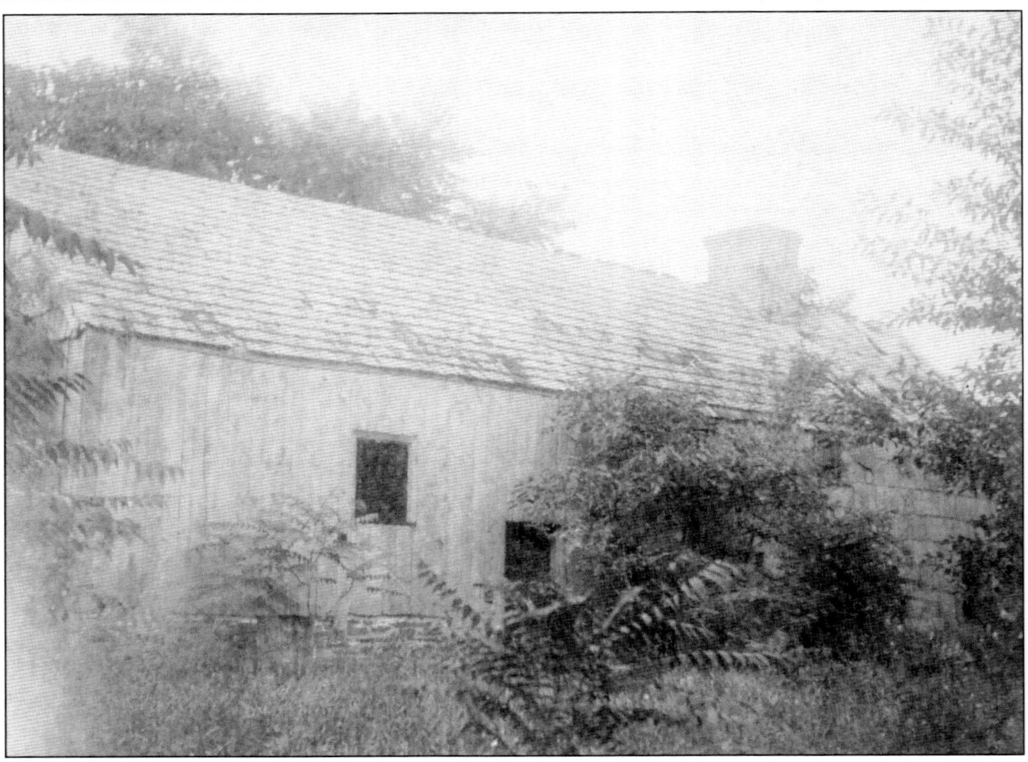

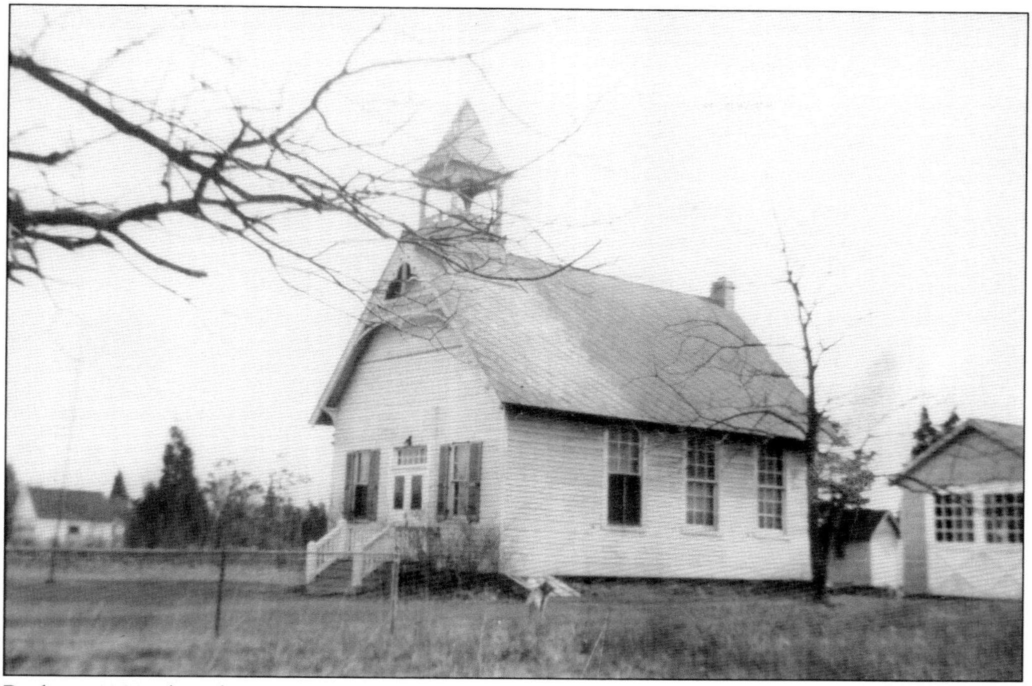

Built in 1889, this classic one-story schoolhouse in Beesley's Point still stands on the east side of US Route 9, where it is now a private residence. It replaced Upper Township's third school, built in 1816 across the road. Designed to hold 48 students, this was one of 20 one-room schools educating pupils throughout the county in 1921. (HPSUT.)

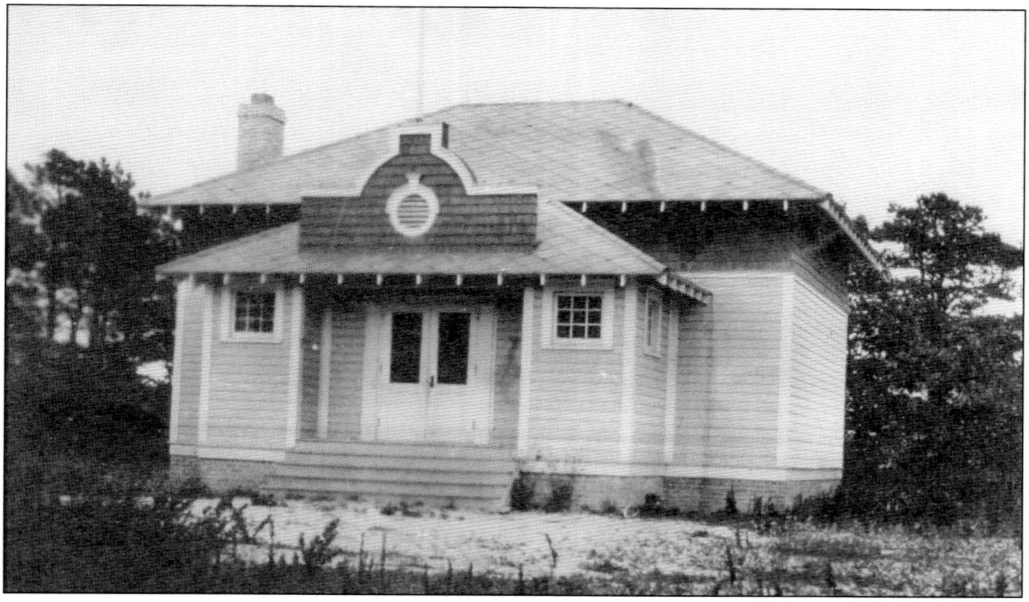

Built in the early 20th century, this one-room school held up to 48 pupils and is located in Palermo on US Route 9. Today, it serves as a day care center. It was one of six schools in Upper Township in the late 19th and early 20th centuries. The others were in Beesley's Point, Seaville, Petersburg, Tuckahoe, and Marshallville. (HPSUT.)

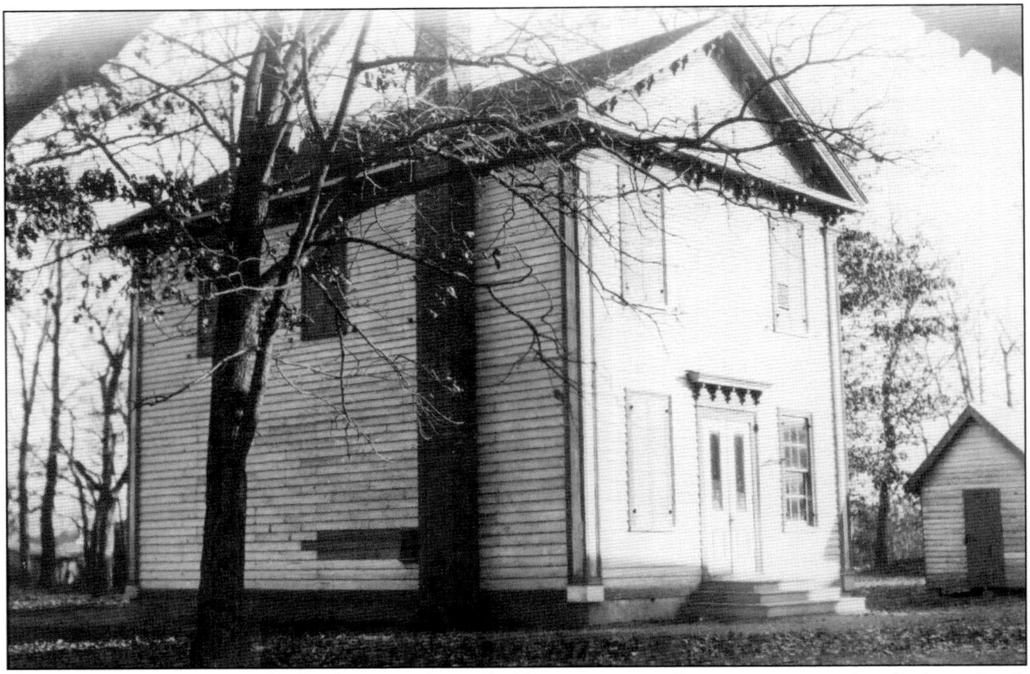

Those parents who could afford it sent their children to an academy, a private school where both academic studies and home arts (for the girls) were taught. This photograph shows the Tuckahoe Academy, a commodious two-story schoolhouse that no longer stands. Cape May County had three other 19th-century academies: in Cold Spring, in Mayville south of Cape May Court House, and in Dennisville. (HPSUT.)

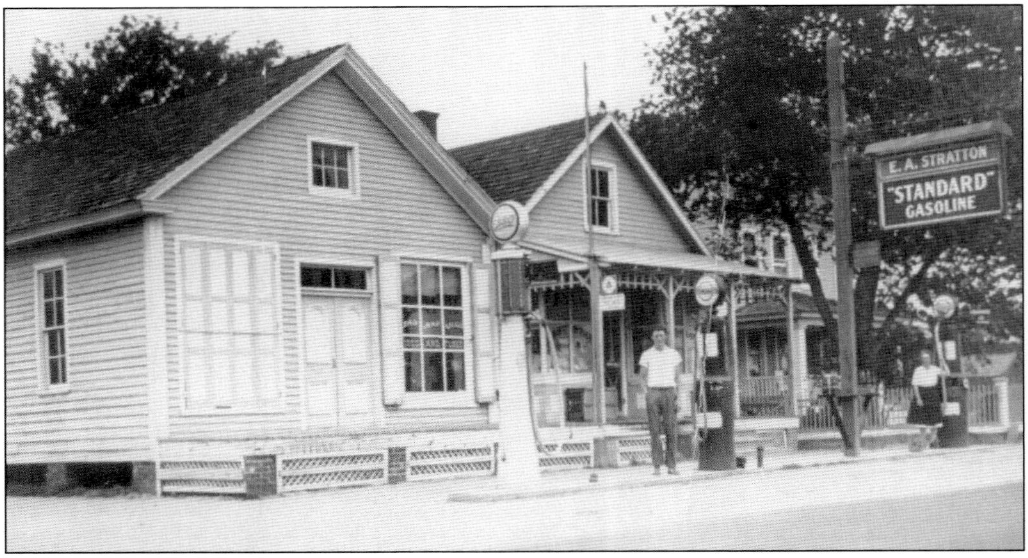

Edward Stratton combined two Victorian-era stores, seen here in the 1930s, into one in Marmora, hosting the post office while selling dry goods, candy, feed, and, later, gasoline. Deliveries were first made by horse and wagon and then by truck. The store was heated by a potbelly stove and featured a "smoking room" in the back for male patrons. Stratton was the postmaster from 1907 until 1941. (HPSUT.)

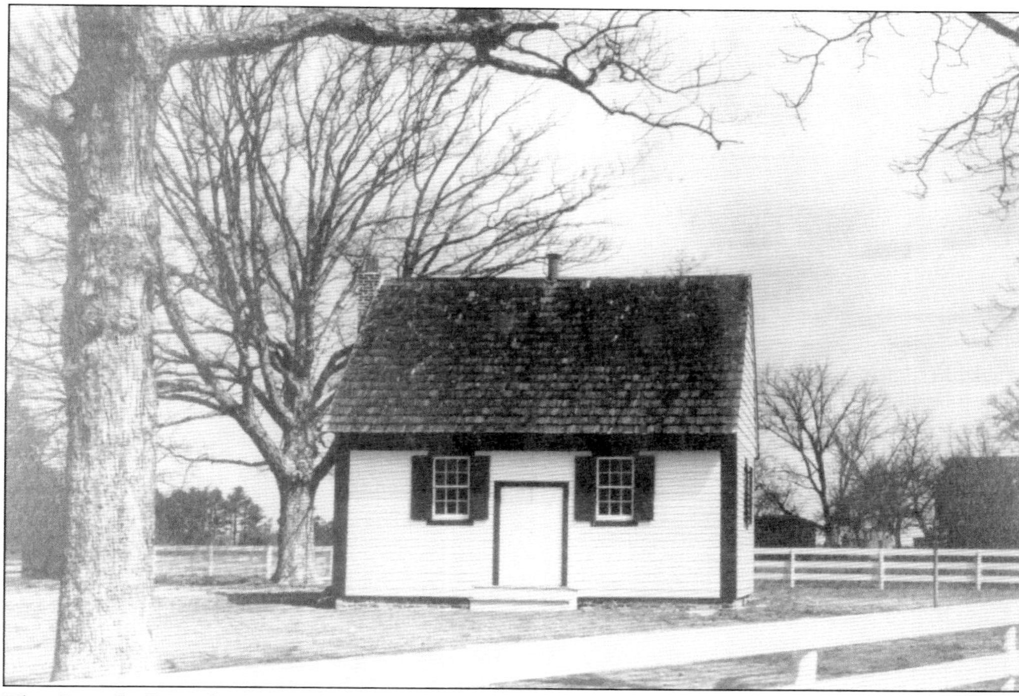

The Seaville Friends Meeting House, seen here about 1930, was built in 1727 in Beelsey's Point, then moved to its present location a mile south of State Route 50 on US Route 9 in Upper Township around 1763. It is the only Quaker meetinghouse in the county and its interior features original, two-inch-thick cedar walls, pews, and exposed framing. The building continues to be used for Quaker worship. (CMCHGS.)

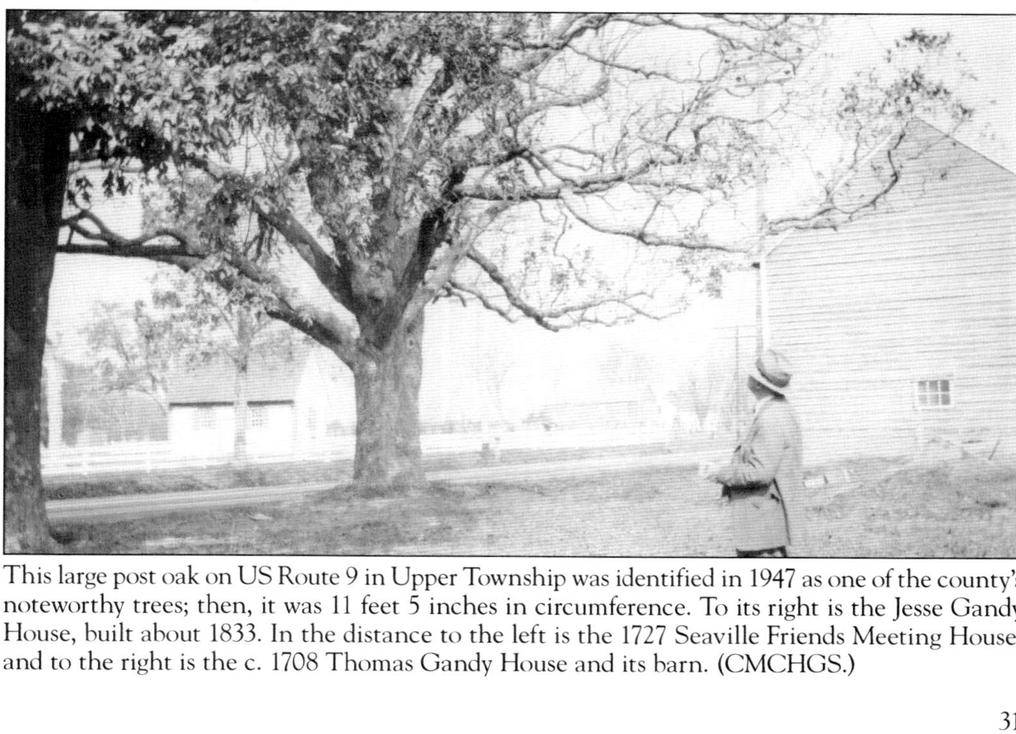

This large post oak on US Route 9 in Upper Township was identified in 1947 as one of the county's noteworthy trees; then, it was 11 feet 5 inches in circumference. To its right is the Jesse Gandy House, built about 1833. In the distance to the left is the 1727 Seaville Friends Meeting House, and to the right is the c. 1708 Thomas Gandy House and its barn. (CMCHGS.)

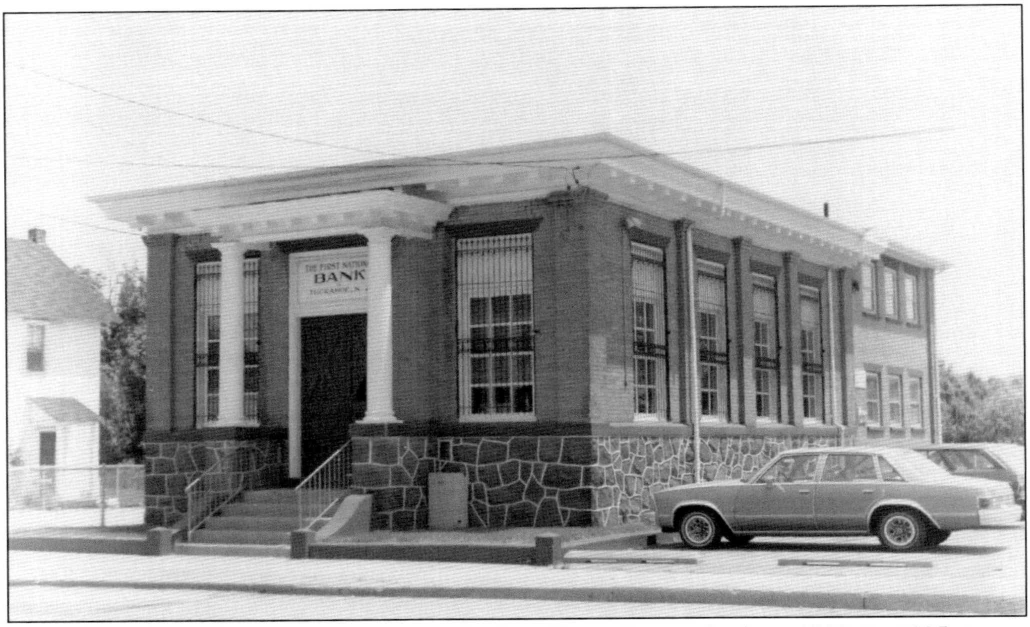

The First National Bank of Tuckahoe, which still stands, was built in 1907. In 1925, it was robbed by three men who shot and killed the bank's vice president and beat two cashiers. After escaping with $7,400, they overturned their car, fled into a cranberry bog, and were captured by a posse of local residents and the state police. All three were convicted of robbery and put in prison. (CMCHGS.)

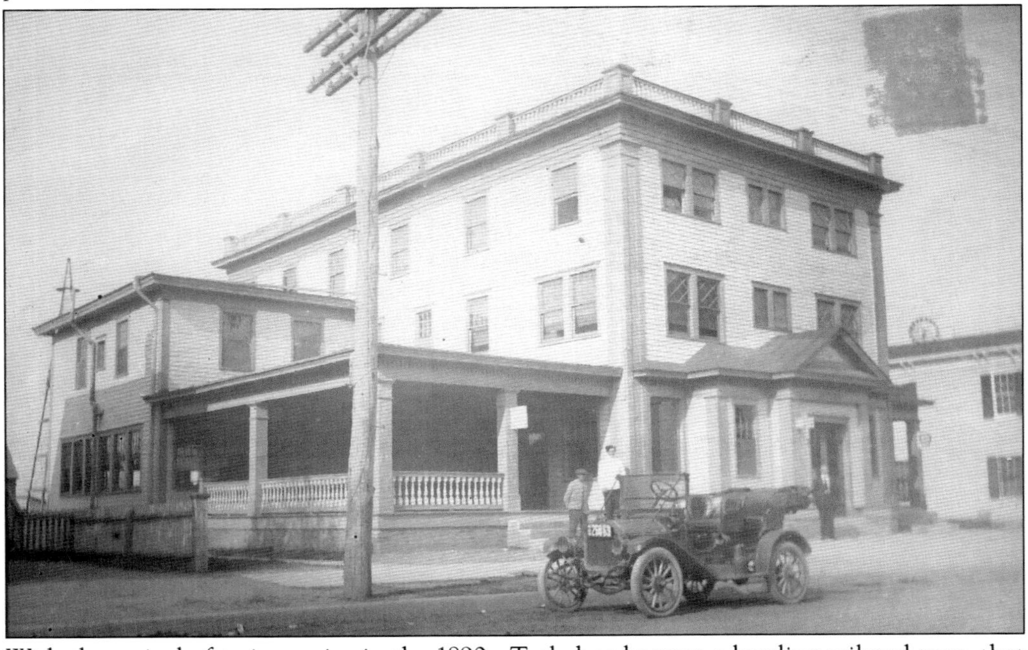

With the arrival of train service in the 1890s, Tuckahoe became a bustling railroad town that catered to shore visitors. The Tuckahoe Hotel, seen here in the early 1920s, was located around the corner from the train station and featured 25 rooms, a dining room, a bar, and a library for its guests. It still stands. (CMCHGS.)

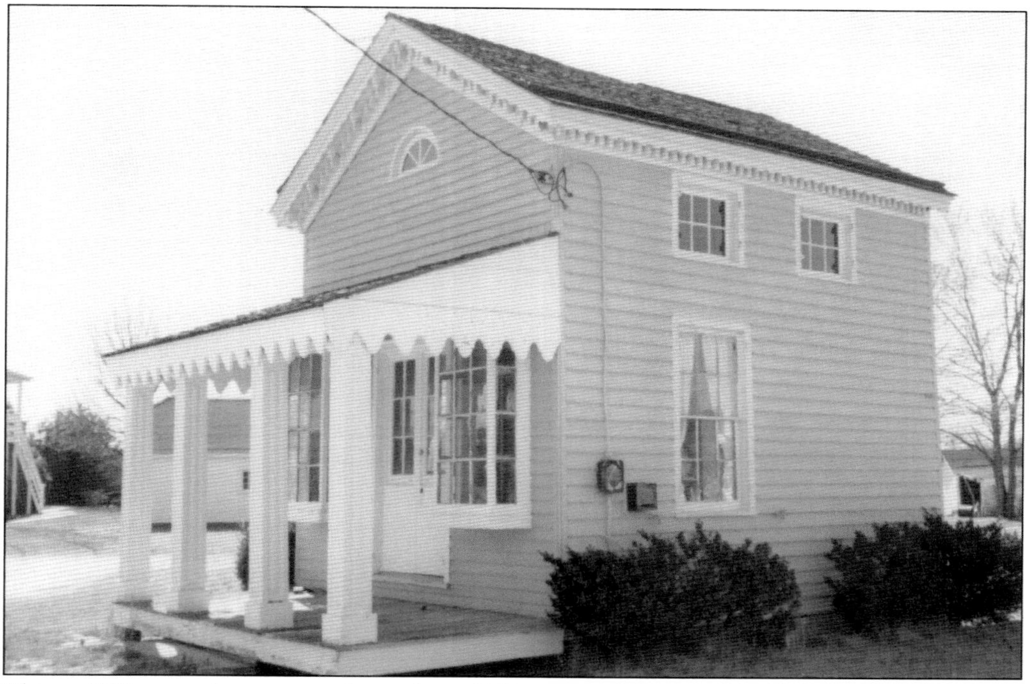

This c. 1855 general store, seen here about 1960, originally stood in Tuckahoe; in the 1870s, it housed a savings and loan, and in the mid-1900s, it was used for township committee meetings. In 1957, it was moved to Beesley's Point, becoming a sandwich shop and motel office. In 1991, it was moved yet again, to Historic Cold Spring Village, where it was restored and is used to demonstrate bookbinding. (CMCHGS.)

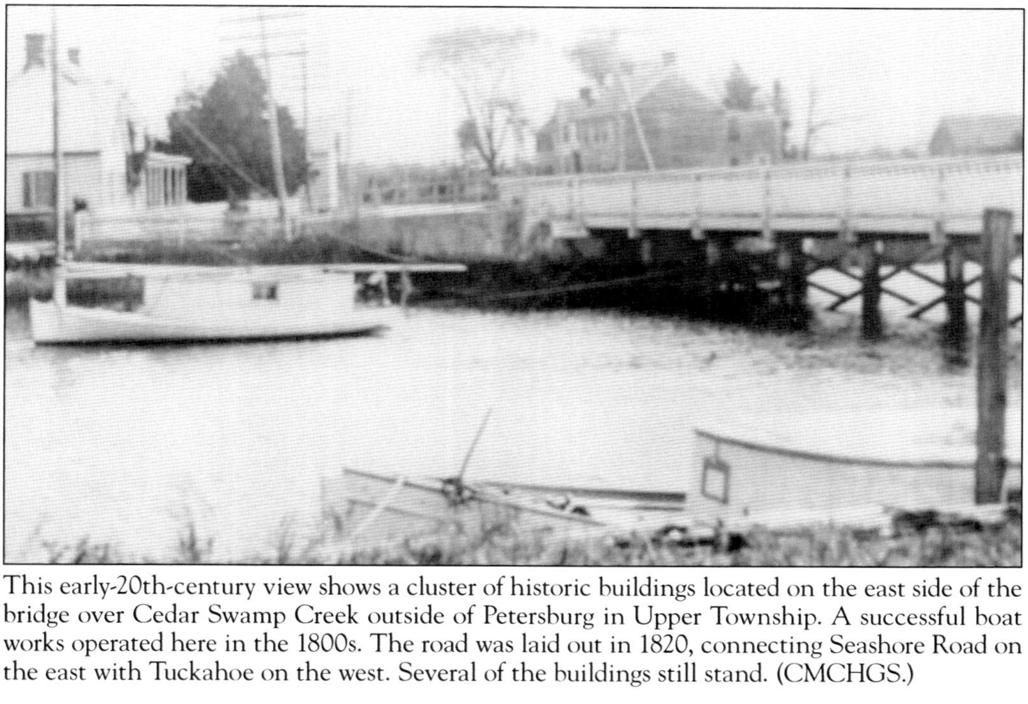

This early-20th-century view shows a cluster of historic buildings located on the east side of the bridge over Cedar Swamp Creek outside of Petersburg in Upper Township. A successful boat works operated here in the 1800s. The road was laid out in 1820, connecting Seashore Road on the east with Tuckahoe on the west. Several of the buildings still stand. (CMCHGS.)

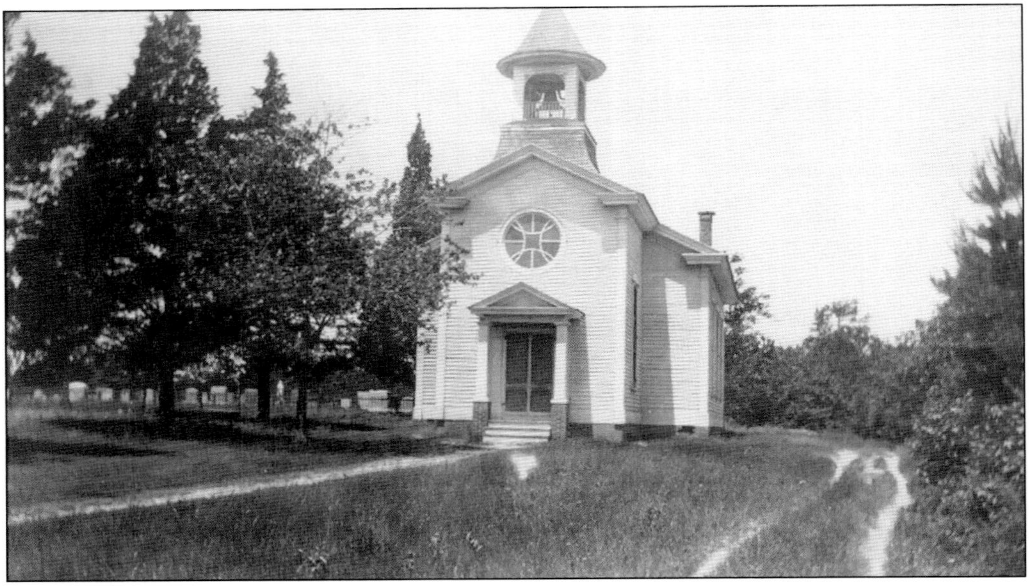

The Seaville United Methodist Church, erected in 1856 on the west side of US Route 9 in Upper Township and shown here in the early 1900s, was one of eleven Methodist churches erected in the Cape May County before the Civil War, more than twice the number of Baptist churches. Methodism dominated the county beginning in the early 1800s, and the first church to be incorporated was in Dennisville in 1802. (George Brewer.)

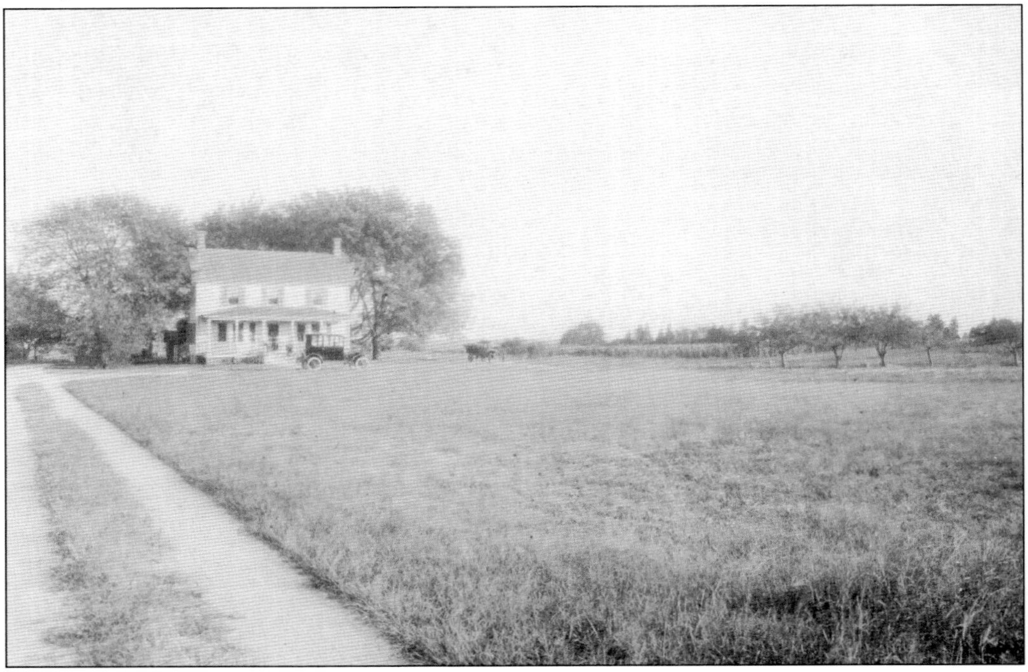

The Amos Corson Farm in Marmora, seen in this 1927 photograph, was a typical Cape May County farmstead with a stately farmhouse sheltered by trees and surrounded by cleared farmland. Corson raised a variety of annual crops and cultivated an orchard as well, seen here to the right. Farmers like Corson sold their fruits and vegetables to the many barrier island hotels. (HPSUT.)

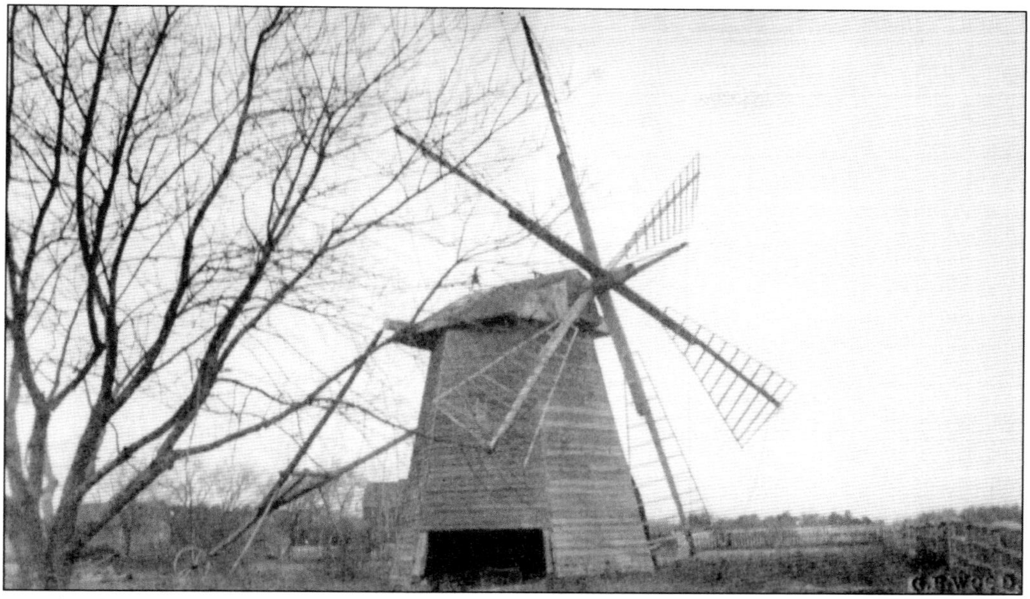

Windmills were a common sight throughout the county in the 1800s. Middle Township resident Jesse Springer built several and patented his design in 1815. The power they created was used to drive either a sawmill or a gristmill. This windmill, seen about 1910, was one of two located on the east side of US Route 9 in Clermont, Dennis Township. (CMCHGS.)

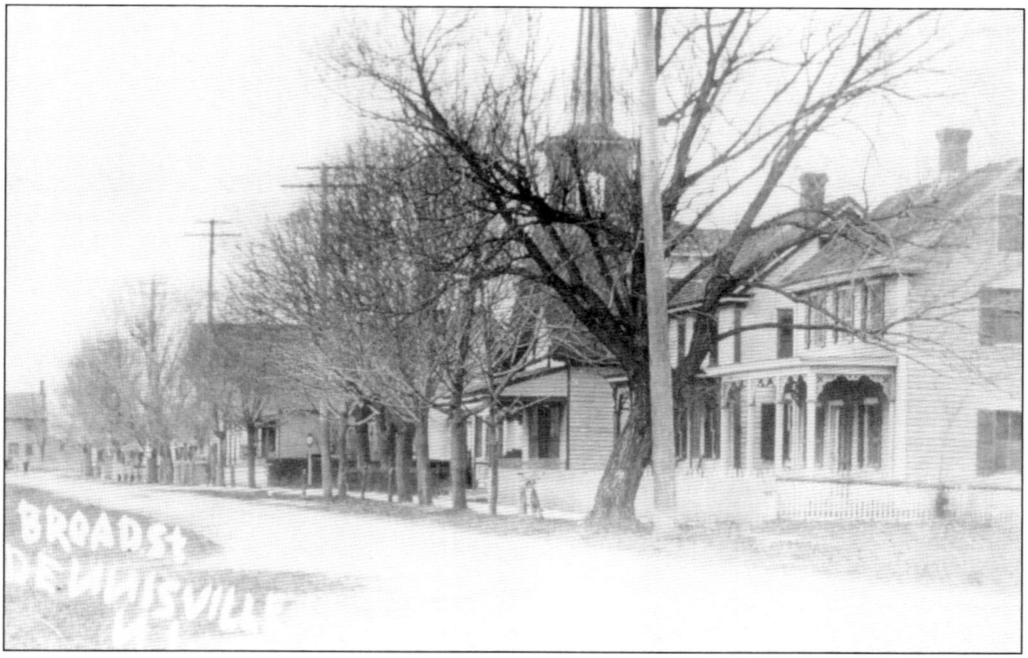

The village of Dennisville, located on the bayside of Dennis Township, prospered through the 19th century as the result of two successful shipyards on nearby Dennis Creek. A movement to make it the county seat, although narrowly defeated in 1848, shows how economically and politically important the village had become. Dennisville was home to sea captains, shipwrights, laborers, and storekeepers and is today a National Register historic district. (CMCHGS.)

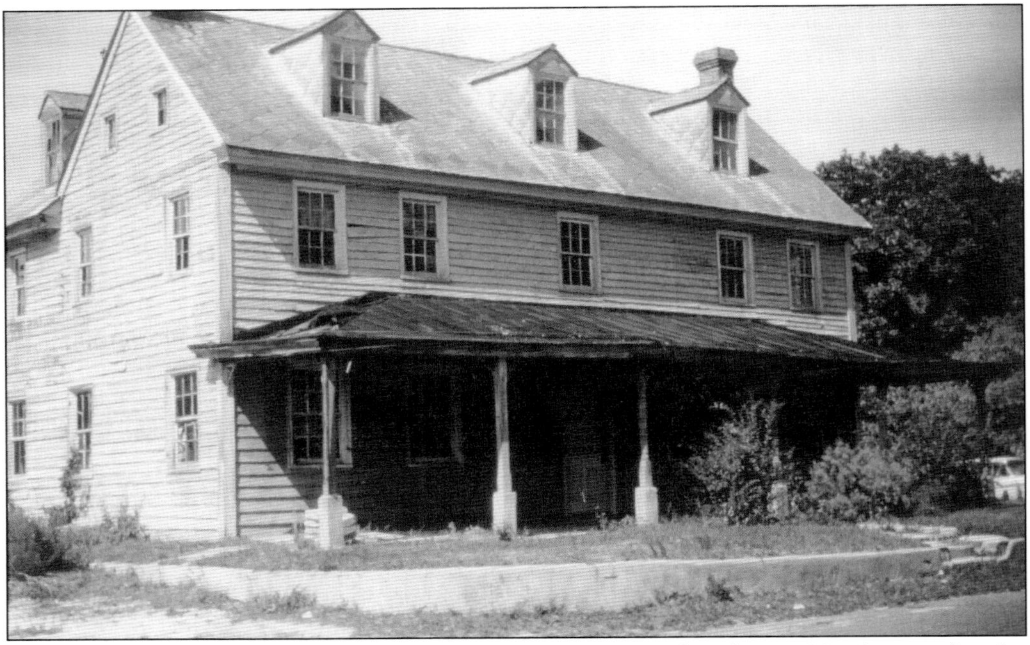

The Dennisville Inn, seen here about 1980, was built in 1836 by Thomas Henderson after the original tavern burned to the ground. It was located a short distance north of Dennis Creek Landing and served travelers arriving by boat, carriage, or horse. In 1985, it was moved to Historic Cold Spring Village, restored, and interpreted as an early American inn. The present Wawa convenience store stands in its place. (CMCHGS.)

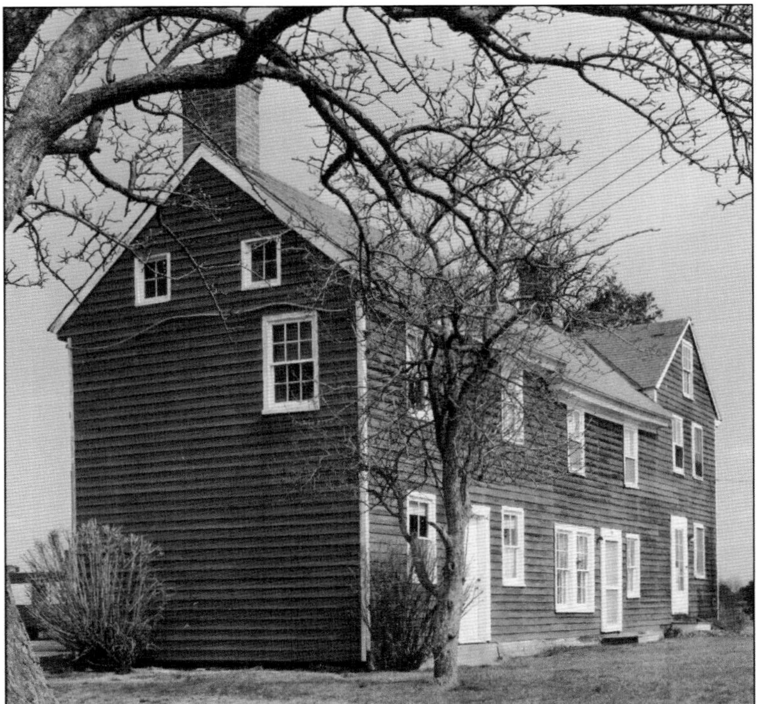

Photographed in 1961, the main block of the Rising Sun Tavern on US Route 9 in Dennis Township consisted of three separate dwellings joined together. The middle section was the earliest, built before 1730. The other two were built in the early 1800s and later moved to the site. John Smith established a tavern here around 1828 and its sign hangs at the county museum. The building was demolished in 2015. (LOC.)

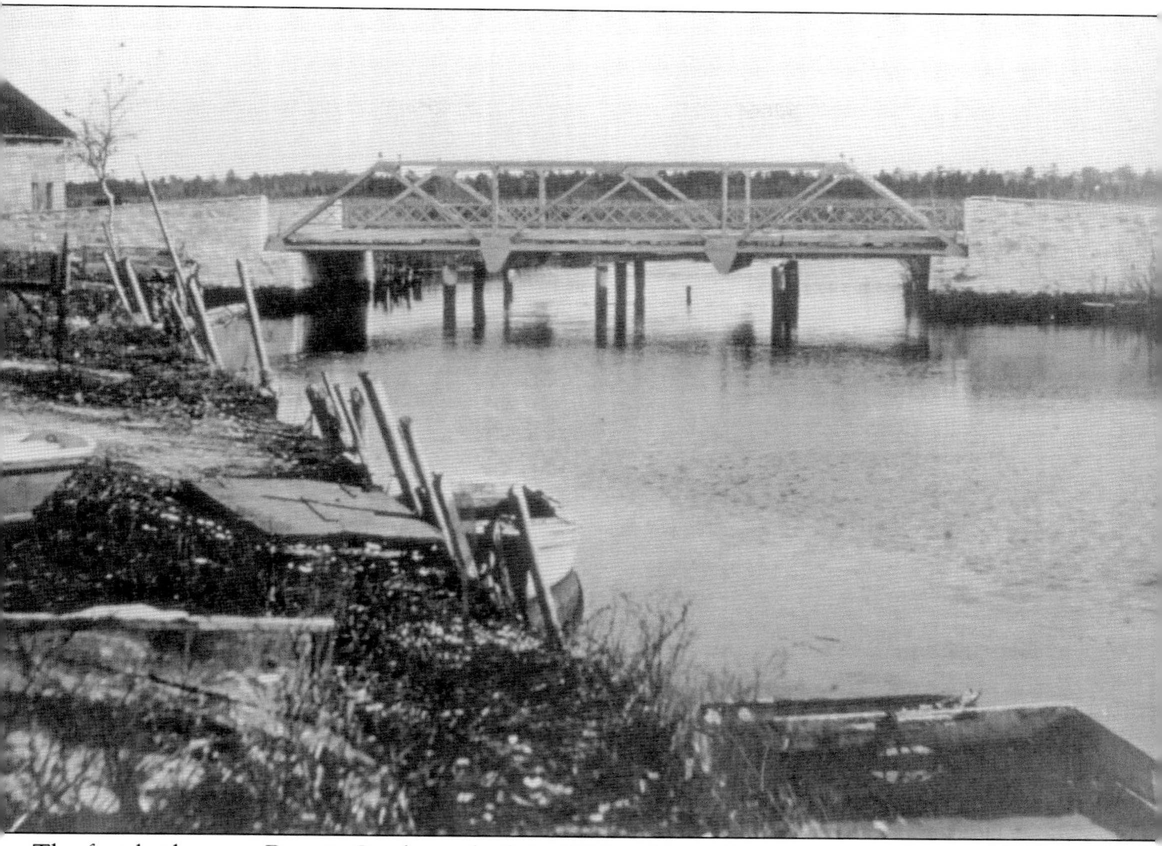

The first bridge over Dennis Creek was built in 1789 and brought an economic boon to both sides of the waterway, spurring the development of the villages of Dennisville on the north side and South Dennis on the south side. Previously, travelers between Camden and Cape May took an overland route roughly five miles northeast of Dennisville that connected with Seashore Road. By the early 1800s, oceangoing schooners were being built at a shipyard located near the bridge, and as the century wore on, hundreds of thousands of shingles and other products made from locally harvested cedar were shipped from the landing. By the 1870s, there was a cluster including stores, houses, a church, and a gristmill near the bridge, as well as another shipyard. This economic prosperity lasted until the railroad came to Dennisville in 1894, signaling the death of the shipbuilding industry. The metal bridge seen here was built in 1907 and replaced in the late 1920s. (CMCHGS.)

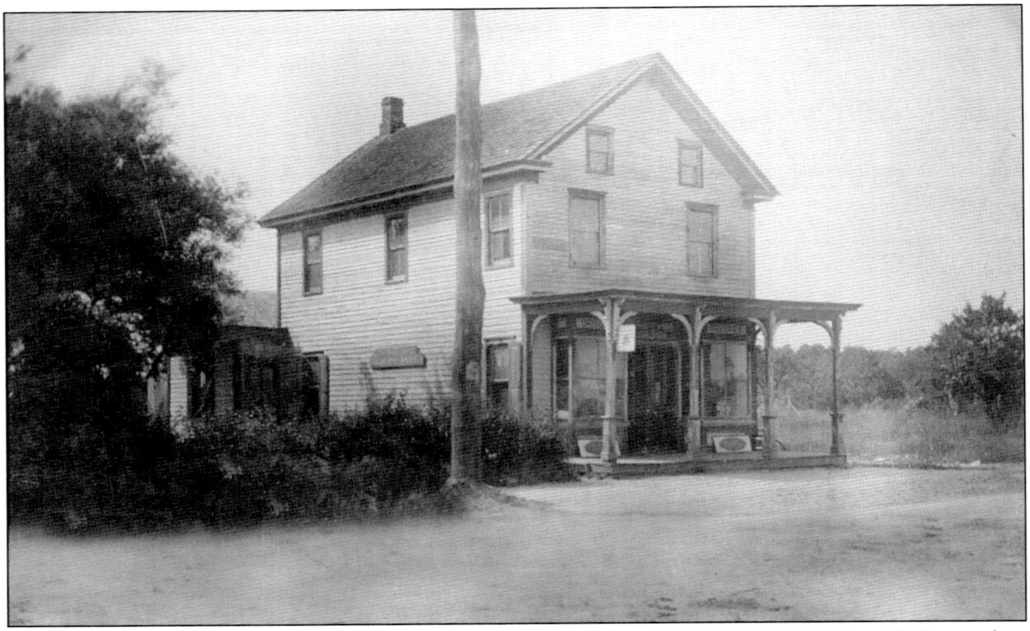

Albert "Bert" Way operated this general store in Ocean View, seen here about 1910, at what is today the intersection of US Route 9 and Sea Isle Boulevard in Dennis Township. General stores were common throughout the county, selling groceries, dry goods, and remedies for most ailments. Many merchants lived with their families on the second and attic stories above their store. (CMCHGS.)

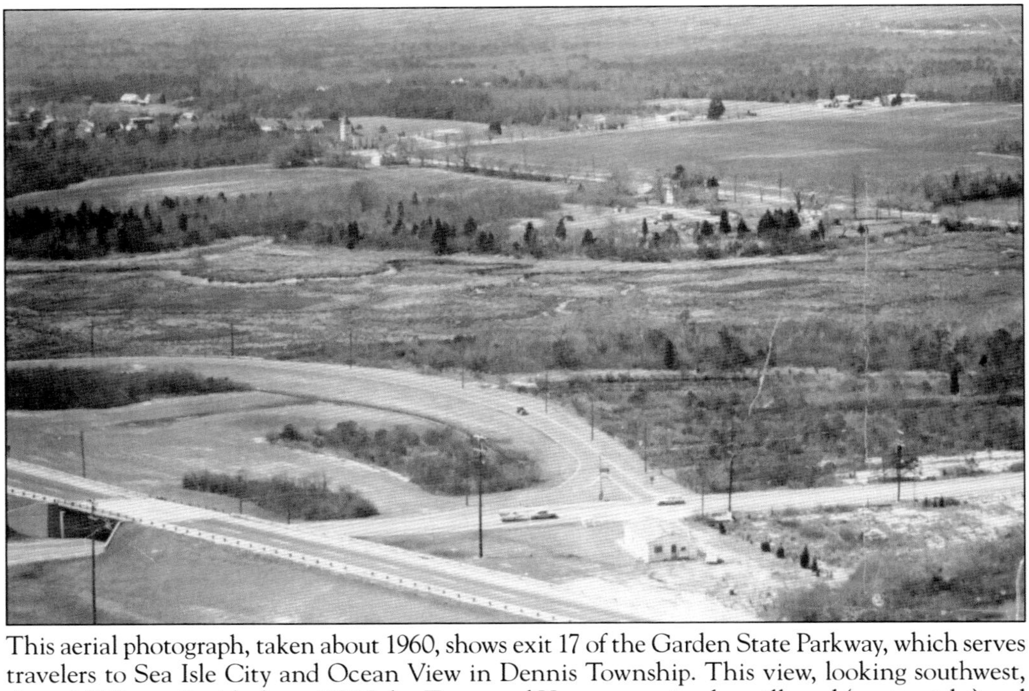

This aerial photograph, taken about 1960, shows exit 17 of the Garden State Parkway, which serves travelers to Sea Isle City and Ocean View in Dennis Township. This view, looking southwest, shows US Route 9 with the c. 1700 John Townsend House opposite the millpond (center right) and the 1855 Cavalry Baptist Church with its tall spire in the distance, center left. (CMCHGS.)

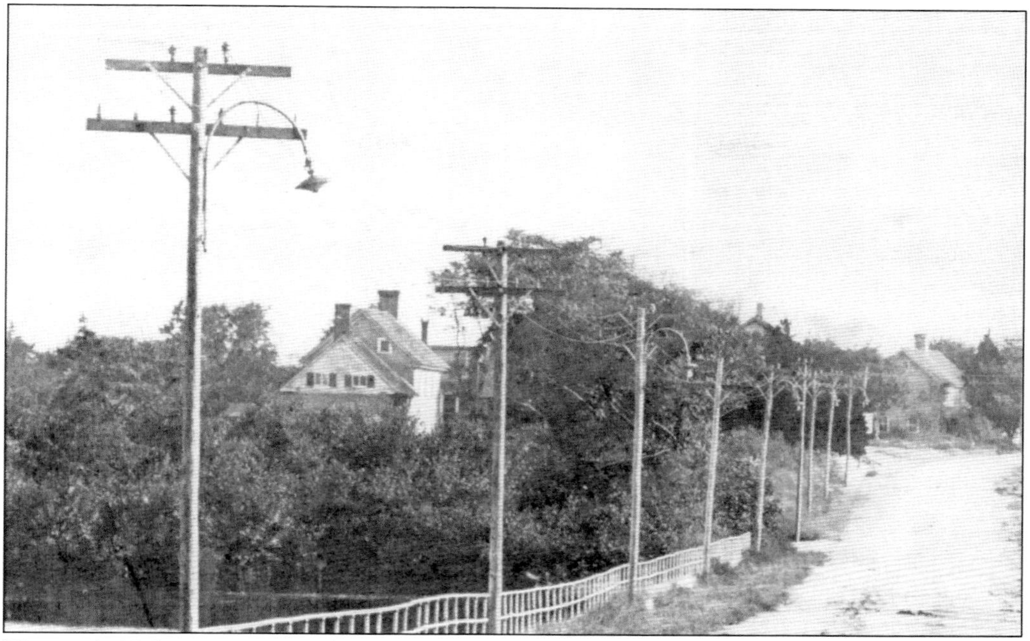

This early-20th-century view shows US Route 9 as it travels north through Ocean View south of Sea Isle Boulevard. The Townsend millpond, bordered by a fence, is to the left. The house immediately beyond the pond is that of Richard Townsend, built before 1730. It burned in the late 20th century, but was rebuilt as an exact copy of the original. (CMCHGS.)

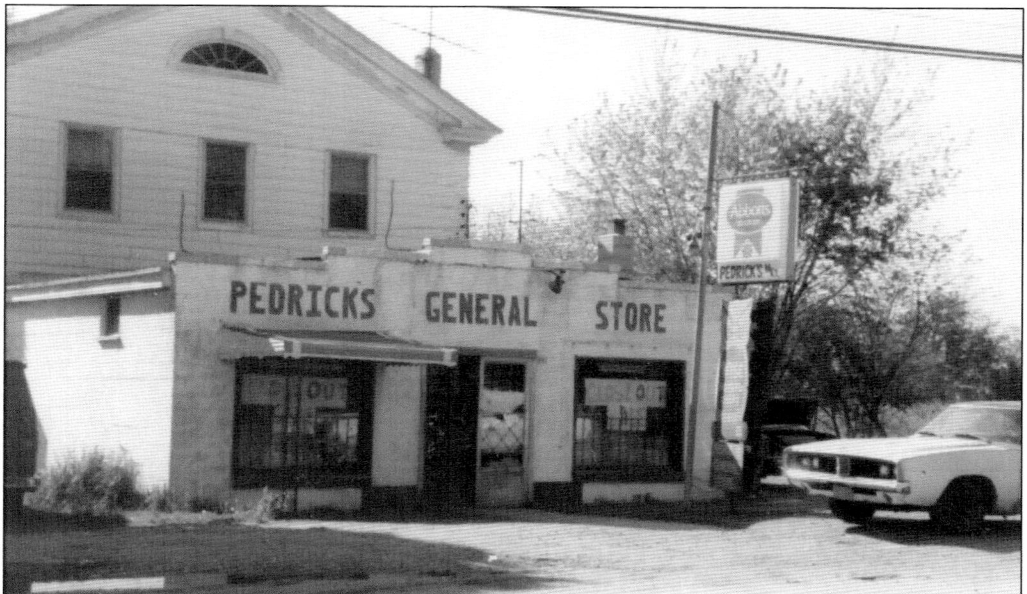

Fred and Thelma Pedrick operated a general store, seen here about 1965, out of a storefront added to the 1839 South Dennis Methodist Episcopal Church in South Dennis. The church's last service was held in October 1935, and the building was then converted into two apartments and given a store addition. Pedrick's closed in the 1970s, and other tenants have since occupied the store. (Donna Matalucci.)

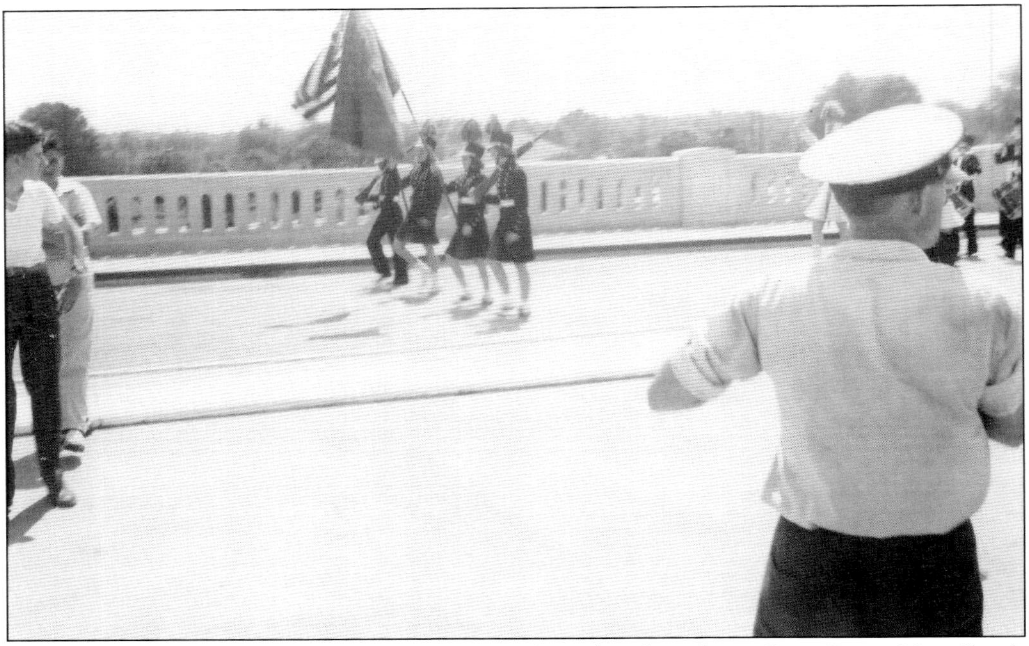

The construction of a new concrete bridge over the railroad tracks on State Route 83 in South Dennis was cause for celebration on June 17, 1941. In the late 1920s, the state laid out that road to connect State Route 47 with US Route 9, rerouting part of Route 47 around Dennisville. At least two houses had to be moved as a result. (Donna Matalucci.)

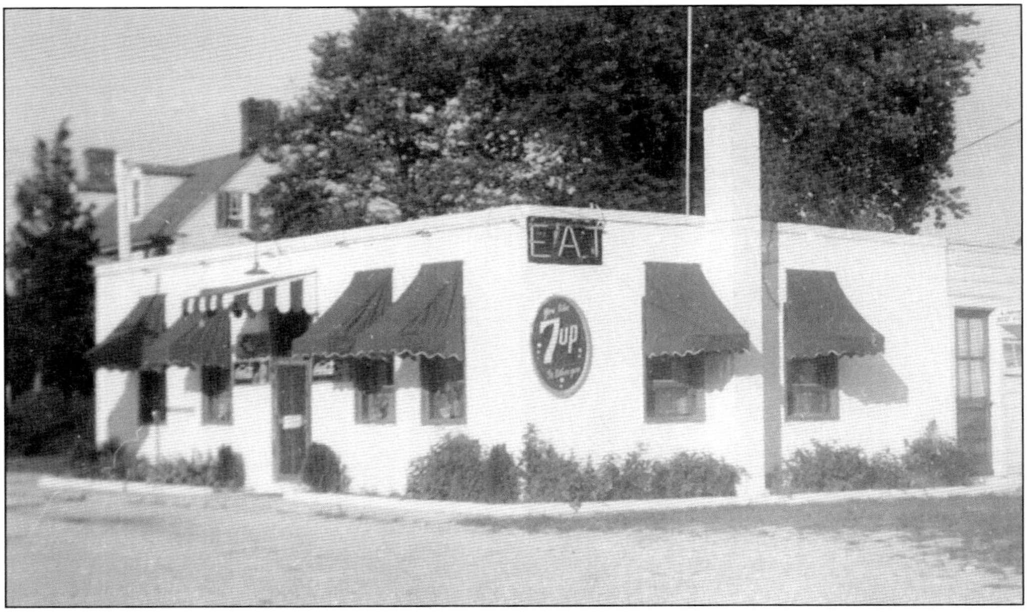

With the advent of travel by car, small roadside eateries like this one were built specifically to cater to the motoring public. The Delsea Inn, seen here about 1950, was located in South Dennis on Route 47, just south of the intersection of Dennisville-Court House Road. Route 47 is also known as Delsea Drive, so named for connecting the Delaware River with the sea. The restaurant no longer stands. (CMCHGS.)

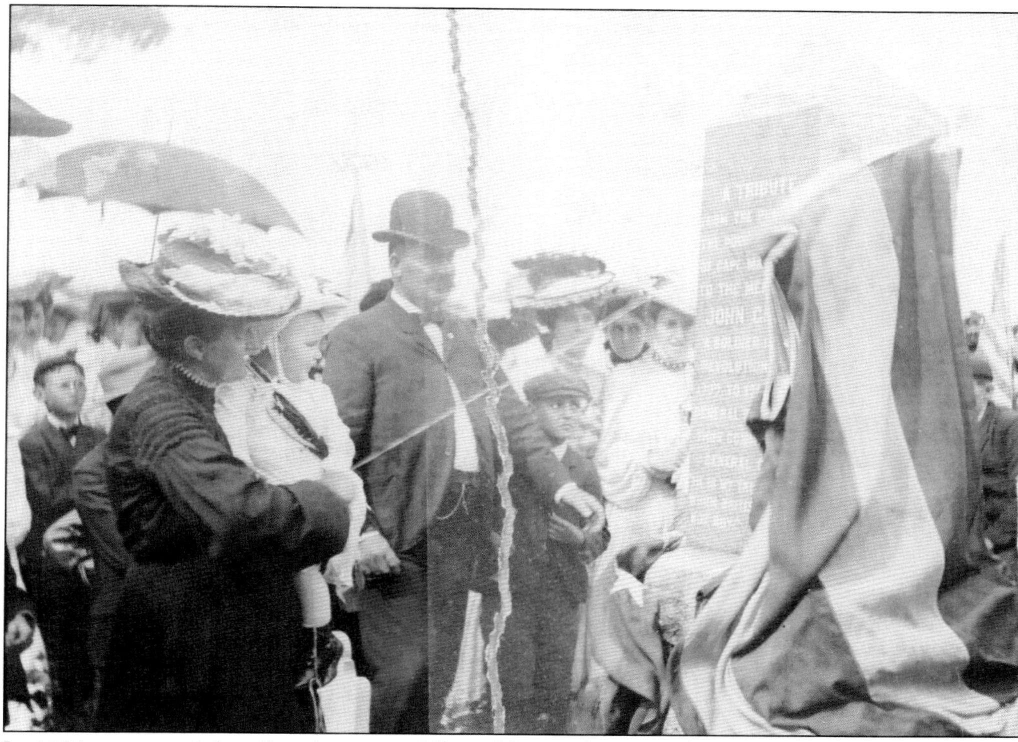

In 1904, a memorial to Revolutionary War soldier and scout John Grace was placed in Union Cemetery, South Dennis, over his grave. Grace, from North Dennis, fought for eight years in several campaigns and was with the New Jersey troops at the Battle of Yorktown. George Washington called him my "trusted scout whom British gold can't buy." The unveiling attracted between 2,500 and 3,000 people. (CMCHGS.)

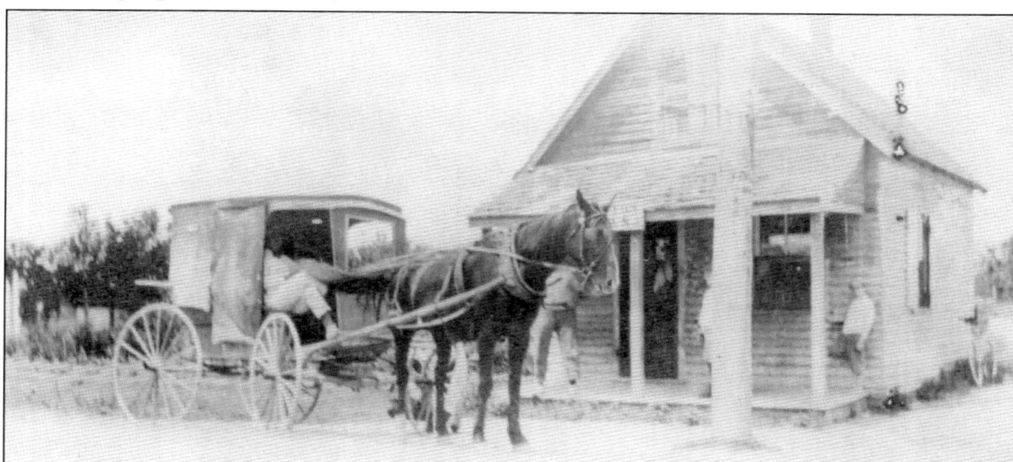

Levi Hand operated a small general store, seen here about 1900, in Eldora at the junction of Paper Mill Road and Route 47. Eldora, located in northwestern Dennis Township, was once a thriving village with a paper mill and pickling plant, but little remains. The store was moved around 1970 to Historic Smithville in Atlantic County, where it joined other moved historic buildings to form a commercial village. (CMCHGS.)

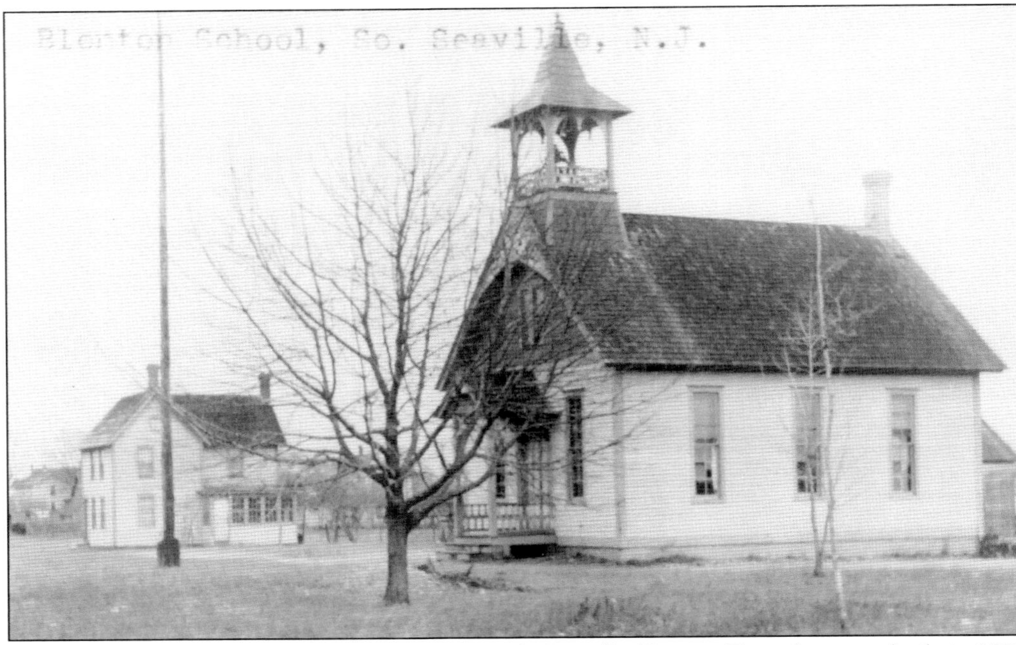

Pictured about 1900, this former school in South Seaville, Dennis Township, was built in 1884 to accommodate 44 pupils. It still stands on Kings Highway, where it has been converted into a house. The small front porch and the bell tower have been removed, but the decorative gingerbread trim on the front remains. (CMCHGS.)

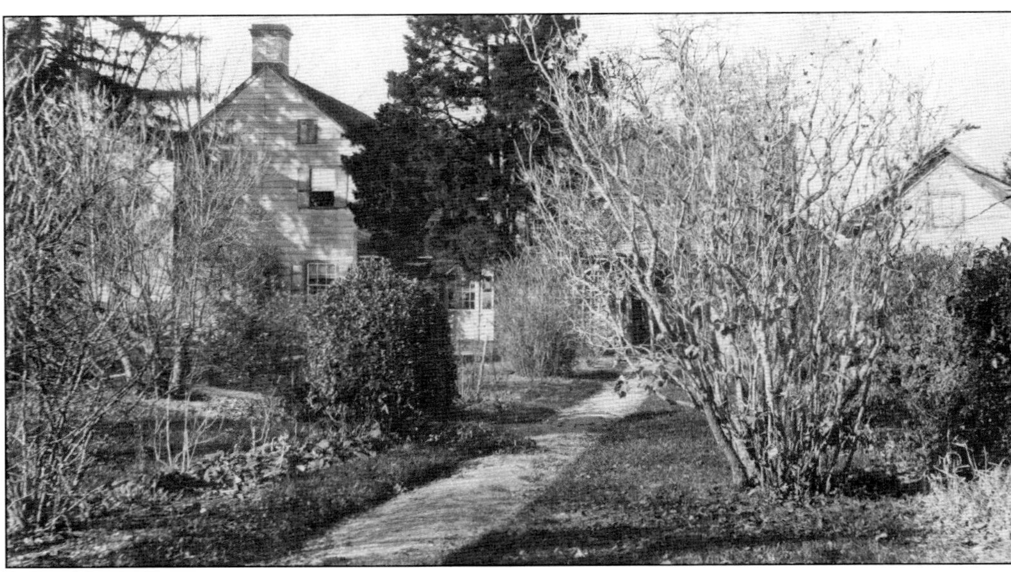

This photograph shows the east side of the William S. Townsend House in North Dennis as it looked on Thanksgiving Day in 1910. The house, built in different sections that range in age from the mid-1700s to the early 1800s, is locally known as "Seven Chimneys," three of which are seen in this photograph. The house still stands. (CMCHGS.)

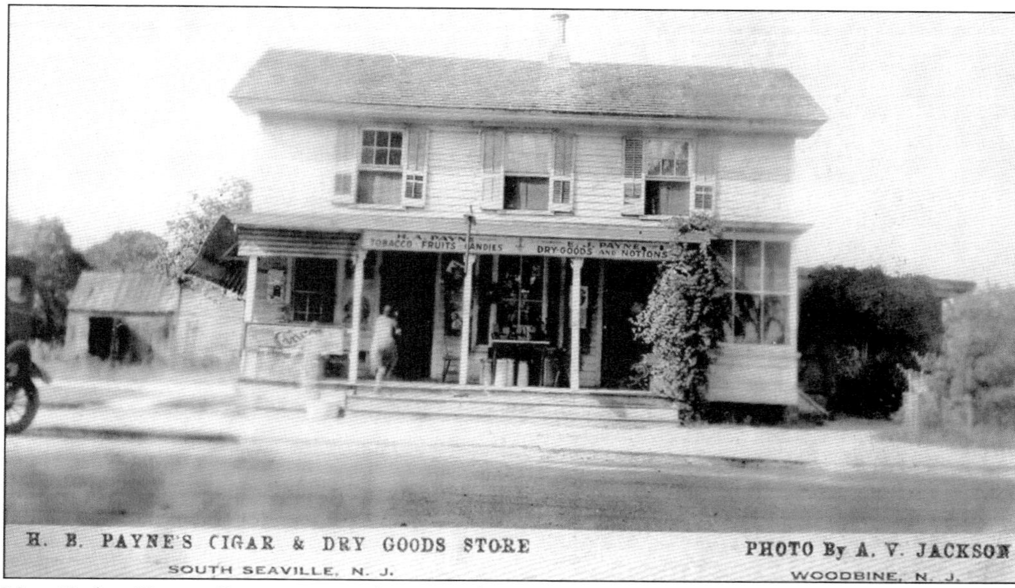

New Yorker Horace Payne operated a general store out of his house in South Seaville, seen here about 1920. His wife, Emma, worked with him in the dry goods section. The house was the birthplace of Frank Wheaton Sr., known as the "dean of American glassware," in 1881. He grew his father's pharmaceutical glass company in Millville, called Wheaton Glass, into the nation's largest family-owned glass business. (CMCHGS.)

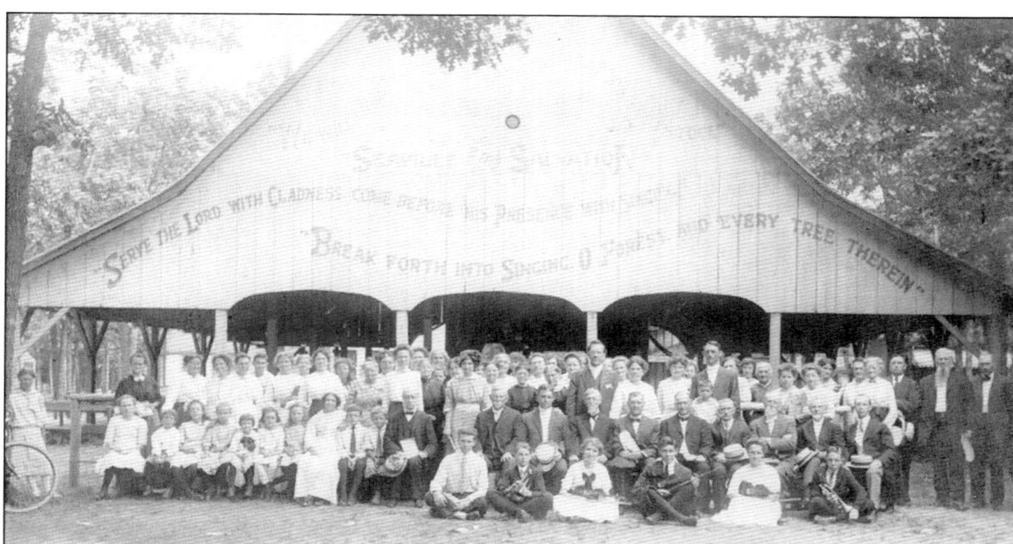

South Seaville Camp Meeting was established as a summertime Methodist pilgrimage in 1863 or 1864, about the time the railroad came through town. Large revival meetings were held in the tabernacle, seen here in the early 1900s, which still stands on the camp's 33-acre grounds. It was built in 1890. Smoking and drinking in the camp were forbidden, as were bicycles and the game of croquet. (CMCHGS.)

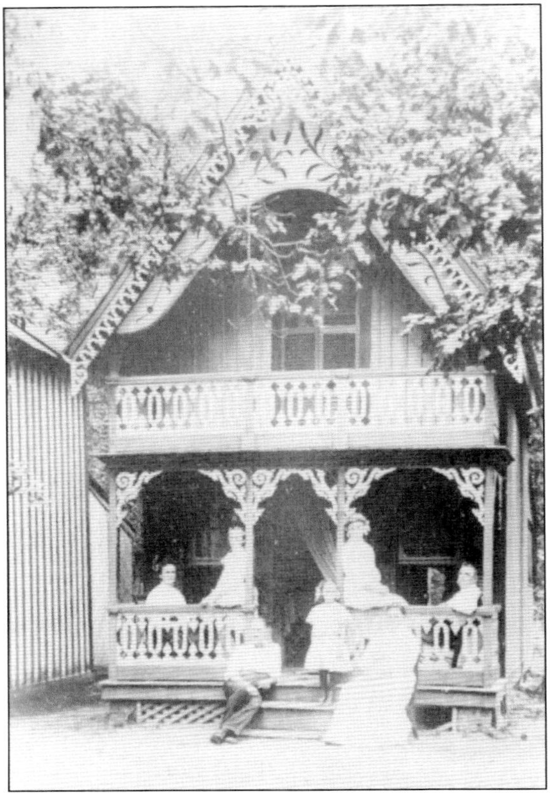

About 200 cottages similar to this one were built at the South Seaville Camp Meeting. Five hundred small lots were available to those willing to build a canvas or frame structure within a year. By 1877, approximately 90 had been erected. Most are two-story, uninsulated dwellings with open porches and Victorian gingerbread trim done in the Gothic Revival style. Today, 89 cottages remain, and camp meetings are still held there. (CMCHGS.)

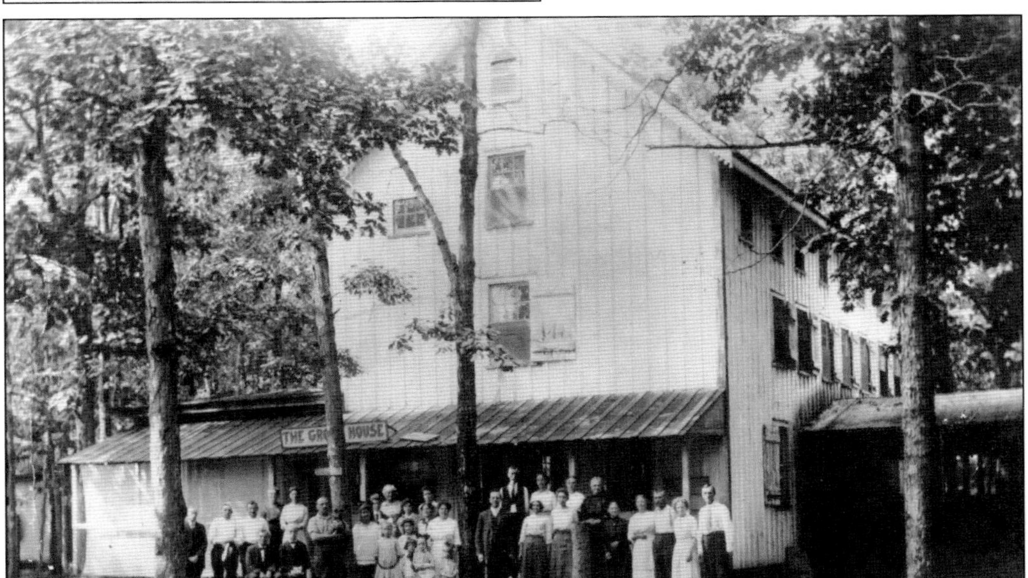

The centrally located Grove House at the camp meeting features communal dining rooms on the first floor and guest rooms on the upper stories, where boarders rented sleeping accommodations during the summer months. Sunday dinners are still served here following services. It is the oldest Methodist camp meeting still in service in New Jersey. (George Brewer.)

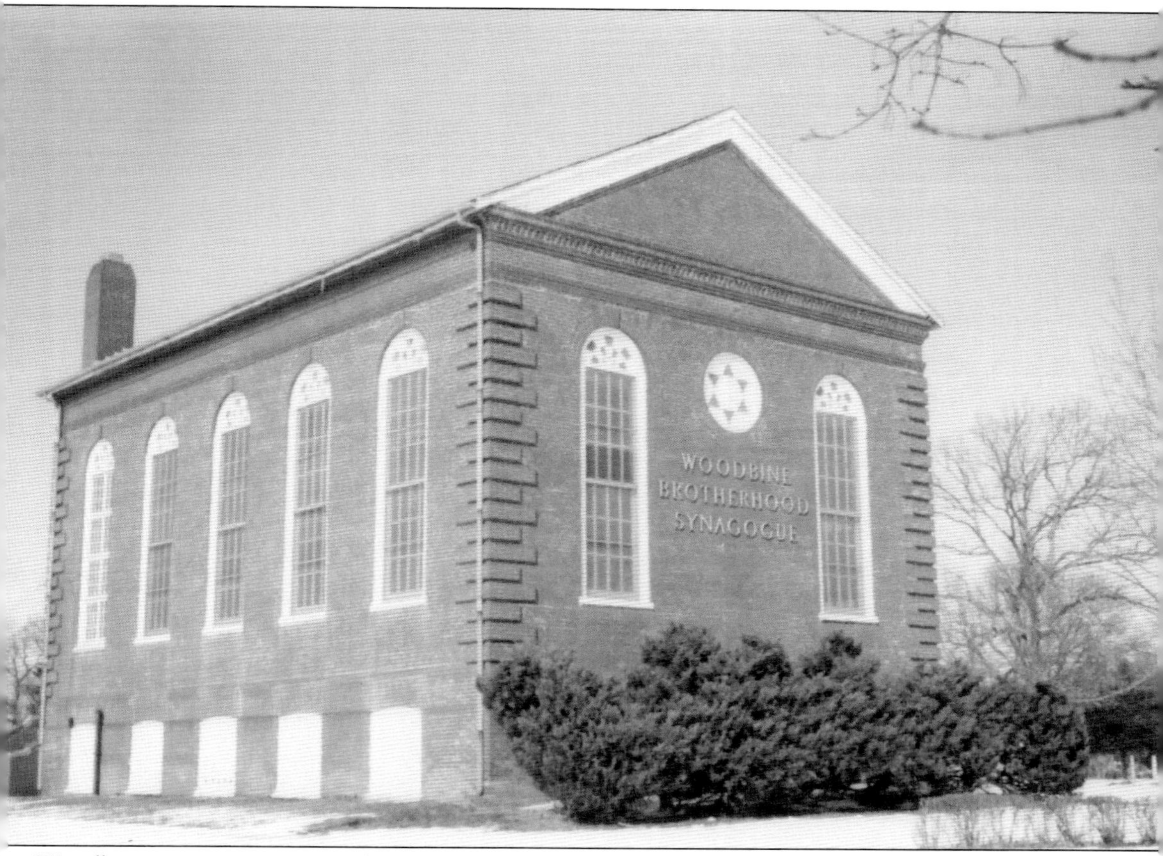

Woodbine was an experimental colony envisioned by the Baron de Hirsch Fund trustees to assist Russian Jews who immigrated to America in the 1890s. The first newcomers tried farming, but poor soil conditions resulted in Woodbine's evolution into a factory town, turning it into the manufacturing center of Cape May County. The synagogue was constructed by its members and consecrated in 1896. It is the largest of the late-19th-century synagogues built in the newly settled "Jewish villages" of southern New Jersey, and its brick walls and rectangular form make it architecturally similar to many 19th-century churches in the region. By 1999, the Jewish population had dwindled and the synagogue closed its doors. Several years later, it reopened as the Sam Azeez Museum of Woodbine Heritage, created to remember and record the town's past. The sanctuary has been restored and is available for special services. The lower level houses the museum's permanent and temporary exhibitions. (CMCHGS.)

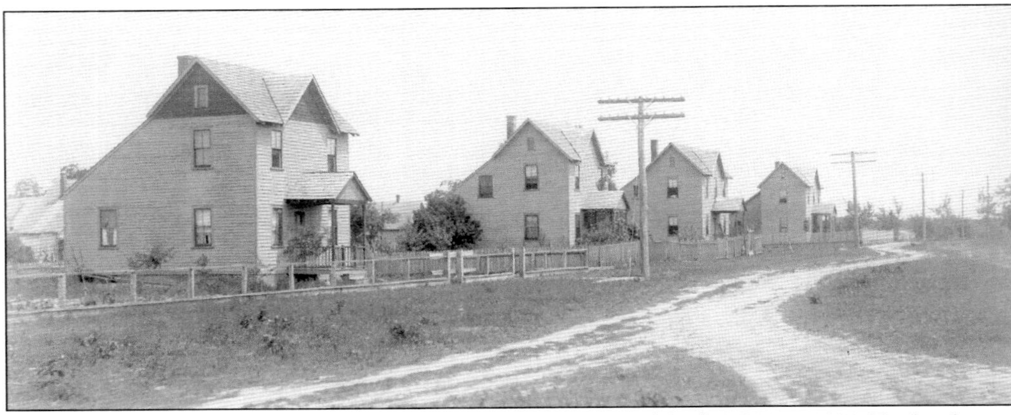

Woodbine was founded on a 5,300-acre site that was purchased for $37,500 in 1891. Twelve farmers and a supervisor arrived that year and began clearing land. The land was surveyed and 62 farms of 30 acres each were laid out. When farming proved untenable, houses like these were built in town for those working in the factories. (CMCHGS.)

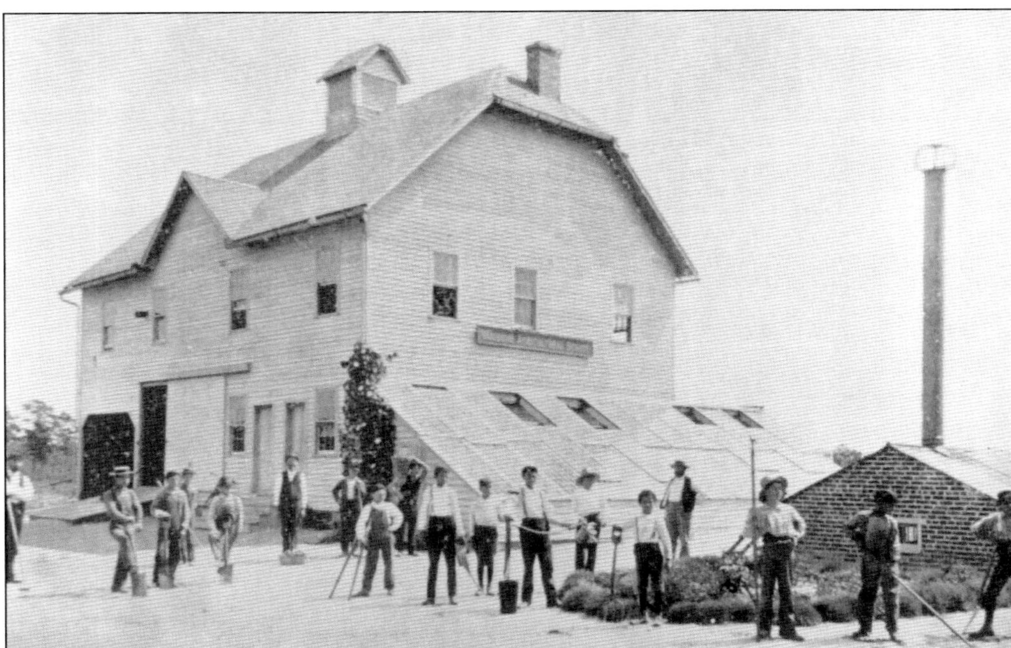

The Woodbine Agricultural School was founded in 1893. Students were given both practical and theoretical introductory classes about agricultural practices that would allow them to get junior positions on existing farms. Graduates could also purchase their own farms if they desired with help from the Baron de Hirsh Fund. The school closed in 1917. (CMCHGS.)

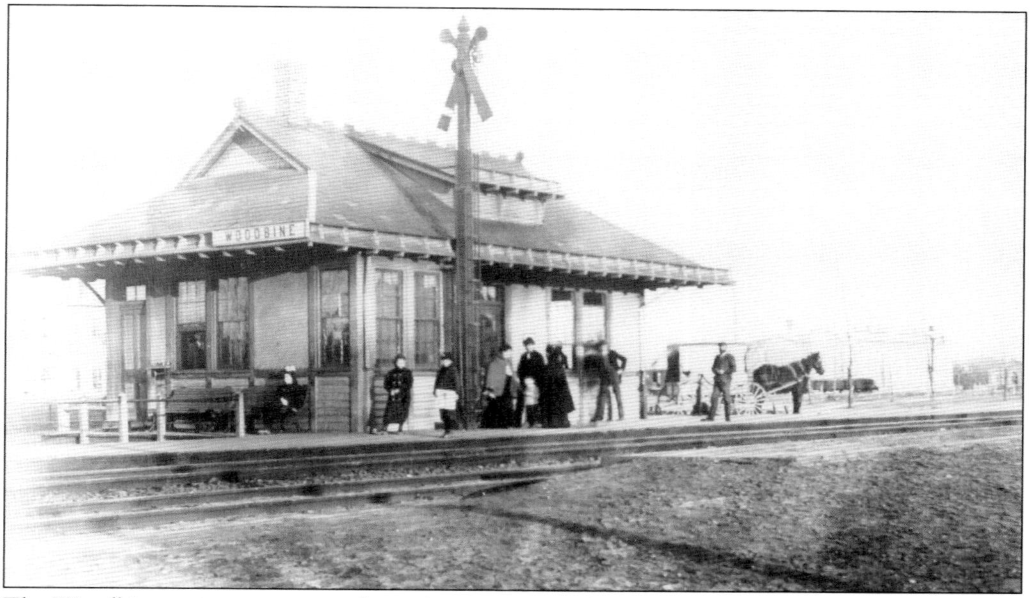

The Woodbine train station, seen here about 1900, was built in 1894. It was initially served by the Cape May & Millville Railroad, later the West Jersey & Seashore Railroad. The stop had been little-used until the Jewish American agricultural and industrial community at Woodbine was established in 1891. The station originally stood on DeHirsch Avenue, opposite the firehouse, but was torn down. (HGM.)

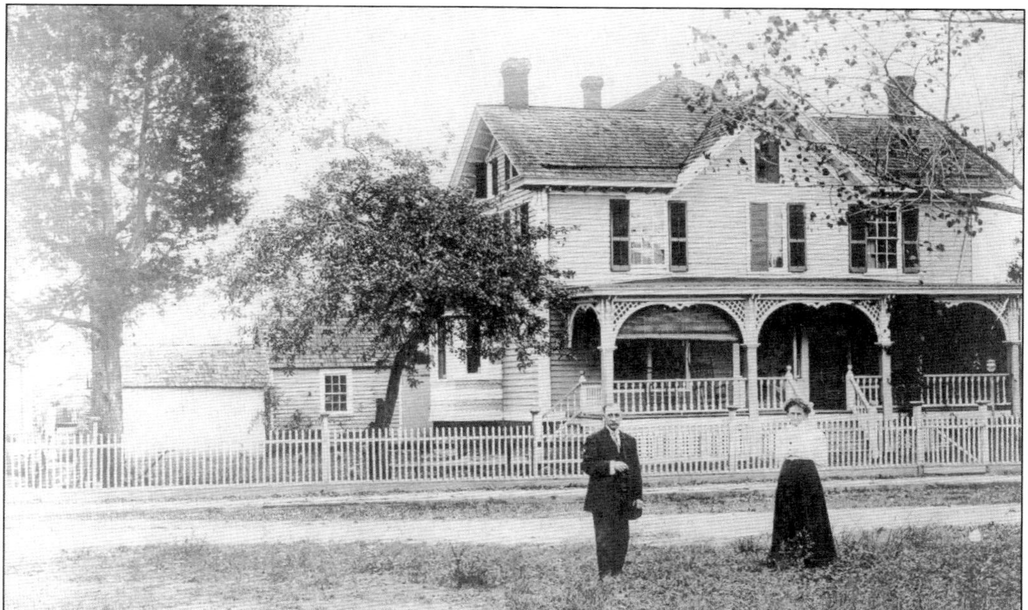

David Blenkow, a shoe dealer, lived in this large two-story house, which still stands in South Seaville. Blenkow had a shoe store on the property not seen in this c. 1900 photograph. The house looks nearly identical today but is missing the elaborate front porch and chimneys. Blenkow fought in Company F, 25th New Jersey Volunteer Infantry during the Civil War, achieving the rank of captain. (George Brewer.)

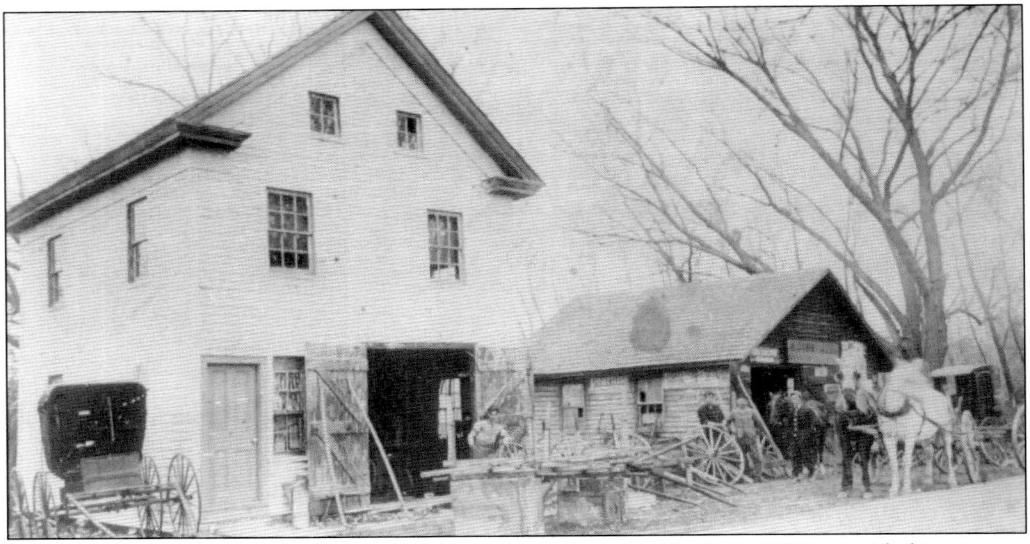

The village blacksmith and wheelwright, like these in Dennisville about 1900, provided important services to area residents. The blacksmith made tools, hardware, and horseshoes and repaired everything from plows to buckets. The wheelwright made wheels for buggies, wagons, and carts. Both trades waned as horseless carriages grew in popularity and modern technology replaced the demand for handmade goods. (CMCHGS.)

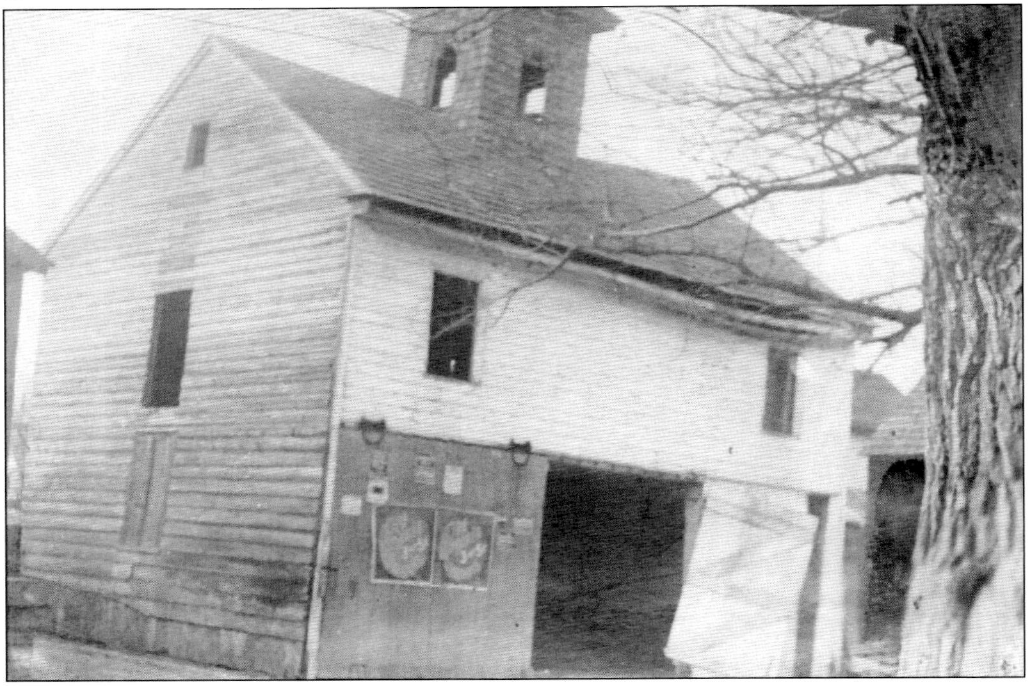

The county's first courthouse was formerly a 1715 Baptist meetinghouse built on land located near Rio Grande in Middle Township and purchased in 1744. Seen here is the second courthouse, built in 1774 in the village of Cape May Court House. It was replaced with a new building, which still stands, in 1850 and appears to have been used as a barn or for storage after its abandonment. (CMCHGS.)

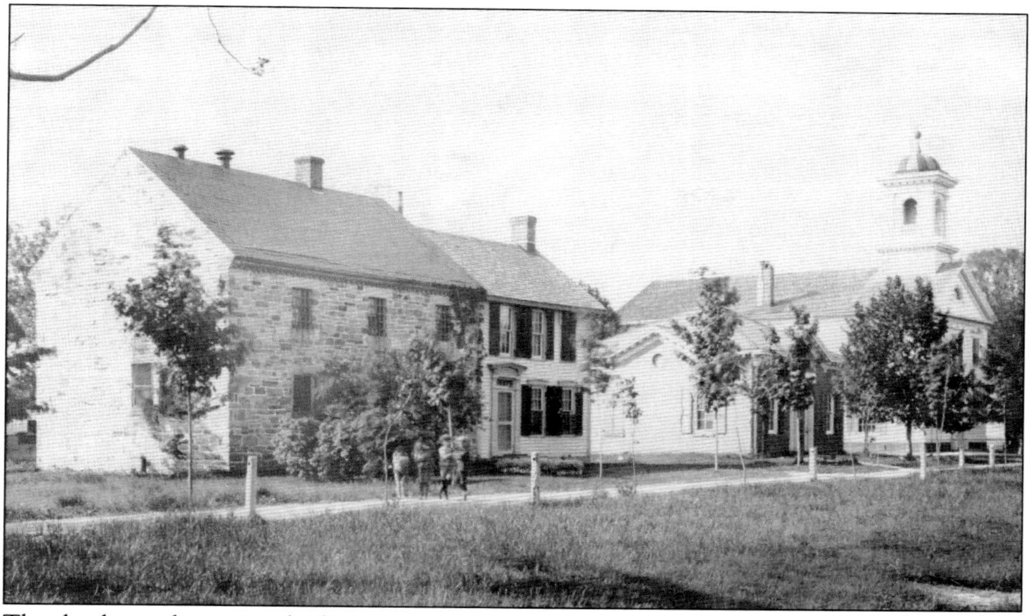

The third courthouse was built in Cape May Court House in 1850 at a cost of $6,200 on a one-acre lot donated in 1774 for that purpose by Daniel Hand. Seen to the far right in this c. 1900 photograph, it stands next to the one-story brick building erected in 1865 that contains both the surrogate's and clerk's offices. At the far left is the sheriff's office with an adjoining stone jail. (CMCHGS.)

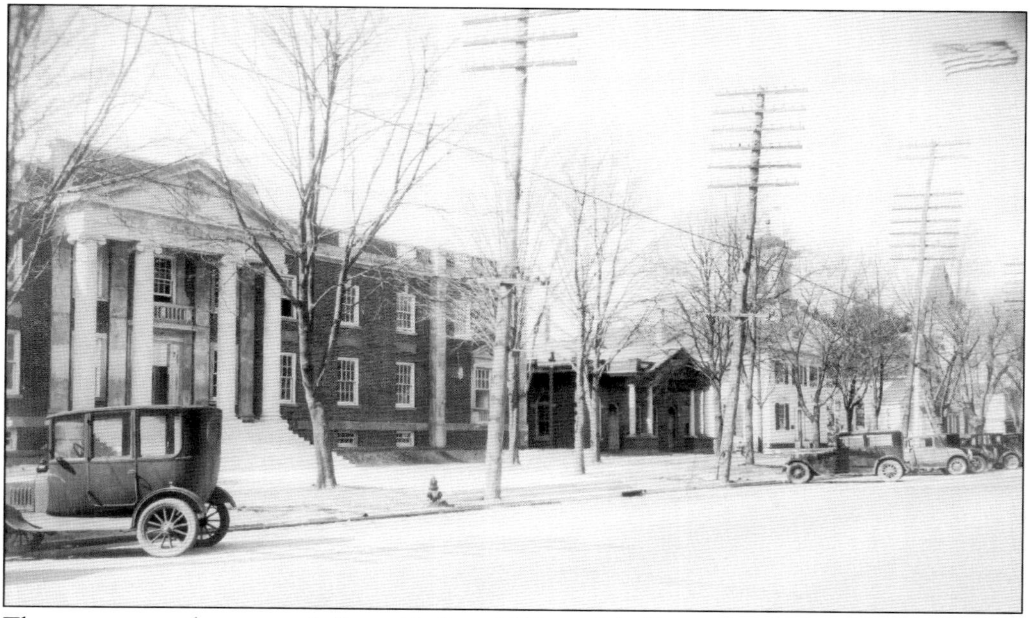

The present courthouse was dedicated in June 1927, roughly 18 months after construction began. The old 1850 courthouse was left on-site and the new one erected just south of it where the former jail and sheriff's office once stood. The dedication in Cape May Court House was marked with speeches, music, a lifesaving demonstration by the Avalon US Coast Guard crew, and several benedictions by local pastors. (CMCHGS.)

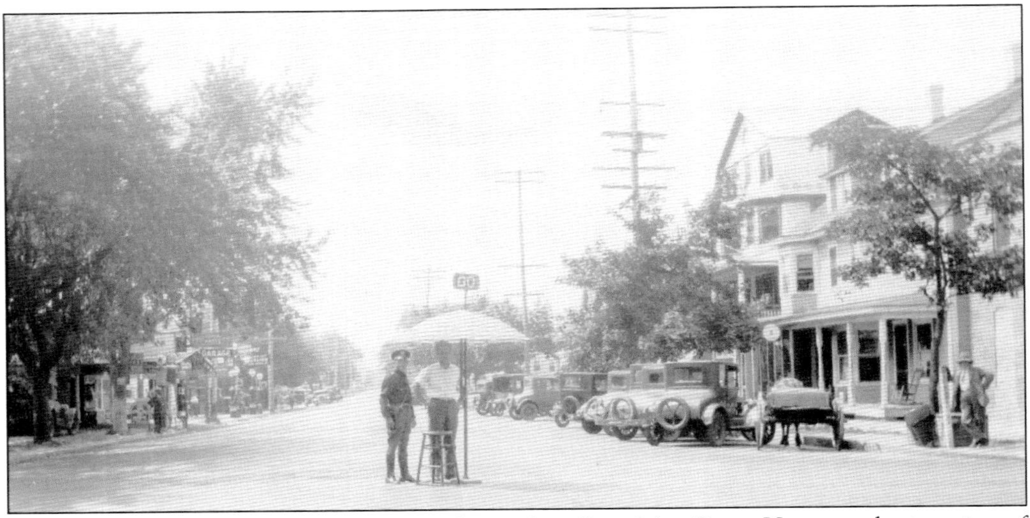

The first traffic "light" in the county was located in Cape May Court House at the junction of Mechanic and Main Streets. It consisted of a policeman who directed traffic by twirling a pole with "stop" and "go" signs mounted on top. This view, taken about 1925, looks south down Main Street and shows Fenton Yearicks manning the stop. (CMCHGS.)

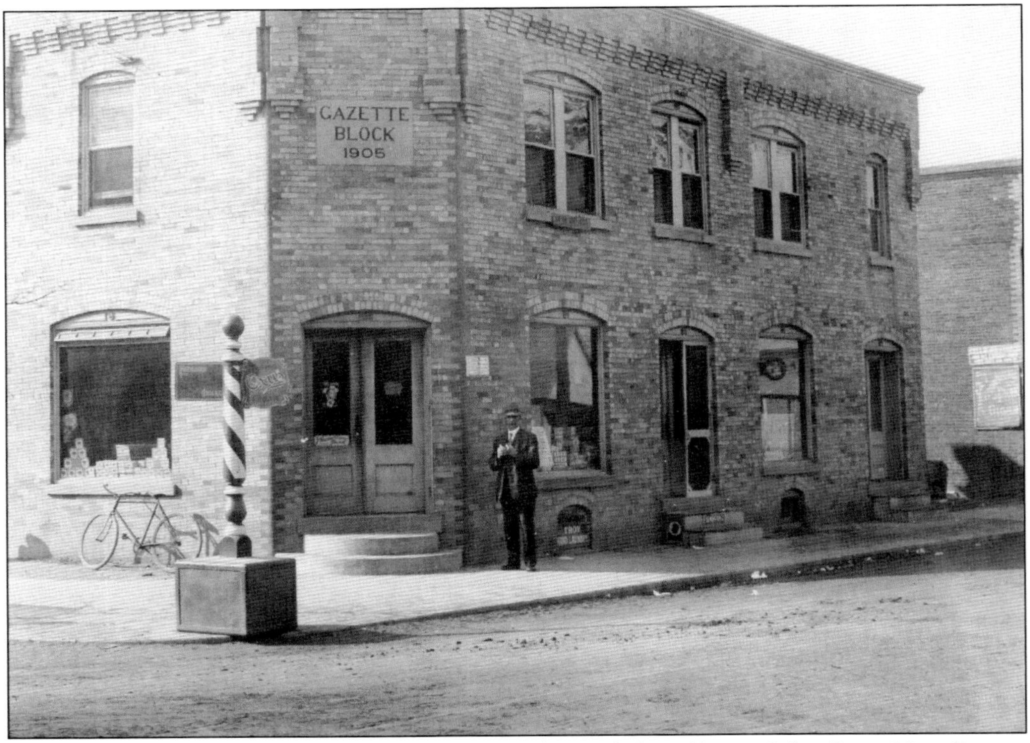

This brick building in Cape May Court House housed the offices of the *Cape May County Gazette*, a countywide newspaper founded in 1880. The original headquarters building, located at the southwest corner of Main and Mechanic Streets, burned to the ground in 1905 and was replaced with this structure. It was then replaced with a similar, but not identical, building in the early 21st century. (CMCHGS.)

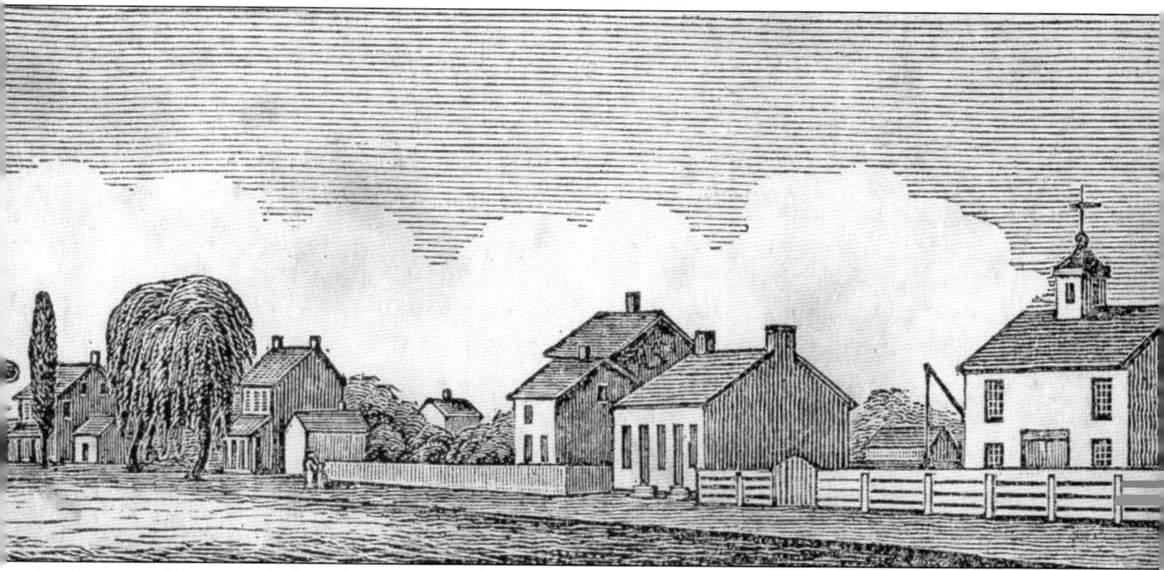

Barber and Howe included this black-and-white etching of Cape May Court House, the county seat, in their 1844 *Historical Collections of the State of New Jersey*. The book describes the village as containing a courthouse, a jail, the county offices, a Methodist and a Baptist church, and 30 or 40 dwellings. The book also comments that the Methodist church is fairly new, but the Baptist church is "ancient." The etching shows the 1774 courthouse at the far right. Next to it is a building with two front doors, with one leading into the surrogate's office and the other into the clerk's office. The next two buildings in the center of the view are probably the sheriff's office and an attached or offset jail. The two houses at the far left may have been taverns or inns, as suggested by the signs in front of them. The county buildings were erected on a one-acre lot donated for that purpose by Daniel Hand in 1774. At that time, the village was called "Middletown" because it was located roughly in the center of the county. (CMCHGS.)

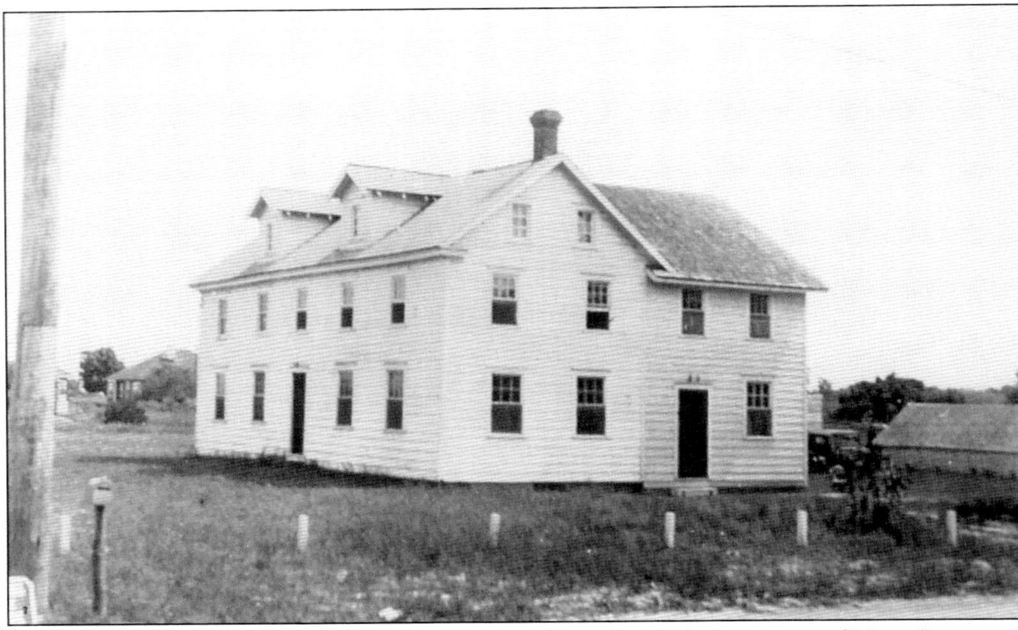

The Cornelius Hand House, built about 1880, stood at the southeast corner of Main Street and Stone Harbor Boulevard, across from the hospital in Cape May Court House. Today, a popular diner occupies the site. The land is part of a 1,000-acre farmstead Shamgar Hand purchased in the 1690s and named Romney Marsh after a marshy area in Kent County, England. (CMCHGS.)

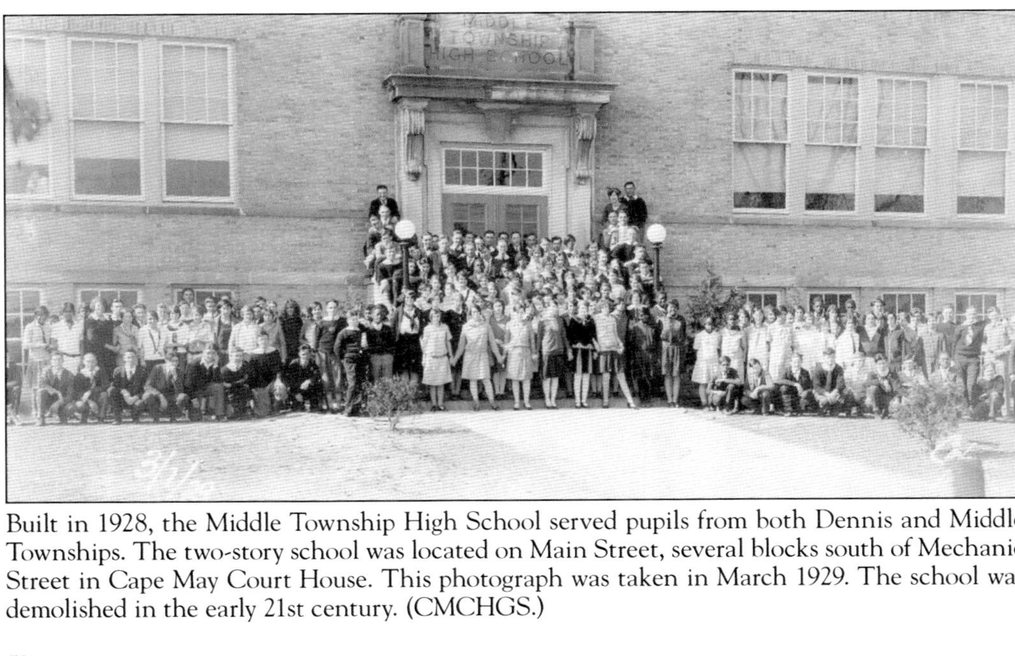

Built in 1928, the Middle Township High School served pupils from both Dennis and Middle Townships. The two-story school was located on Main Street, several blocks south of Mechanic Street in Cape May Court House. This photograph was taken in March 1929. The school was demolished in the early 21st century. (CMCHGS.)

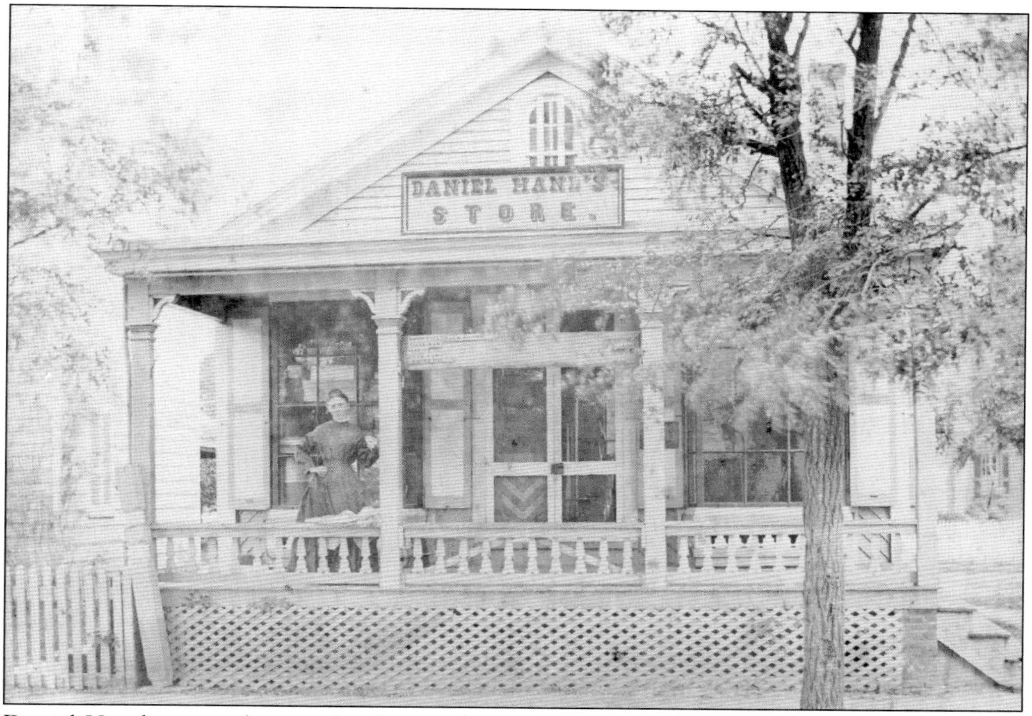

Daniel Hand operated a popular dry goods store, seen here about 1900, in Cape May Court House at the busy intersection of Mechanic, Dias Creek, and Goshen Roads. The identity of the young woman posing on the front porch is not known. Hand willed it to his wife in 1881 to operate or rent as she desired. The building is now a house, highly altered from its original appearance. (CMCHGS.)

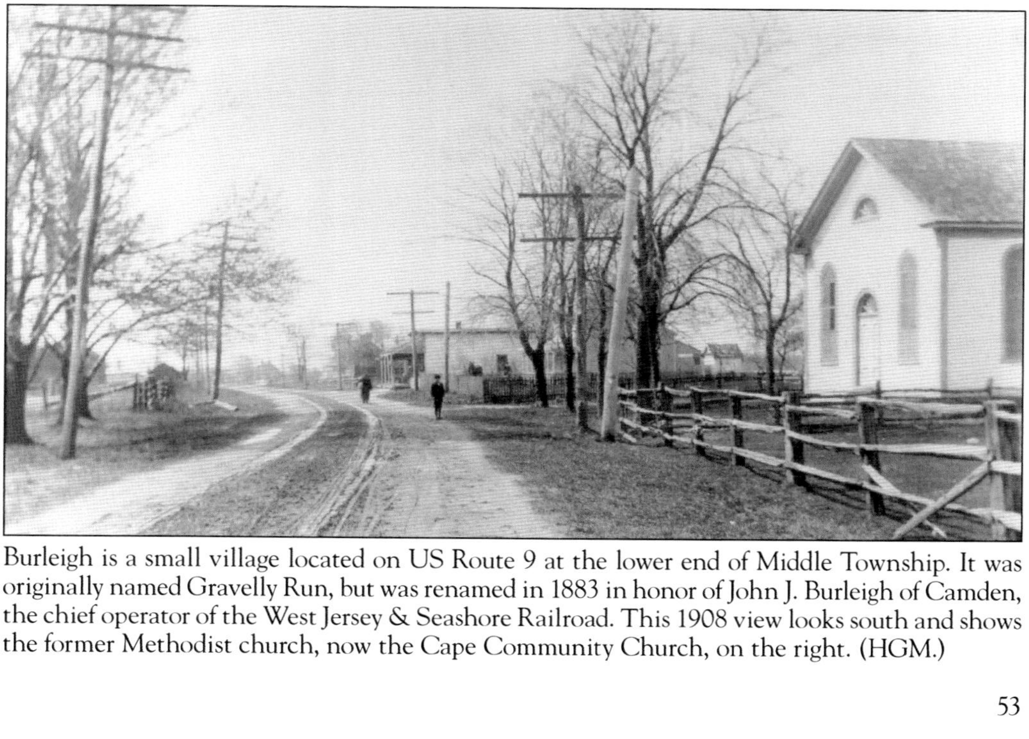

Burleigh is a small village located on US Route 9 at the lower end of Middle Township. It was originally named Gravelly Run, but was renamed in 1883 in honor of John J. Burleigh of Camden, the chief operator of the West Jersey & Seashore Railroad. This 1908 view looks south and shows the former Methodist church, now the Cape Community Church, on the right. (HGM.)

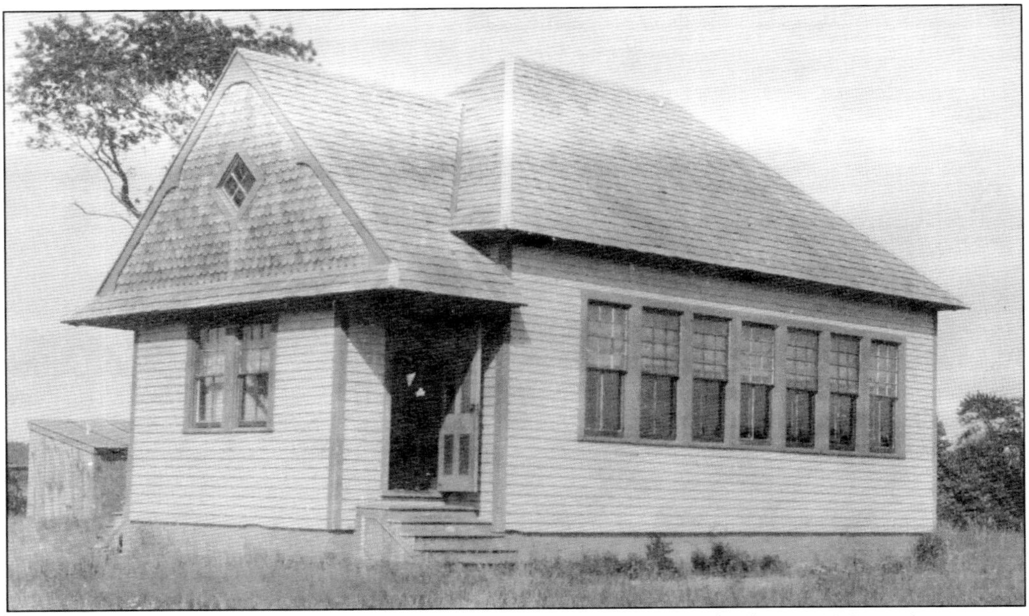

The one-room schoolhouse in Burleigh, Middle Township, was built in 1896; at the time, it was described as "neat and commodious." It was designed according to common architectural practices of the day for schools and featured a bank of windows that would provide proper lighting, tall ceilings for adequate ventilation, and separate entrances for boys and girls. It no longer stands. (CMCHGS.)

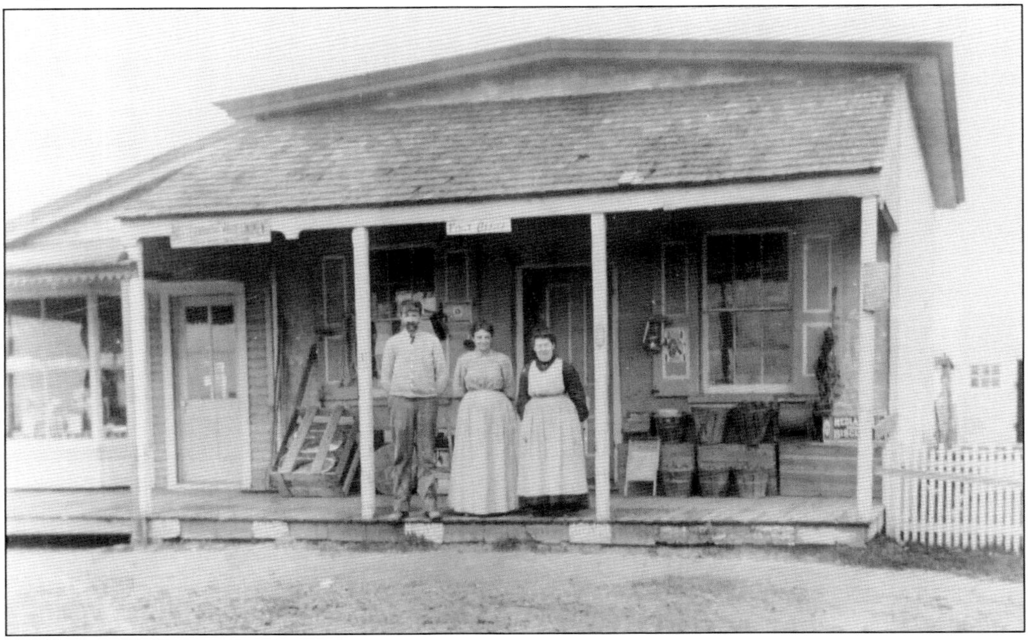

Taken in 1908, this photograph shows the general store in Burleigh that also acted as the post office, a typical commercial arrangement at the time. Burleigh's first post office had been established in 1886. The man seen here might be Garner T. Hand, who is cited as the postmaster of Burleigh in 1907. The two women are unidentified. (HGM.)

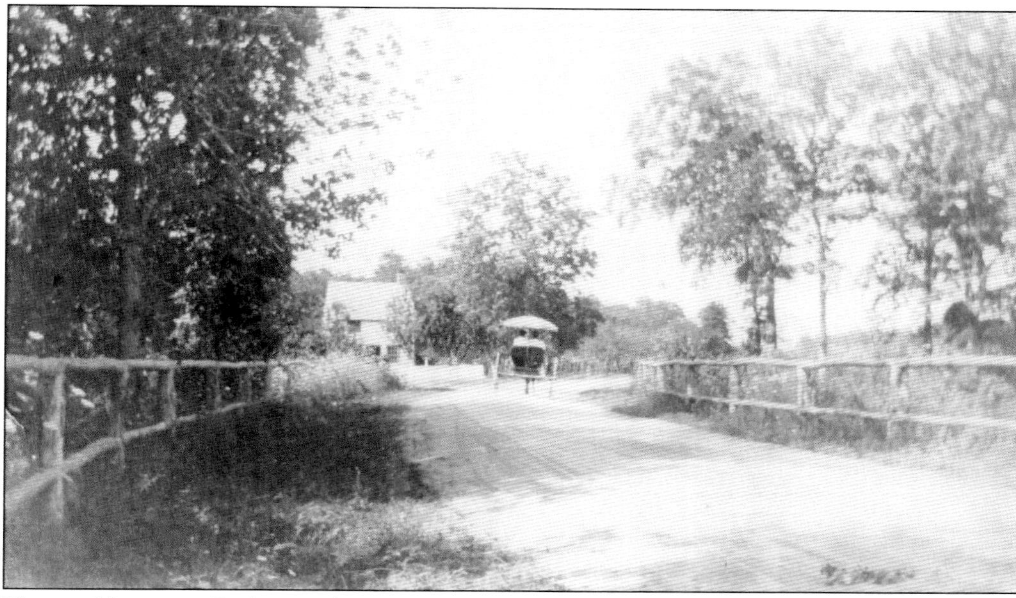

The road between Goshen and Cape May Court House is as picturesque today as when it was photographed about 1900. The exact view is not identified on the photograph, but it appears to show the sharp turn in the road where a gristmill once stood halfway between these two Middle Township villages. (CMCHGS.)

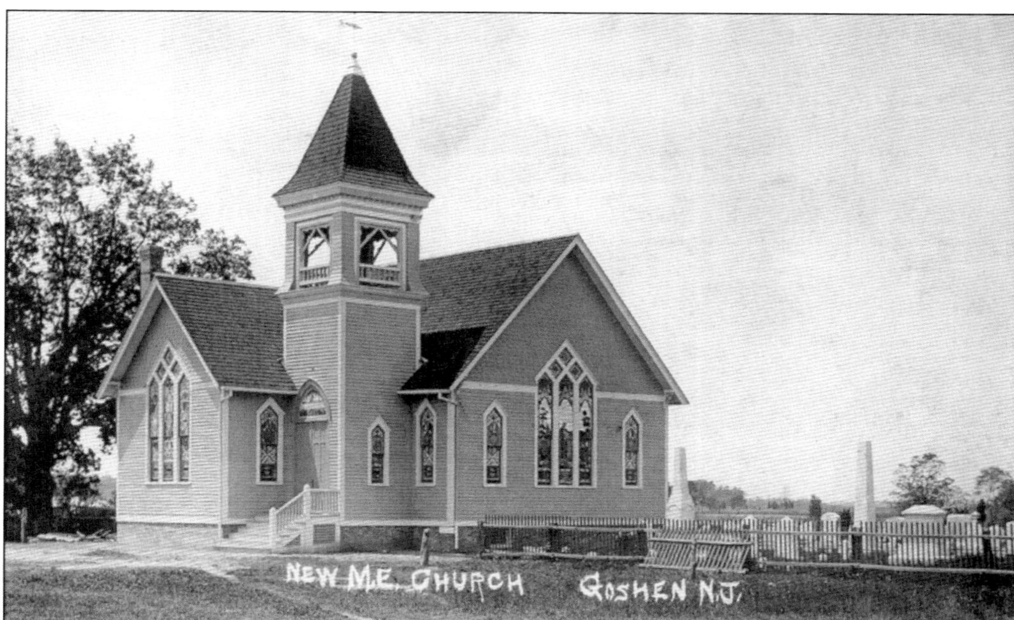

The first Methodist Episcopal church in Goshen was organized in 1839 as the spread of Methodism through Cape May County led to the construction of 11 churches before the Civil War, more than twice the number of Baptist meetinghouses. The new Methodist Episcopal church, seen here, was built in 1910. Now the Goshen United Methodist Church, it still stands. (George Brewer.)

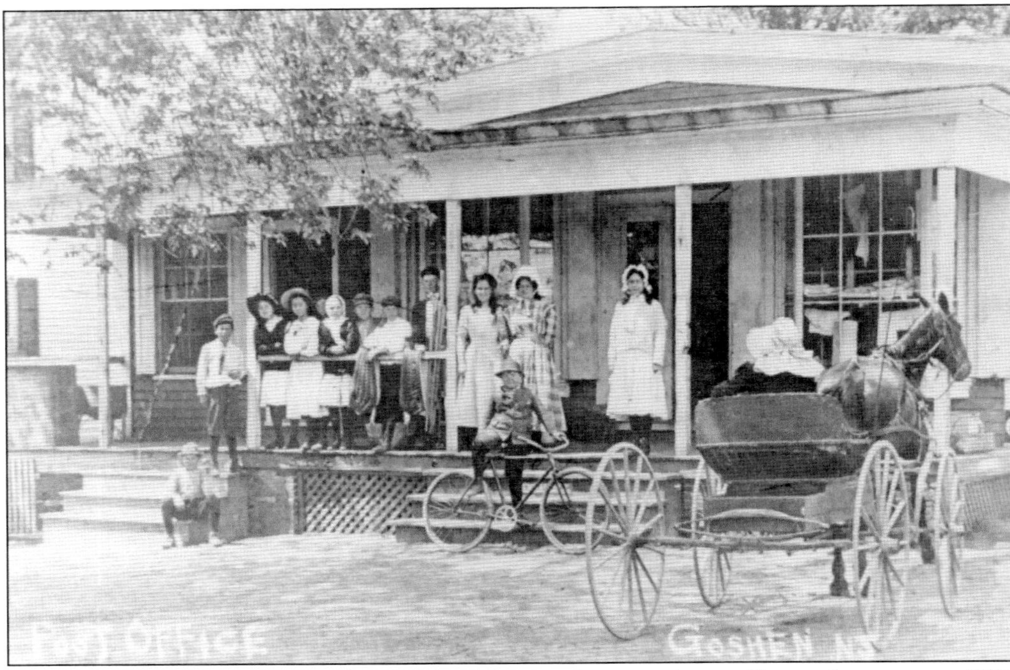

Youngsters from Goshen pose in front of Smith's general store and post office in the summer of 1917. The post office operated out of this building from 1909 until it burned in the winter of 1922. A new store erected on the same site continued to serve as the post office until 1949. (CMCHGS.)

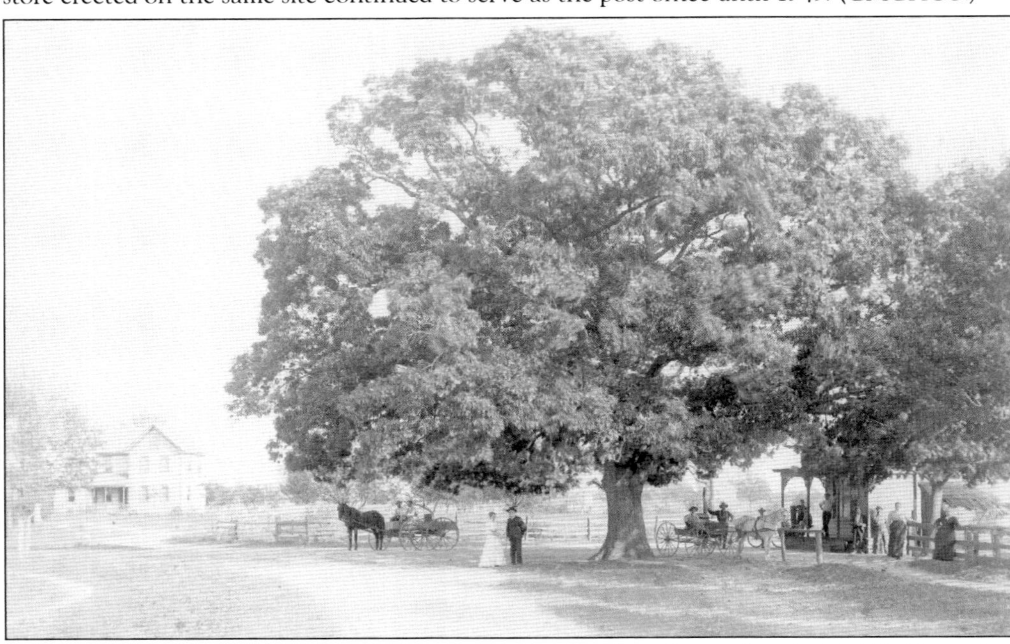

This great oak tree originally stood on Bayshore Road in Green Creek, Middle Township. Woodrow Wilson reportedly gave a campaign speech under its boughs, probably when he was running for governor of New Jersey, a position he held from 1911 until 1913. He then served as the 28th president of the United States from 1913 until 1921. (CMCHGS.)

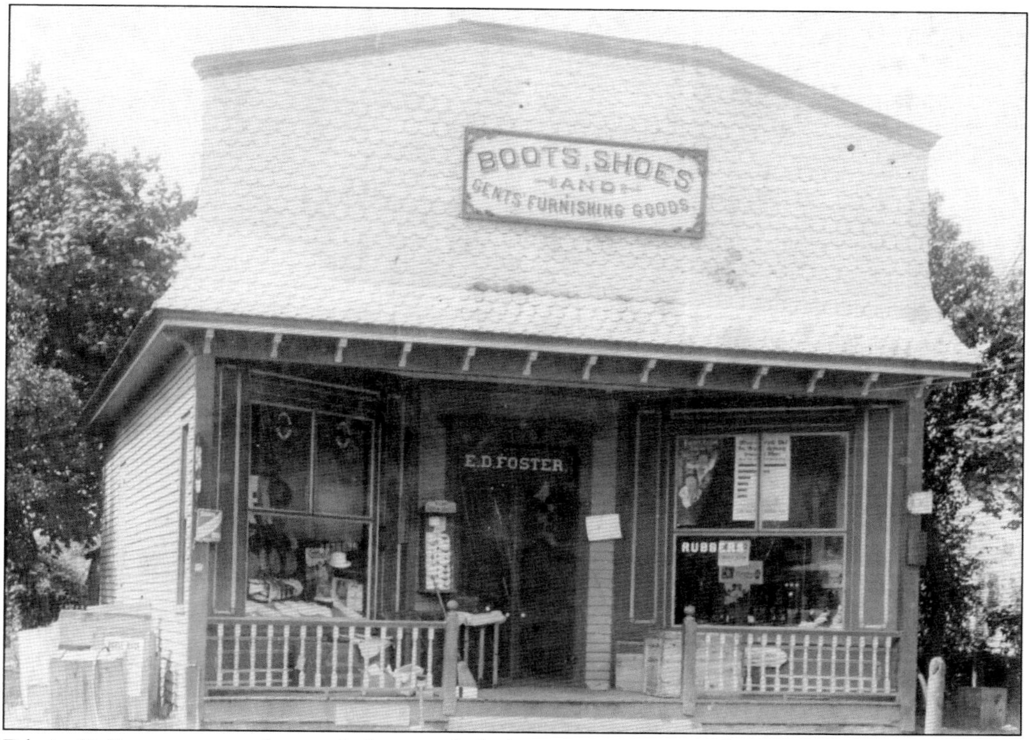

Edwin D. Foster operated a men's shoes and clothing store opposite the site of the present county library on Mechanic Street in Cape May Court House in the early 1900s. On display in the shop windows are a variety of men's shoes, caps, hats, "Arrow Brand" collars, and neckties. A sign in the window advertises "Educator shoes," made by Rice & Hutchins, a large Boston shoe manufacturer. (CMCHGS.)

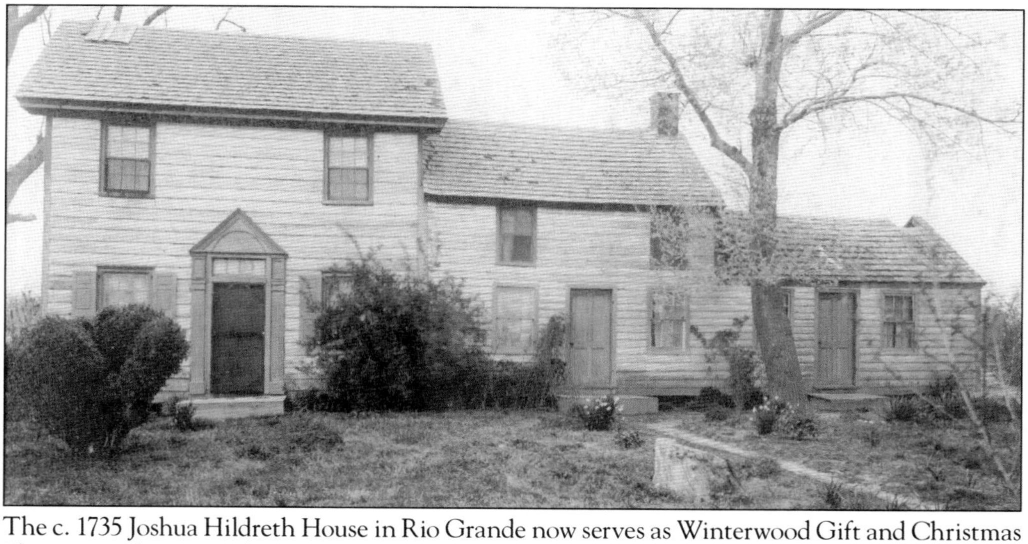

The c. 1735 Joshua Hildreth House in Rio Grande now serves as Winterwood Gift and Christmas Shoppe on the west side of US Route 9. Local lore claims that the mantel in the tallest section was carved by a British deserter who was given refuge in the house during the Revolutionary War. (CMCHGS.)

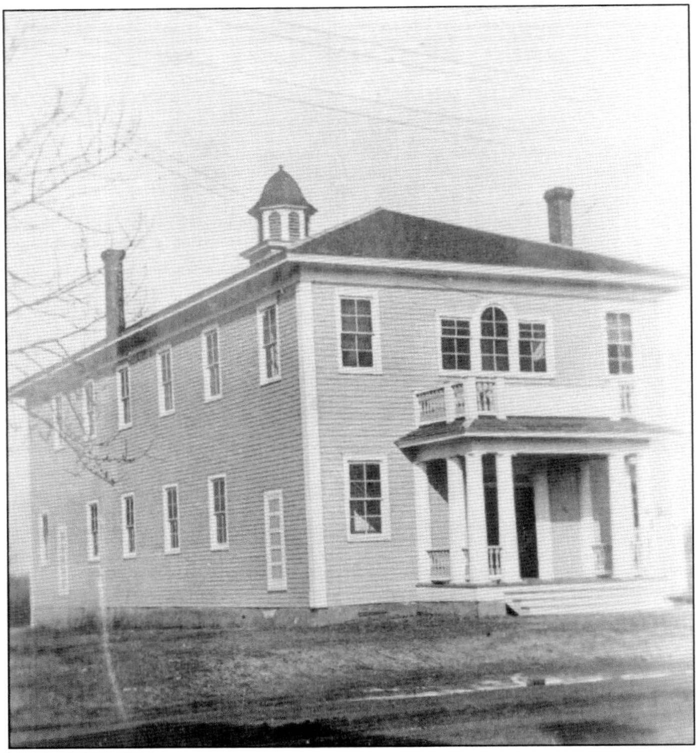

This building, pictured in 1923, was built about 1910 for the Rio Grande Chapter of the National Grange of the Order of Patrons of Husbandry. Locally, it was known as the Grange. This fraternal organization promoted the economic and political well-being of the community and agriculture. Granges were also community centers, hosting dinners, meetings, and parties. (CMCHGS.)

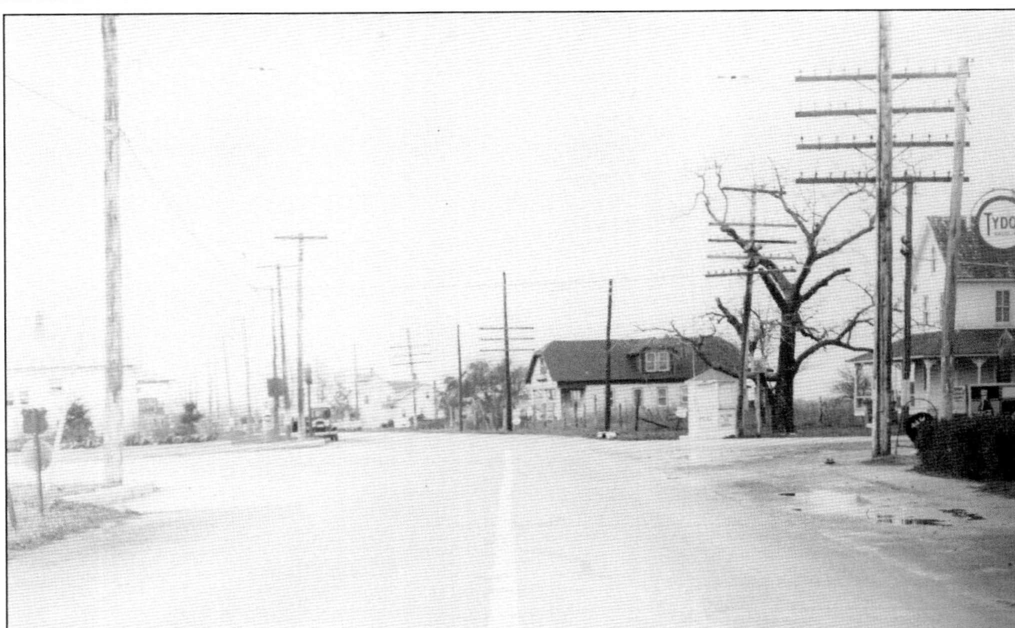

This photograph, taken November 29, 1935, shows the intersection of State Route 47 and US Route 9, and looks north on Route 9 in Rio Grande. Today, this area houses the largest concentration of commercial buildings in Cape May County, including Lowe's, Wawa, Kmart, and Walmart. None of the buildings seen here still stand. (CMCHGS.)

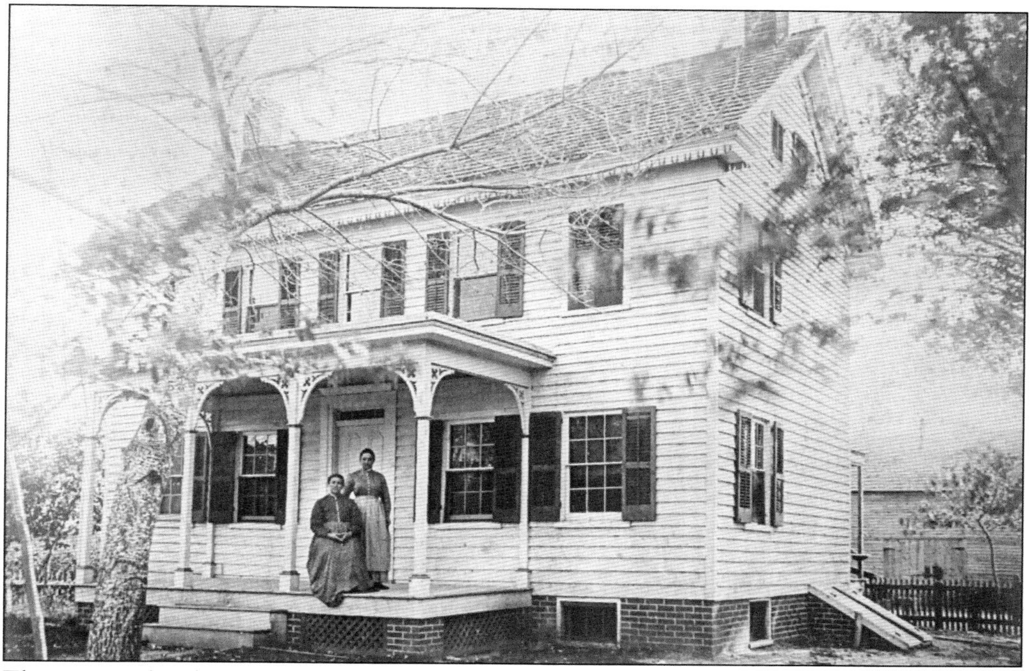

This c. 1850 farmhouse and barn, built by Ephraim Hildreth III, once stood where the present Walmart is located in Rio Grande, Middle Township. The women posing on the front porch in this c. 1900 photograph are Tabitha Hildreth (left) and her daughter, Allena (right). (J.P. Hand.)

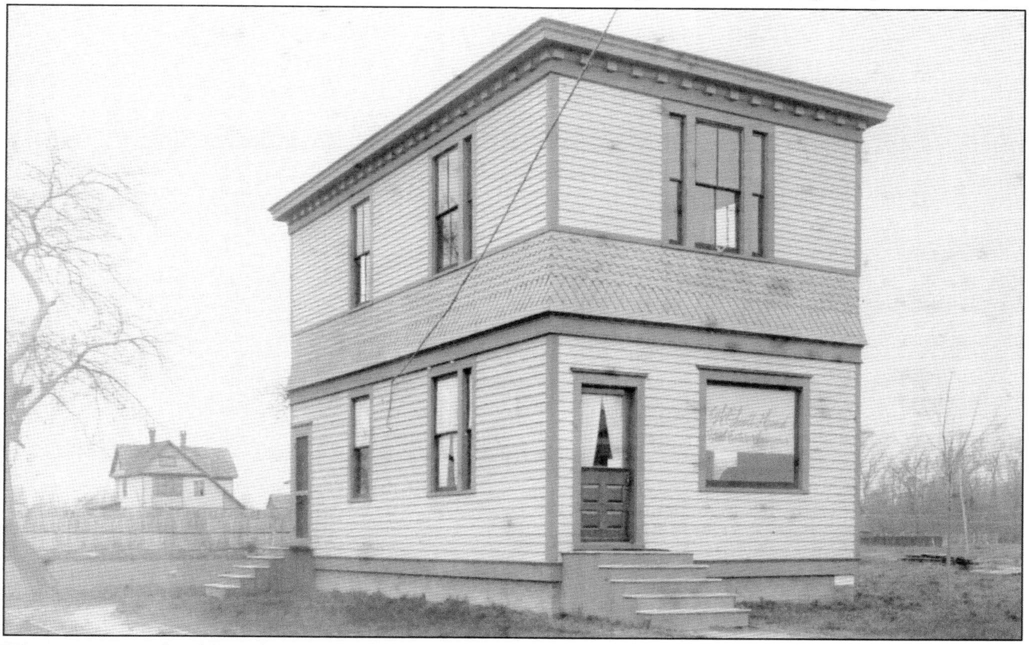

W. Scott Hand sold real estate and insurance out of this two-story office located in Cape May Court House, seen here in the 1880s. Hand also worked in the county clerk's office for a number of years before moving to Ocean City around 1890. The building still stands at the corner of Church and Main Streets and houses an insurance company. (CMCHGS.)

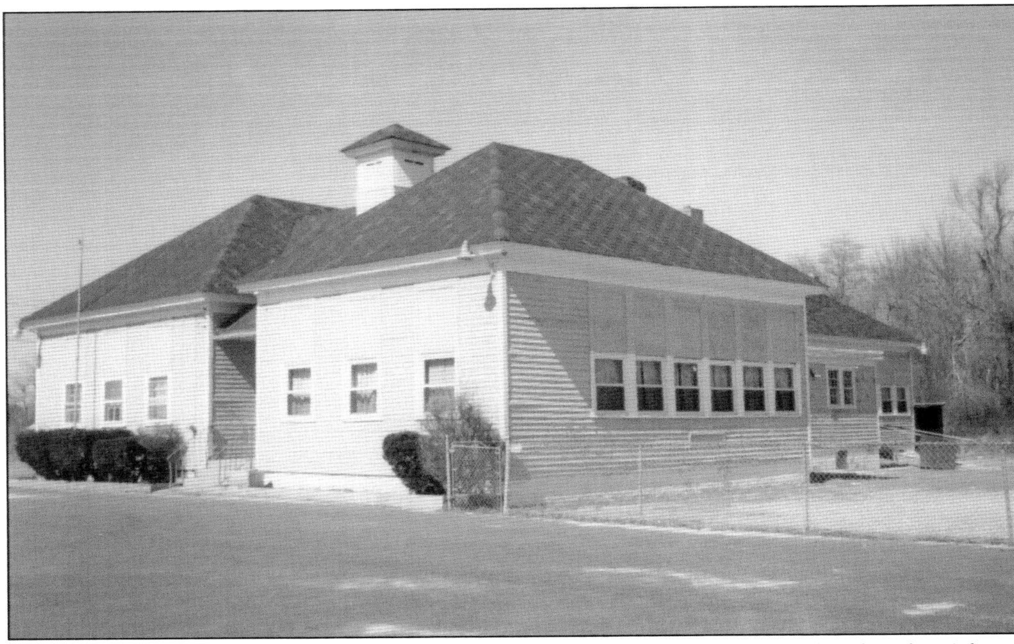

The Whitesboro public school was built about 1911 to serve the children who lived in this African American community just north of Rio Grande in Middle Township. The town was founded in 1901 by George Henry White, an African American from Philadelphia who bought about 2,000 acres here expressly to create a "rural settlement of Negroes." (CMCHGS.)

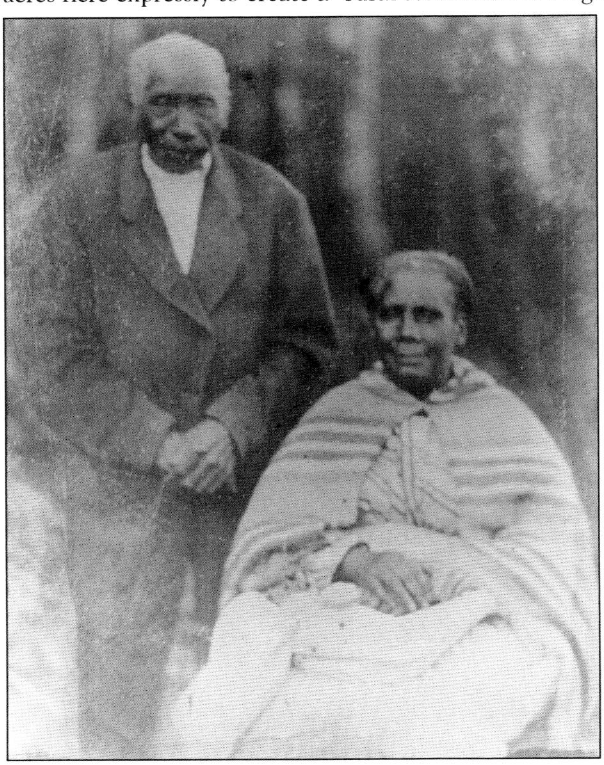

Ishmael Armour and his wife, Julia, pose for the camera about 1880. Armour was born a slave in 1801, but was manumitted in 1826 by his owner, John Townsend, who lived in Middle Township. Ishmael and Julia raised a family of seven children near Goshen and are buried in Old Wesley Cemetery, a few miles east of that small village. (CMCHGS.)

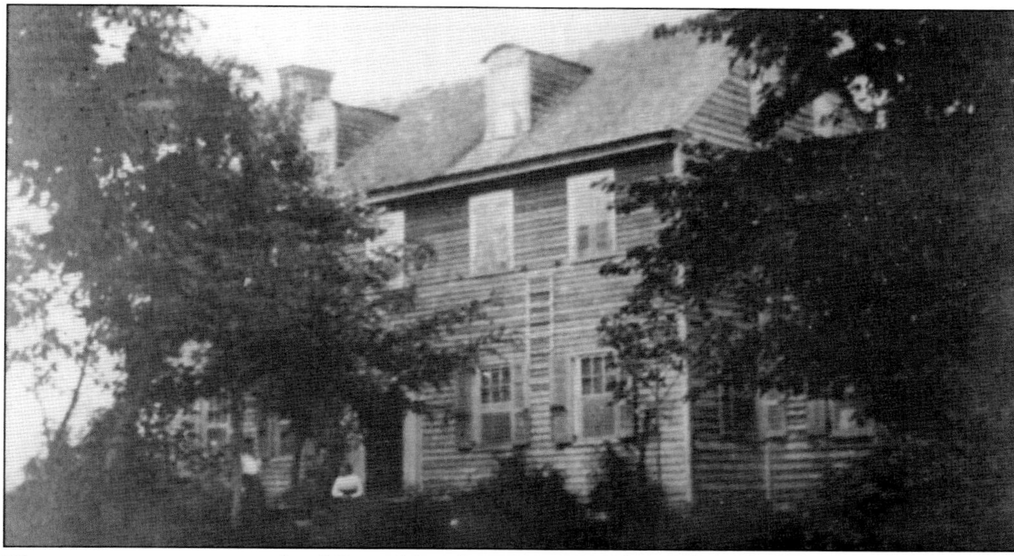

The county museum north of Cape May Court House is housed in the Cresse-Holmes House, seen here about 1890. The rear section was built about 1704 by John Cresse while the two-and-a-half-story main block (shown here) was built about 1815 by Robert Morris Holmes. Holmes was an innovative farmer and state assemblyman, and he held a patent on a self-righting surfboat made of cedar and used for lifesaving. (CMCHGS.)

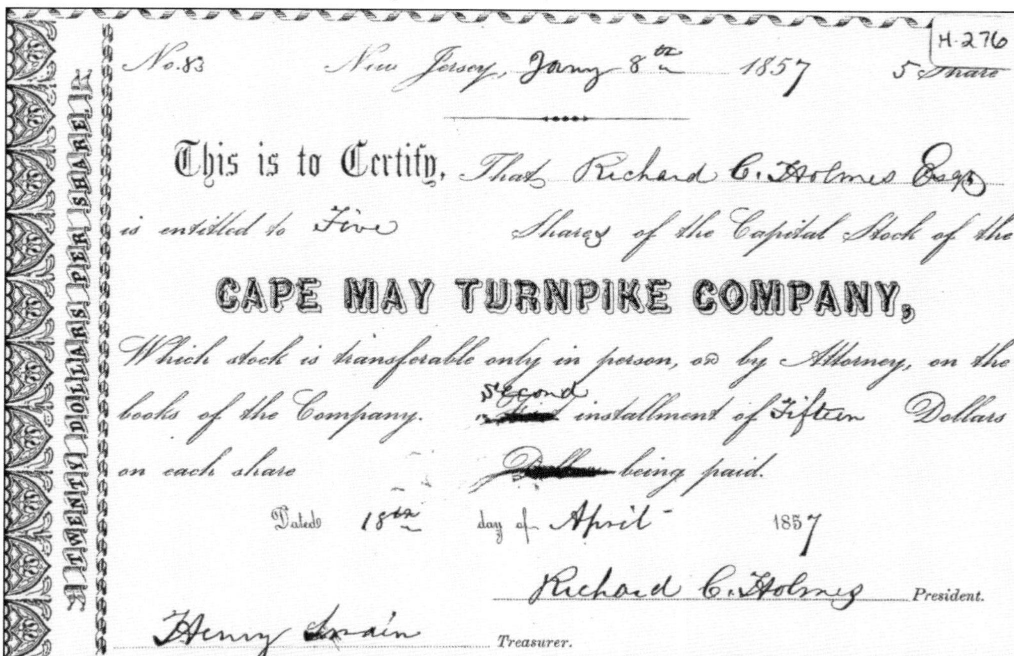

H-276

No. 83 New Jersey, Jany 8th 1857 5 Share

TWENTY DOLLARS PER SHARE

This is to Certify, That Richard C. Holmes Esqr is entitled to Five Shares of the Capital Stock of the

CAPE MAY TURNPIKE COMPANY,

Which stock is transferable only in person, or by Attorney, on the books of the Company. Second installment of Fifteen Dollars on each share being paid.

Dated 18th day of April 1857

Richard C. Holmes President.

Henry Swain Treasurer.

A group of influential county businessmen incorporated the Cape May Turnpike Company in 1854, building a toll road between Cape May Court House and Cape May City, roughly along the path of present-day US Route 9. Opponents of the new road built a toll-free road called the "Shunpike," which still exists. The turnpike was not highly profitable because the roadbed continually washed away, requiring costly repairs to rebuild it. (CMCHGS.)

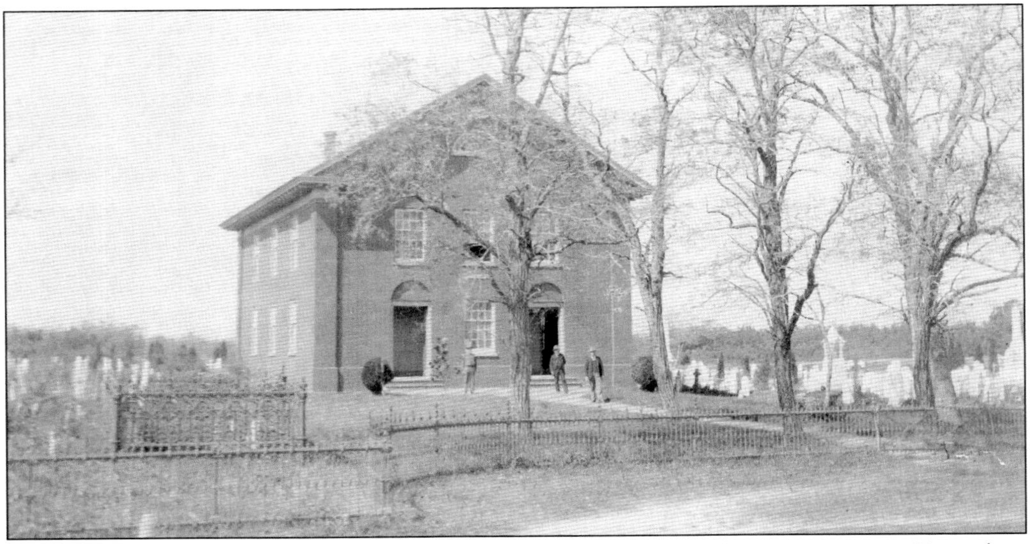

Cold Spring Presbyterian Church, known as Old Brick, was founded in 1714 in Lower Township. Its current building, seen here in the early 1900s, was built in the Federal style in 1823 and stands on the west side of Seashore Road. Legend says that five presidents worshipped here—Benjamin Harrison, Lincoln, Pierce, Taft, and Wilson. More Mayflower descendants are buried in its cemetery than anywhere outside of Massachusetts. (CMCHGS.)

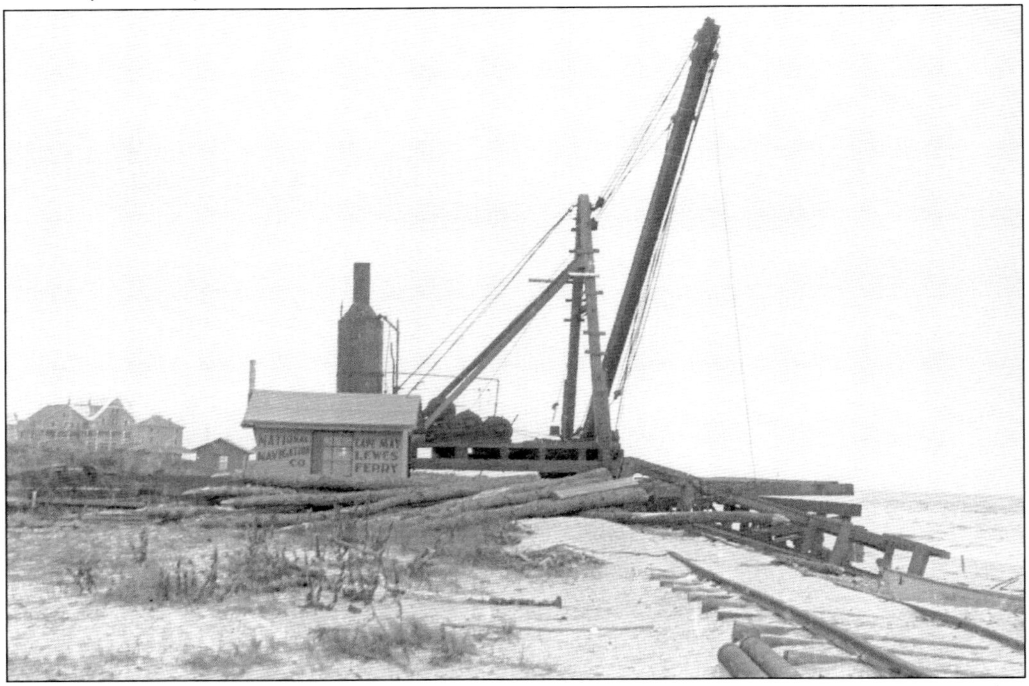

Baltimore entrepreneur Jesse Rosenfeld formed the National Navigation Company, seen in this c. 1926 photograph by Isaac Zwalley, and purchased the *Atlantus,* one of several World War I concrete ships. He moored her near the former steamboat landing site in Lower Township with plans to use her as part of a ferry terminal. However, she broke free during a storm and partially sank just off the beach where she still rests. (HGM.)

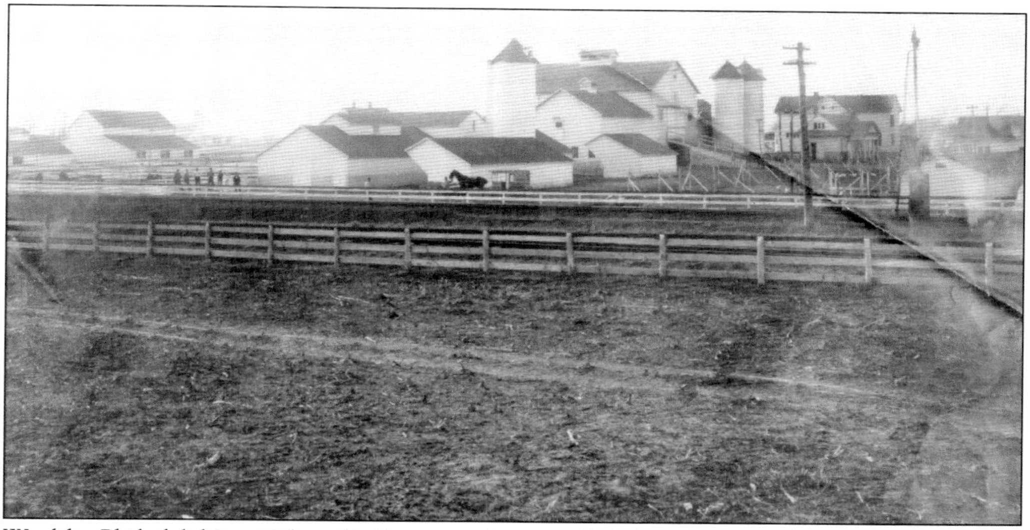

Wealthy Philadelphian Nelson Z. Graves took over a failed housing development in East Cape May around 1910 and also built a large farm in Lower Township on the east side of Seashore Road. This view, looking west over his farm, shows tracks for both the Atlantic City and the West Jersey Railroads that ran parallel to each other here on their way to Cape May. Graves went bankrupt, losing everything. (CMCHGS.)

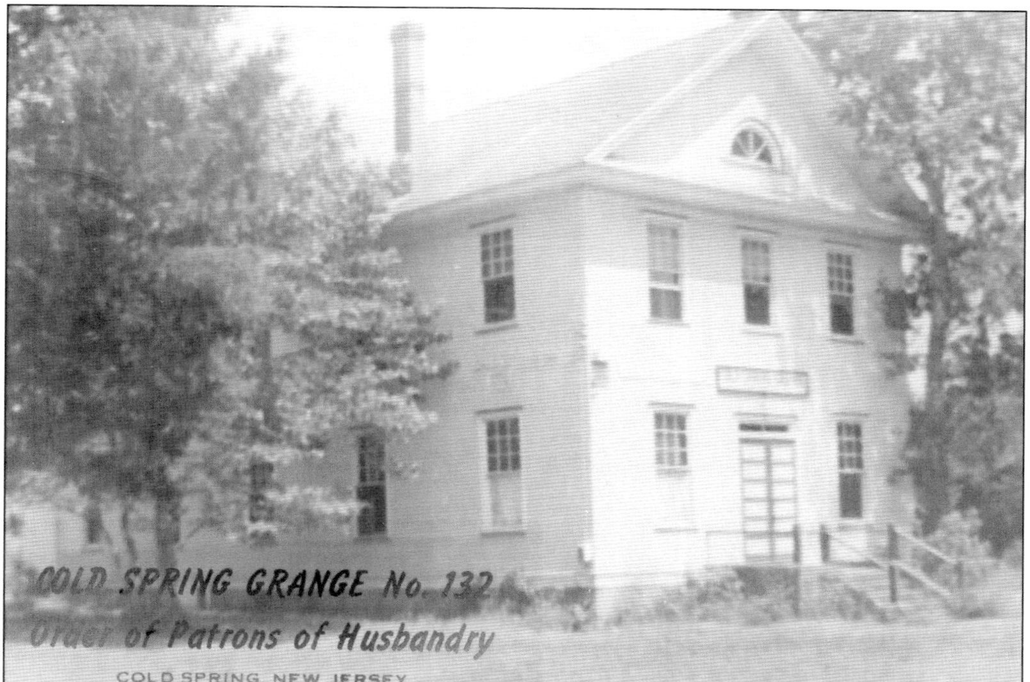

Cold Spring Grange No. 132 was built in 1912 as a meeting hall that served as a political, business, educational, and social organization for local farmers and residents until about 1970. Lecture topics included poultry raising, potato growing, and manure saving. Today, the building serves as a restaurant at Historic Cold Spring Village, a living history museum village listed in the New Jersey Register of Historic Places. (CMCHGS.)

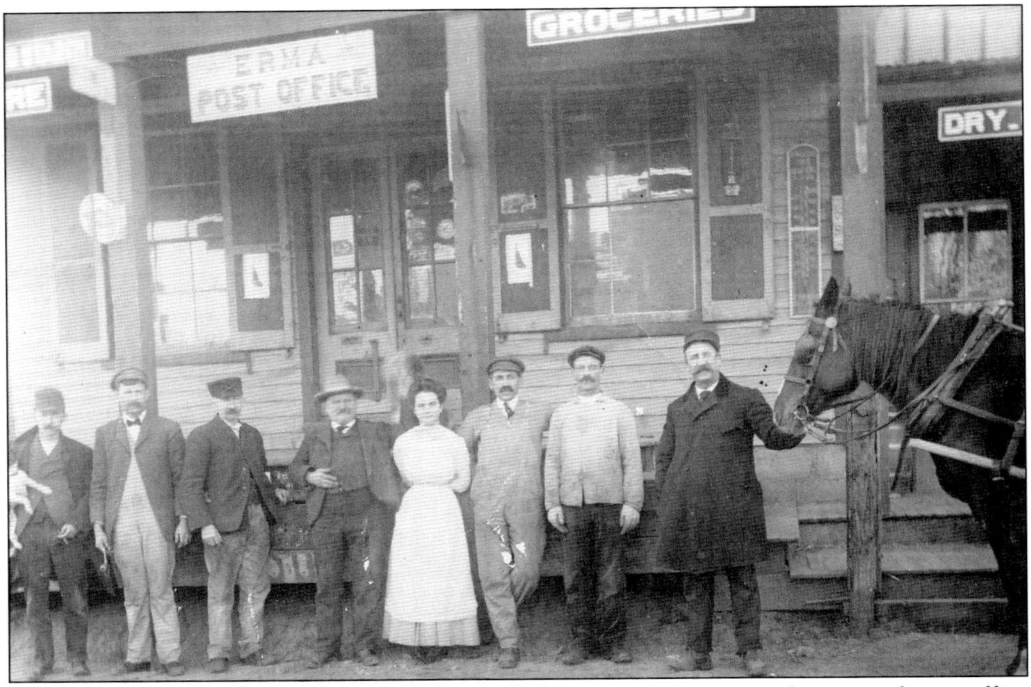

Reuben Townsend Johnson (fourth from the left) operated this general store and post office at Bennett's Station near Erma in Lower Township. Standing next to him is Edna Weeks, and next to her is Augustus H. Swain, Johnson's son-in-law. Levi Dickinson holds the horse; the others are unidentified. The photograph was taken after the 1898 opening of the Erma Post Office. (CMCHGS.)

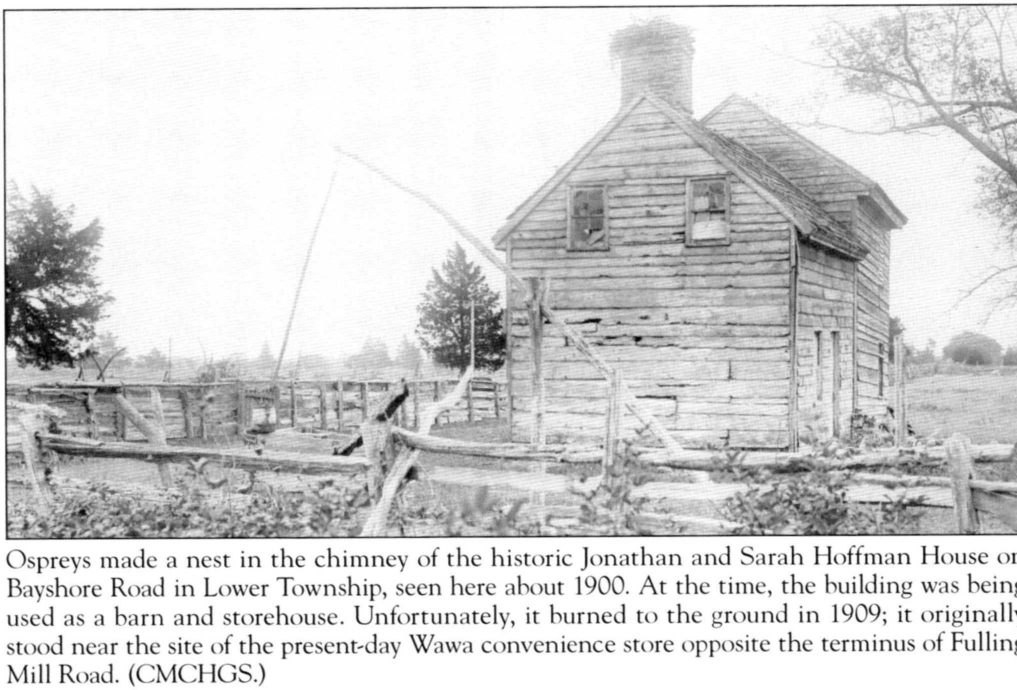

Ospreys made a nest in the chimney of the historic Jonathan and Sarah Hoffman House on Bayshore Road in Lower Township, seen here about 1900. At the time, the building was being used as a barn and storehouse. Unfortunately, it burned to the ground in 1909; it originally stood near the site of the present-day Wawa convenience store opposite the terminus of Fulling Mill Road. (CMCHGS.)

Four

Seaside Resorts

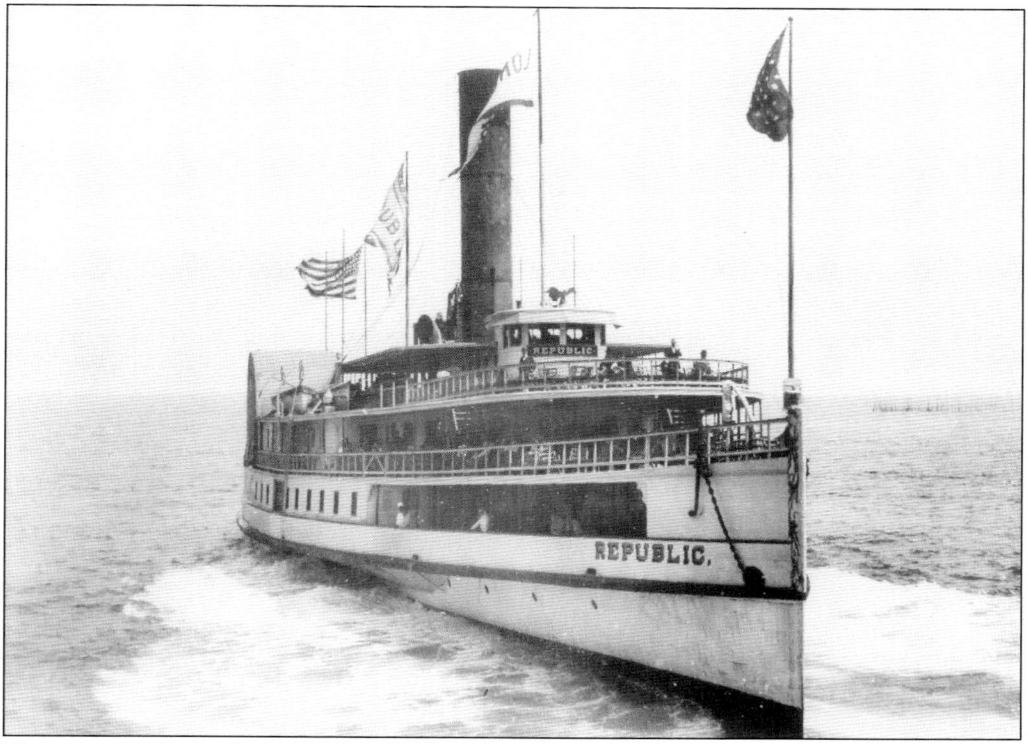

The elegant sidewheel steamer *Republic* took her maiden voyage from Philadelphia to Cape May in March 1878. Vacationers paid $1 (round-trip) for the six-hour journey while enjoying fully furnished salons, 16 staterooms, and 2 private parlors on its three decks capable of handling 2,500 passengers. The return trip offered an oyster supper, a full brass band, and orchestra music for dancing. She was retired in 1903. (HGM.)

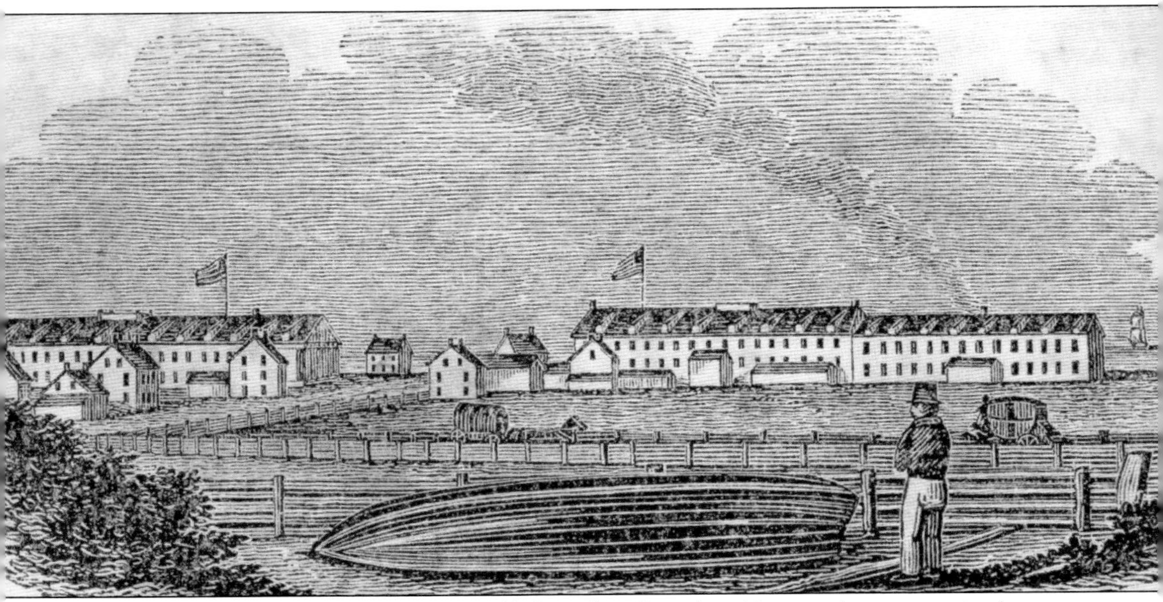

Cape Island, as Cape May City was called until 1869, is the oldest seashore resort in the country. During the Revolutionary War, Lower Township resident Robert Parsons advertised the sale of a house and 254 acres "open to the sea . . . and within One Mile and a Half of the Sea Shore; where a Number resort for Health, and bathing in the Water; and this Place would be very convenient for taking in such people." This 1844 etching is the earliest depiction of Cape May's first hotels. The view faces the ocean, where two tall ships sail. Seen are several two-story private residences, many of which boarded visitors in the summer months. Also seen are two of the city's hotels. Their plain, bland architecture was typical of the resort's early lodging. In 1844, the city was described as having about 50 houses, many of them occupied by Delaware River pilot boat captains. (CMCHGS.)

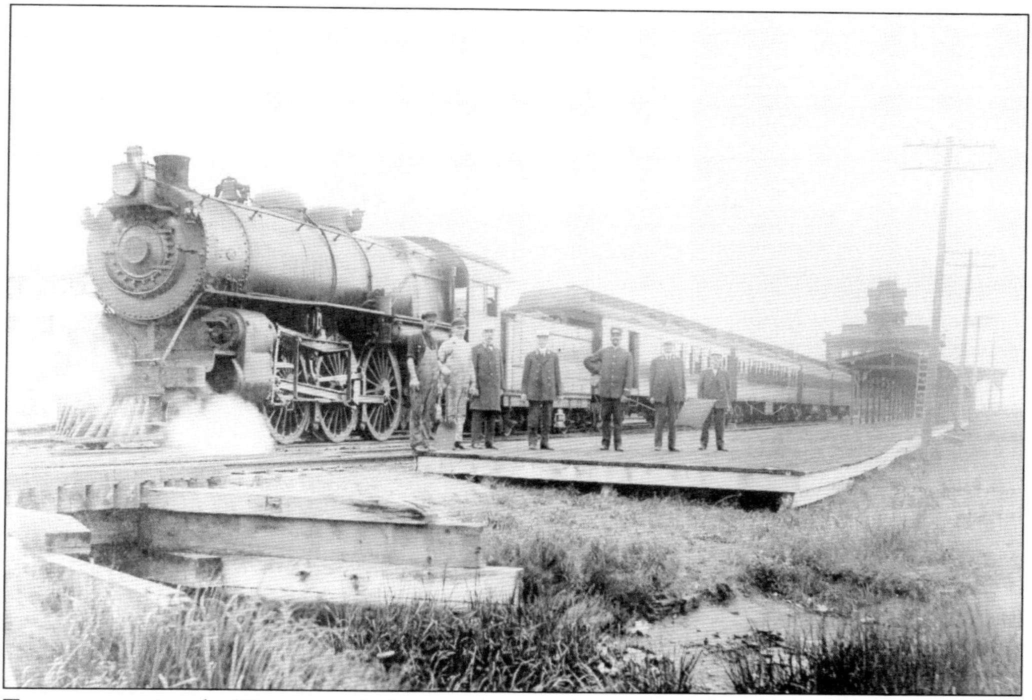

Trainmen serving the West Jersey & Seashore Railroad stand on the platform at Cape May's Grant Street Station next to Pennsylvania Railroad locomotive No. 2125 about 1912. The station, seen in the distance, was built in 1876 by the railroad at a cost of $20,000. Used only in the summer, it became known as the "summer station." It was demolished in 1934. (HGM.)

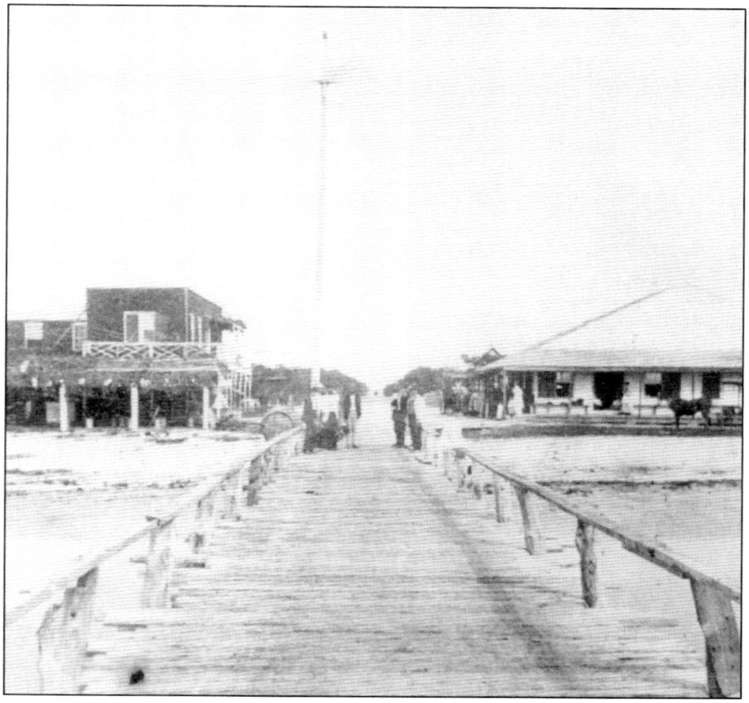

Steamboat Landing, a wharf located at the west end of Sunset Boulevard, is seen here in the 1870s. These two buildings catered to passengers arriving by boat, offering them accommodations, food, and spirituous liquors as they waited for carriages to take them overland to Cape May, a distance of about three miles. By the 1880s, the trip was accomplished by rail instead of horse-drawn carriage. (CMCHGS.)

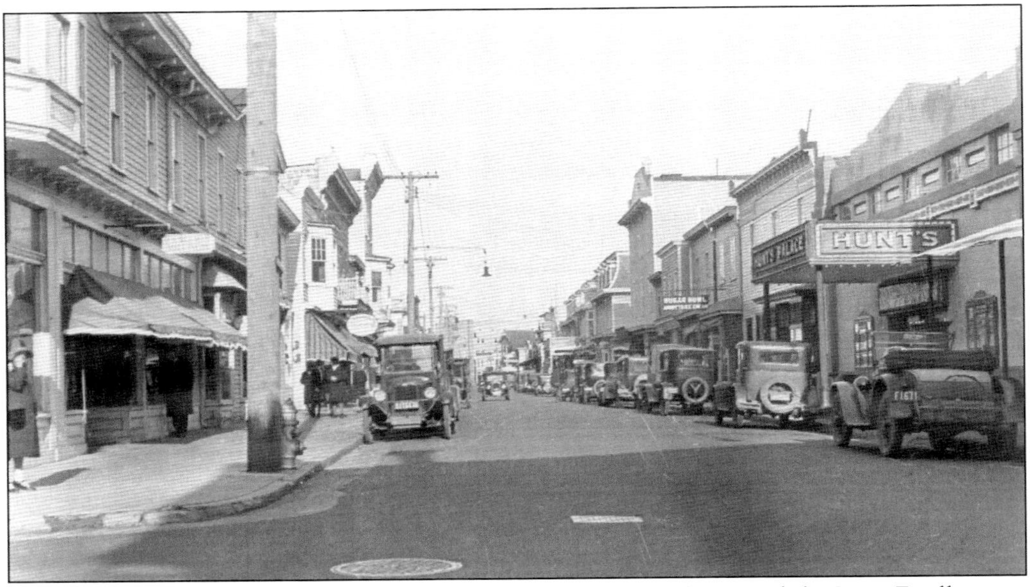

Hunt's Palace movie theater, seen to the right in this c. 1930 photograph by Isaac Zwalley, was located on Washington Street near Congress Hall in Cape May City. This view looks almost north up Washington Street and shows the great variety of shops, stores, and entertainment available to locals and visitors alike. Many of these buildings still stand, but most have been highly altered. (HGM.)

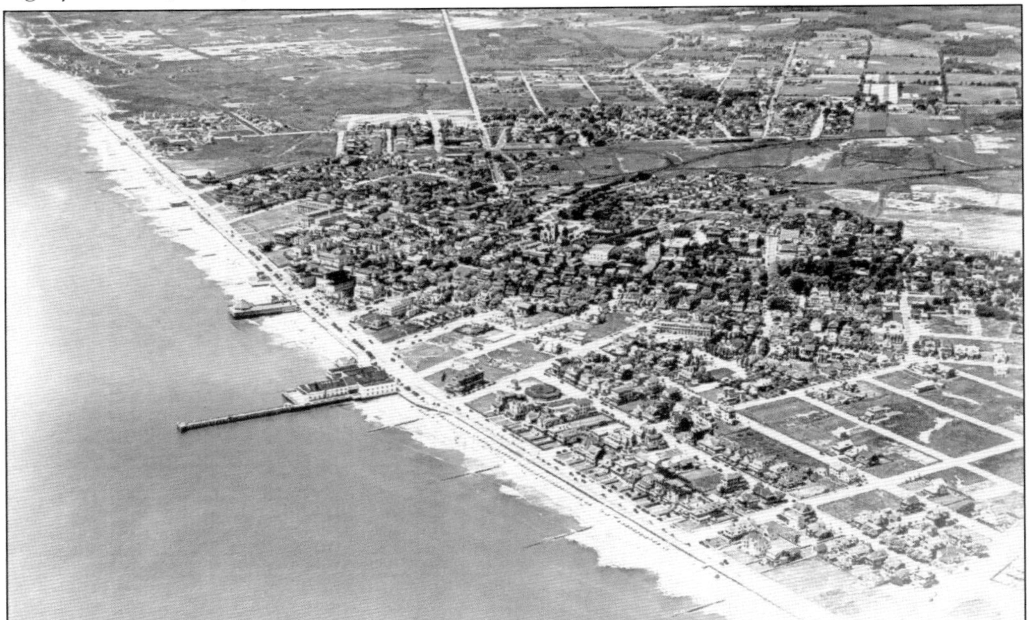

This aerial photograph, with a view looking west, shows Cape May City and environs in August 1932. Convention Hall and its pier stand opposite the former site of the Stockton Hotel—demolished in 1910—upon which only a few new buildings had been erected. The road to Steamboat Landing, now Sunset Boulevard, makes a straight line from the city to the shores of the Delaware Bay. (HGM.)

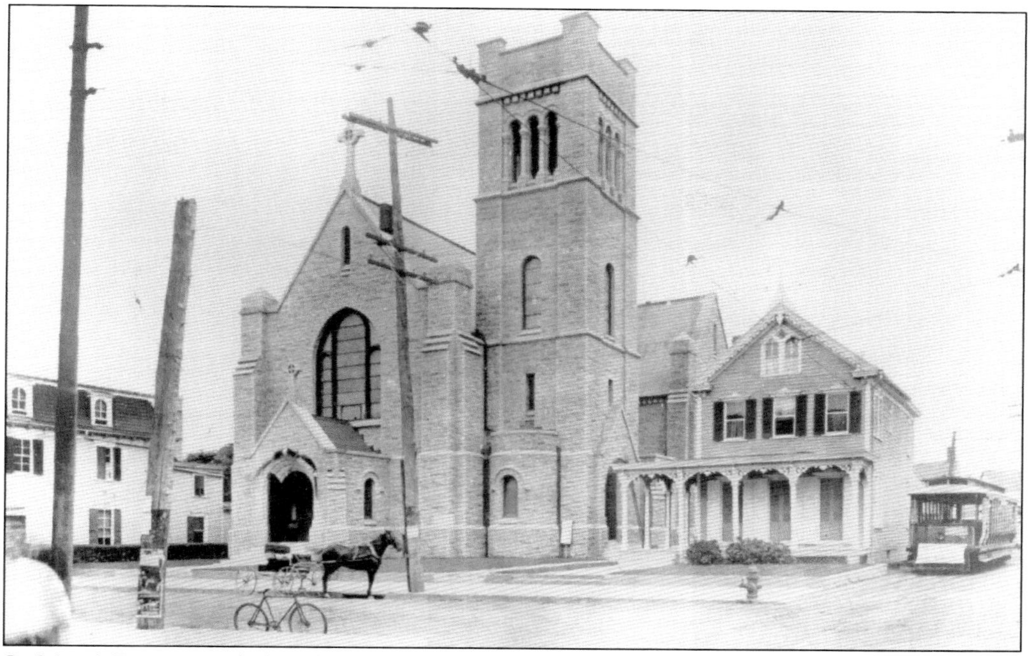

St. Mary's Roman Catholic Church, seen here about 1915, was built in 1911 and still stands at the corner of Washington and Ocean Streets in Cape May City. It was designed by George Lovatt, the architect of many of Philadelphia's most important Catholic churches. William McShane, a Philadelphia building contractor, oversaw the construction. The buildings on either side of the church no longer stand. (HGM.)

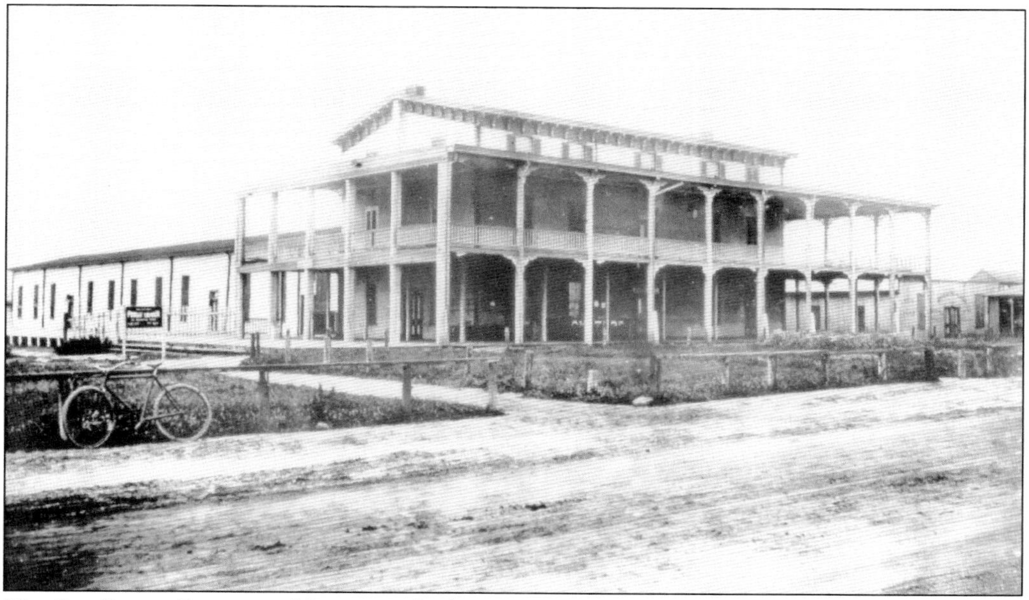

The Sea Breeze Excursion House was built in 1868 by the West Jersey & Seashore Railroad to accommodate day-trippers who visited the resort by the thousands after the railroad to Cape May City was completed. It held 1,500 people, who used its several drawing rooms, a dining room, a general reception room that doubled as a ballroom, and washrooms. It no longer stands. (HGM.)

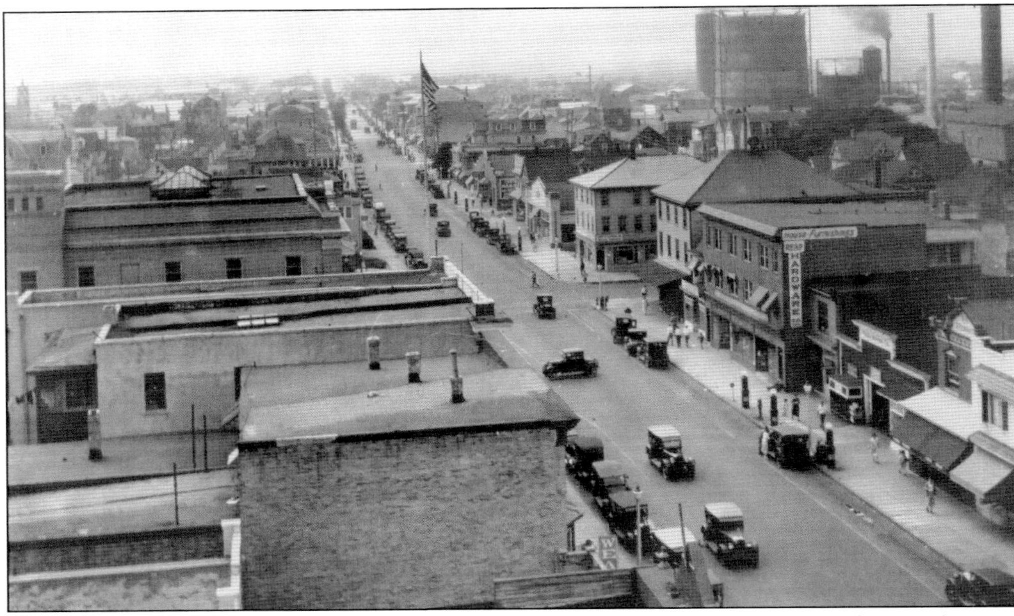

The view in this 1930s aerial photograph looks south down Asbury Avenue at the Ninth Street intersection in Ocean City, which was founded in 1879. The flag waves in front of the city hall, completed in 1914. Many of the buildings shown on the west side of Ninth Street still stand, although most have been altered, especially at the street level. (CMCHGS.)

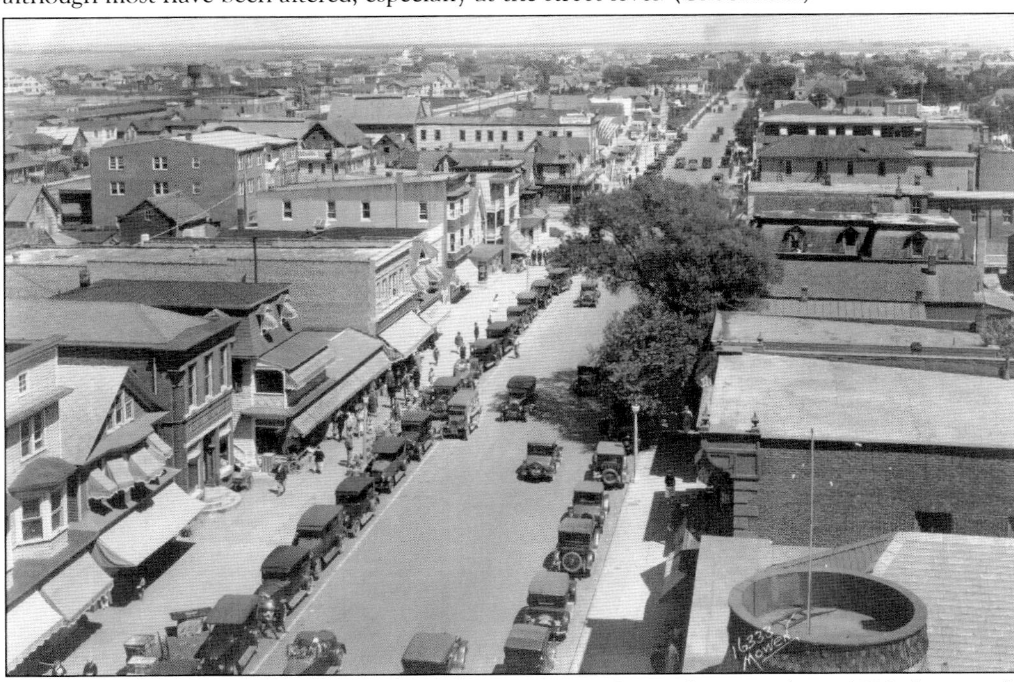

The west side of the 700 block of Asbury Avenue in Ocean City is shown in this c. 1930 photograph, which has a view that looks north. Only a handful of the original buildings are still standing. The brick building with the circular steps housed the *Sentinel* newspaper offices. Its front has been drastically changed and it is now home to the Pappagallo store. (CMCHGS.)

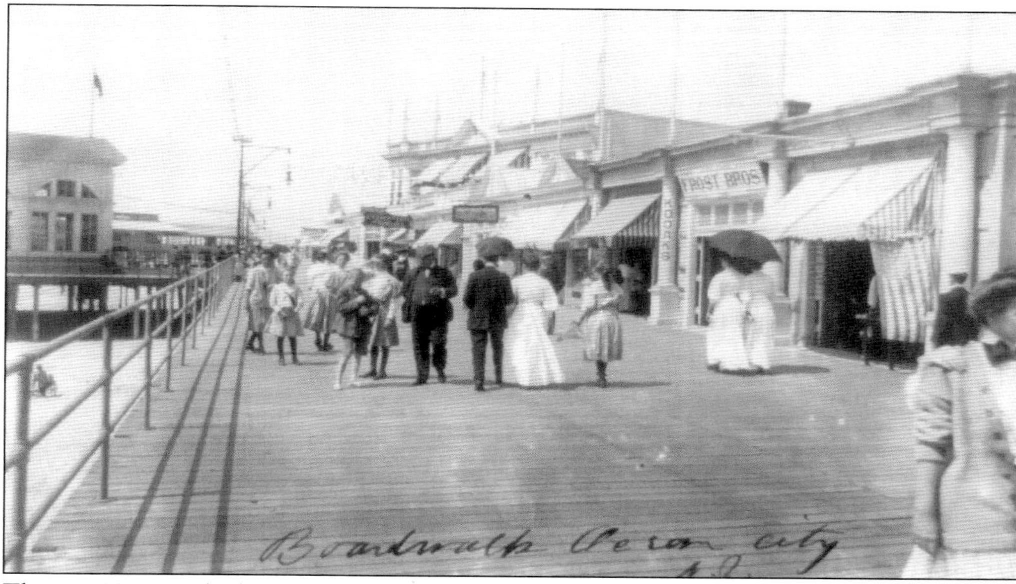

This c. 1908 view looking south along the Ocean City boardwalk was taken at Eighth Street. Built over pilings to protect it from being washed away in large storms, the public pavilion is seen to the left. A fire in 1927 destroyed 300 feet of the boardwalk between Eighth and Tenth Streets, but spared many of the stores and shops seen here. (LOC.)

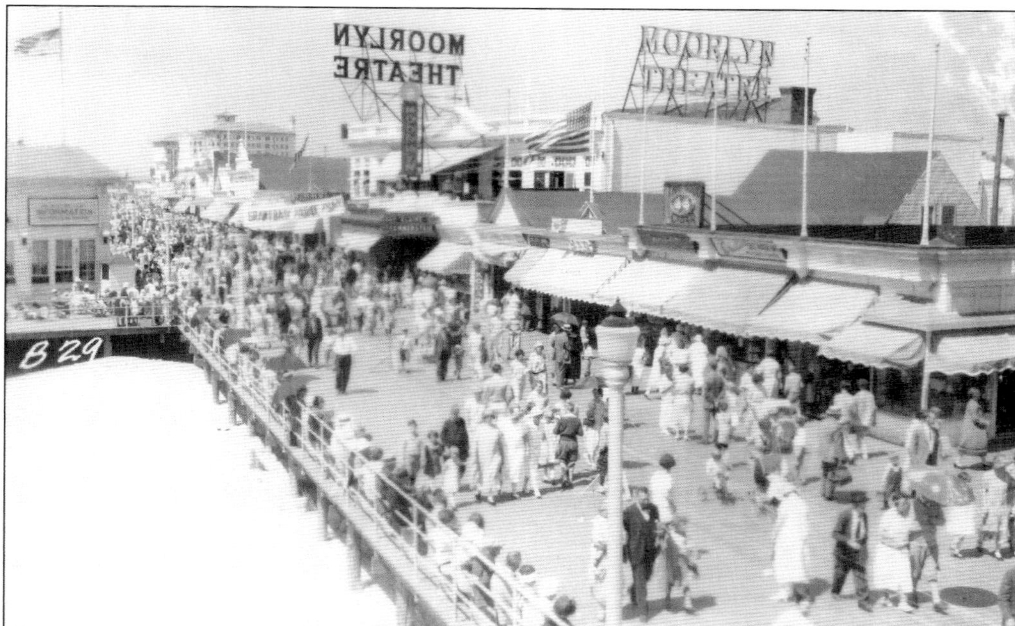

Capable of seating nearly 2,000, the Moorlyn Theatre, directly across from the music pier, was the largest of Ocean City's four movie theaters. Known originally as Moore's Bowling Casino, it opened in 1901 and later became a 200-seat movie house called Nickelodeon, playing silent movies for 5¢. It took its current name in 1922, featuring vaudeville acts and silent movies with live organ accompaniment. (CMCHGS.)

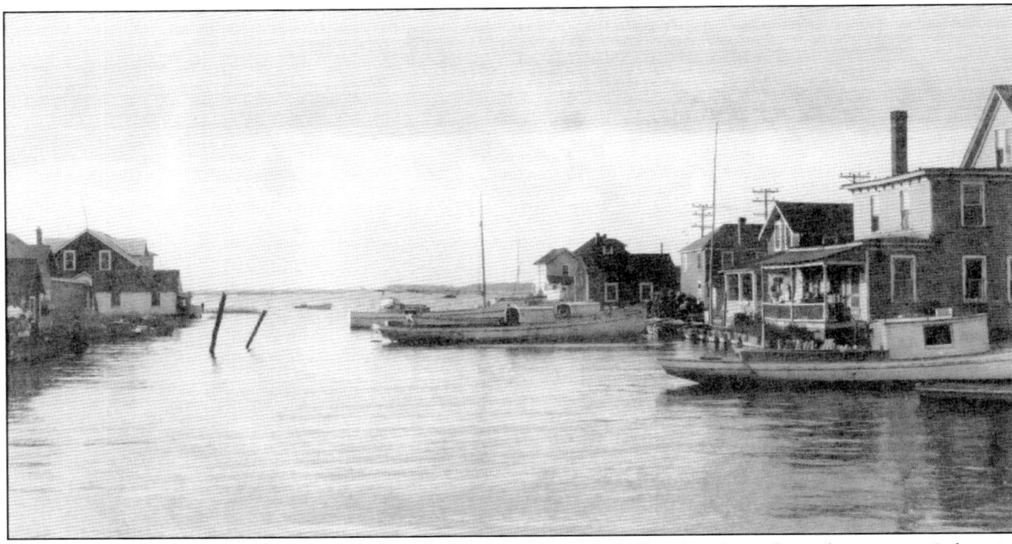

Oceanfront lots were not the only waterfront properties to be developed in the county's barrier island communities. Scenes like this one, showing modest cottages built along man-made or natural back-bay waterways, were common. Many offered docks where pleasure boats could be moored. This scene is thought to be of Ocean City. (CMCHGS.)

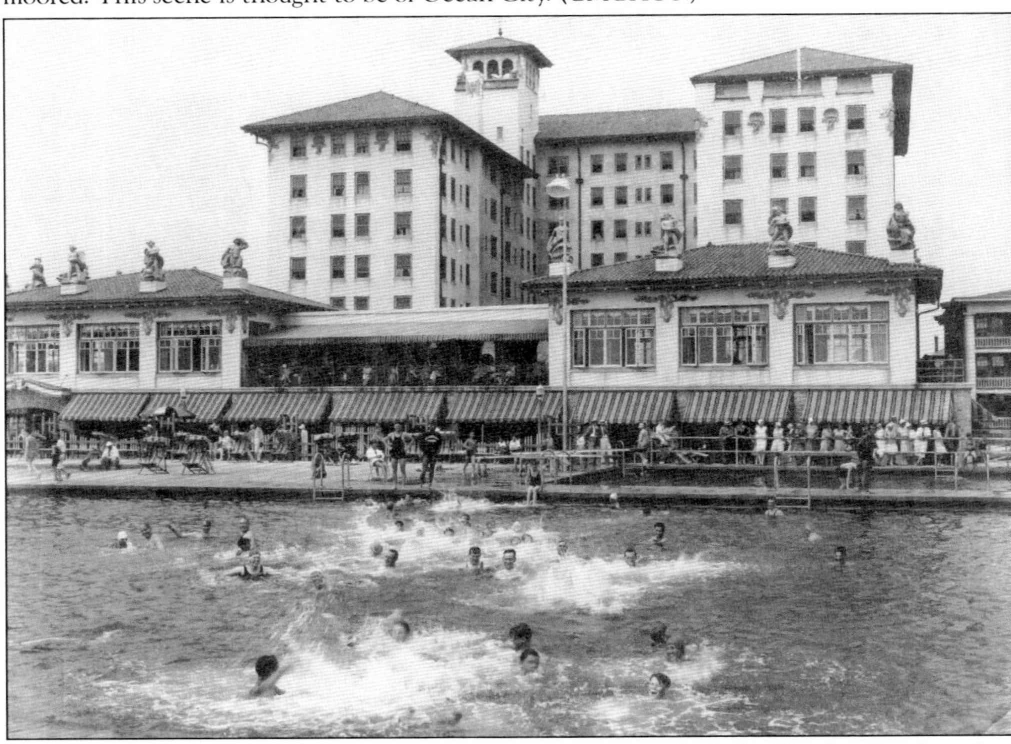

Designed by Vivian Smith, who also designed Ocean City's city hall, the Flanders Hotel was built in 1923 as an elegant, seaside hotel on the boardwalk at Eleventh Street in Ocean City. It featured 232 rooms, each with its own bathroom and an outside view, hot and cold saltwater baths, and several open-air pools. The building still stands, now offering luxury suites. (CMCHGS.)

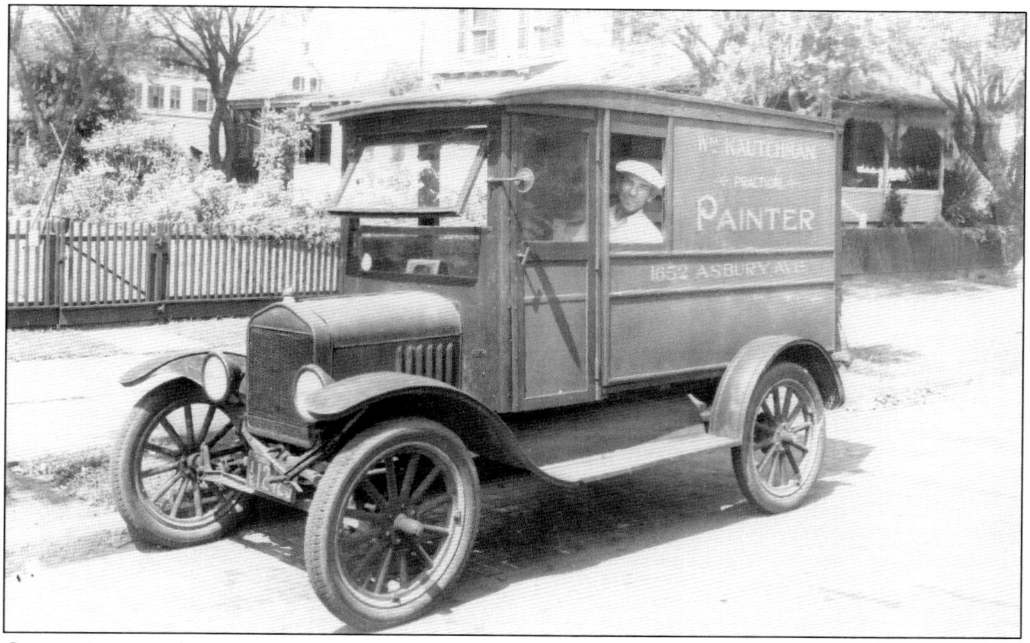

Ocean City resident William Kauchman poses in his 1920s Ford Model T panel body truck with several of the city's more substantial houses behind him. A painter, Kauchman found plenty of work in the city because the majority of its houses were built of wood and needed routine painting to keep them protected from the salt air. (CMCHGS.)

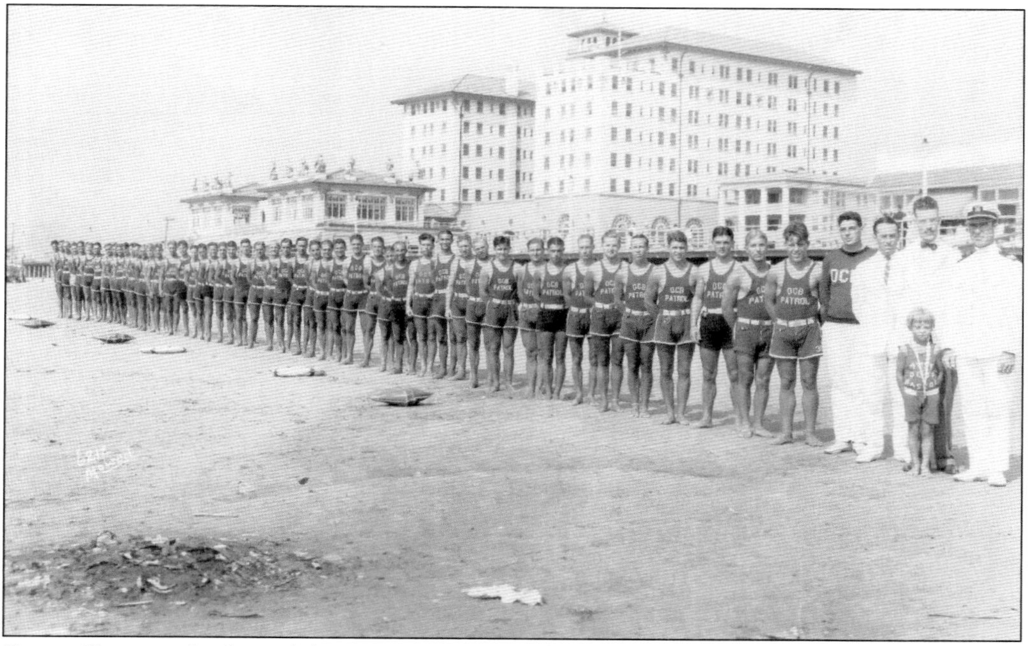

Ocean City was the first of the county's resorts to hire paid lifeguards—the Ocean City Beach Patrol, created in 1898. Lifeguards were paid $40 per month and worked each day from 9:00 a.m. until 3:00 p.m. This photograph, taken around 1925, shows the patrol posing on the beach near Tenth Street with the Flanders Hotel in the background. (CMCHGS.)

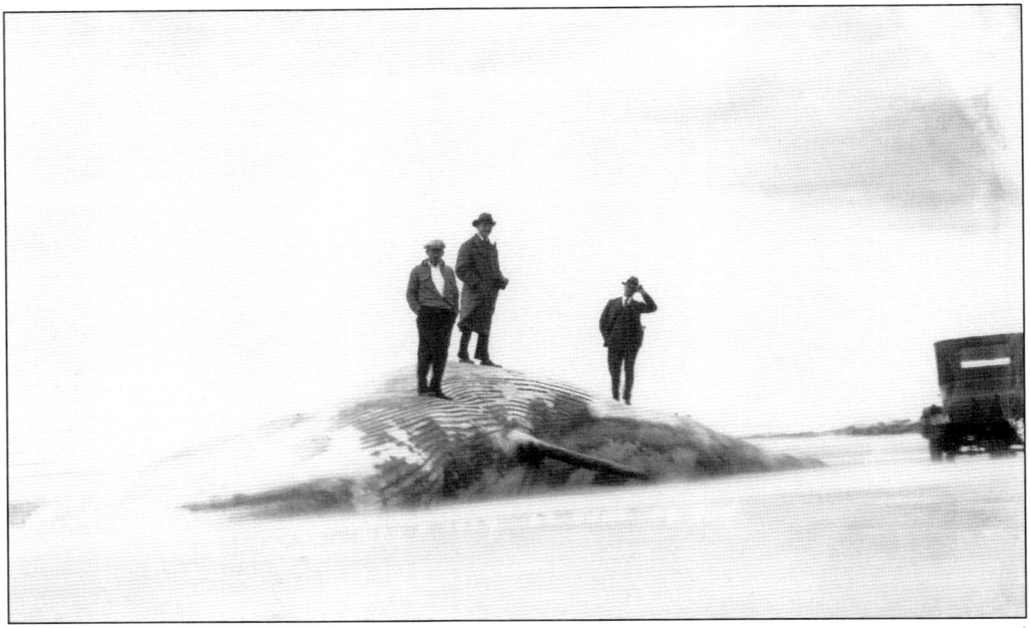

A 60-foot-long dead whale washed ashore in Ocean City in May 1929. The newspaper reported that its carcass was going to be towed to sea by the Coast Guard and then used as a target for one-pound guns. Whales were commonly seen along the Jersey coast in the 1700s but became scarcer as they were hunted to near extinction. (CMCHGS.)

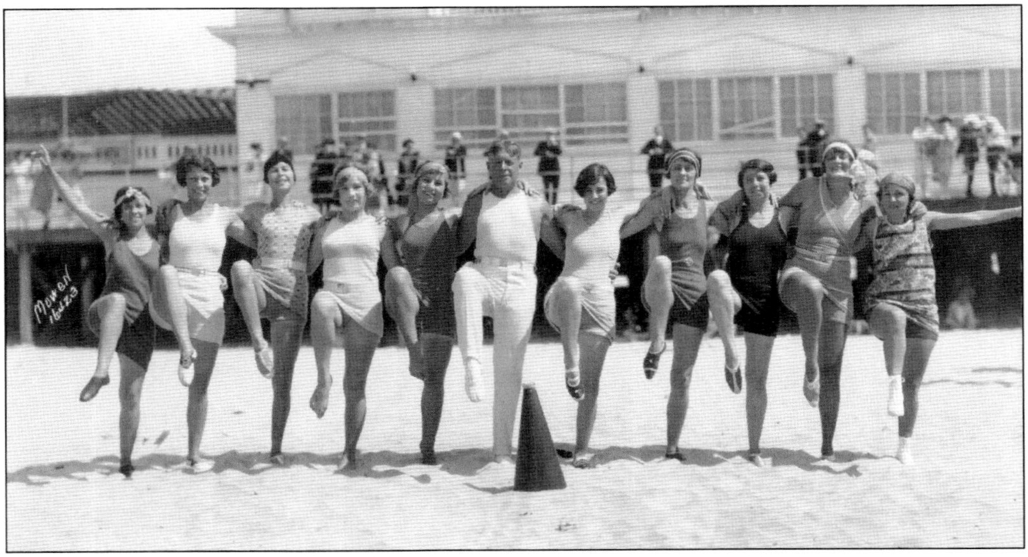

By the 1920s, bathing costumes like those worn by these young women posing in Ocean City featured a long knit top, almost like a dress, over attached shorts. As the century progressed, women's swimwear became shorter and tighter, with necklines dropping to deep boatnecks or V-necks. The more fashionable wore beach shoes of duck canvas or rubber slippers. (CMCHGS.)

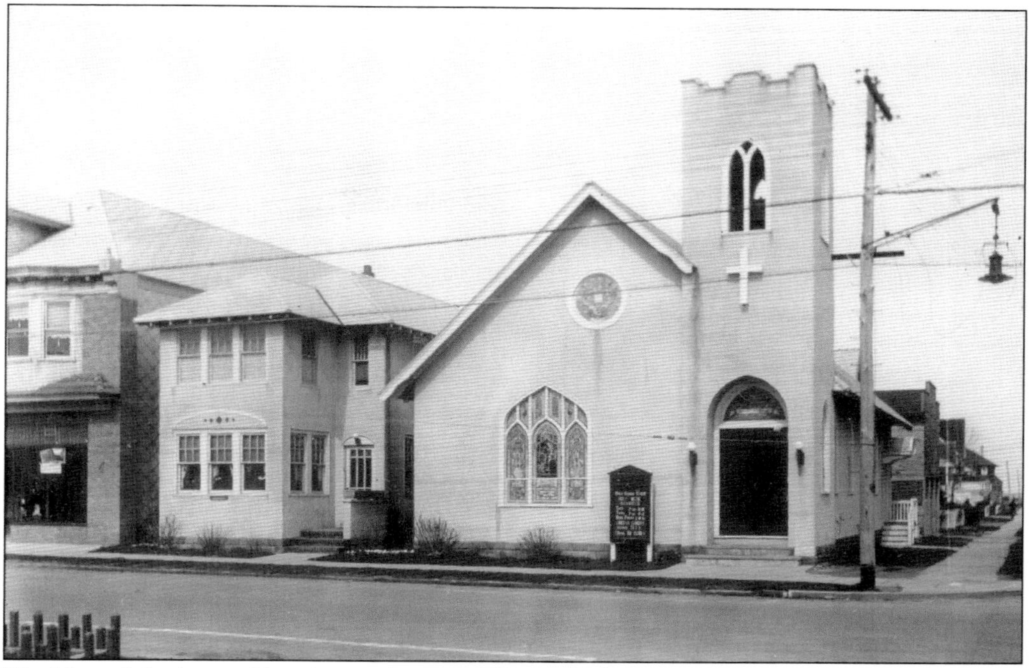

The Messiah Lutheran Church, seen here in 1930, was built in 1915 at the corner of Landis Avenue and Forty-Second Street in Sea Isle City. The one-story church featured a two-story bell tower and had a stucco-covered exterior. Services were held here until about 2007, when the congregation sold the building and erected a new one on the mainland in Ocean View. (CMCHGS.)

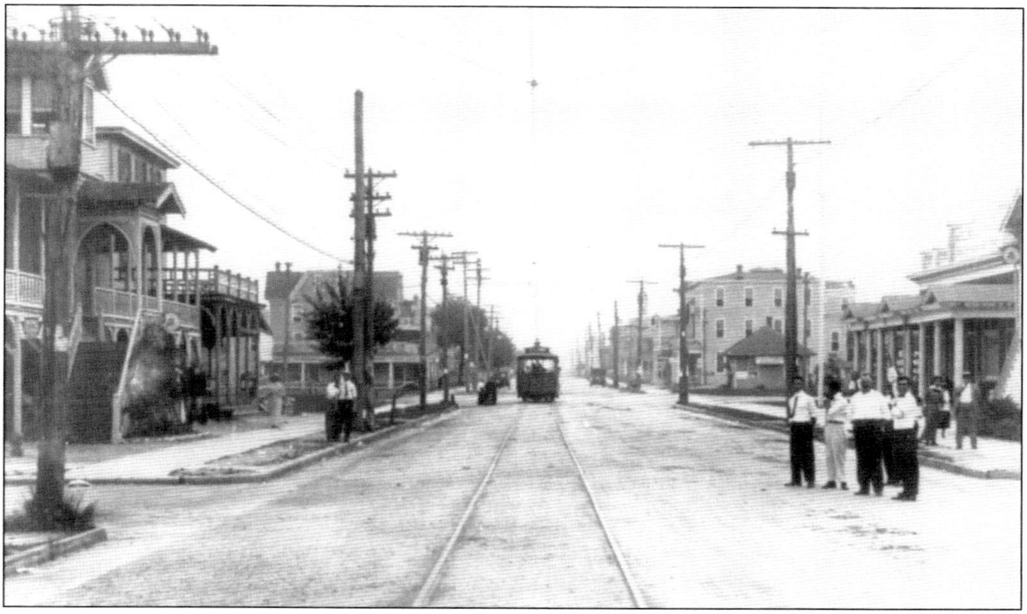

This busy intersection at Fortieth Street and Landis Avenue in Sea Isle City featured three hotels in the early 1900s: the 1887 Hotel Bellevue with its c. 1914 café (seen to the right), the Philadelphia Hotel, and Petersen's Hotel (seen to the left). Of these, only the Philadelphia Hotel still stands, highly altered and now known as the Ocean Drive Hotel. (HGM.)

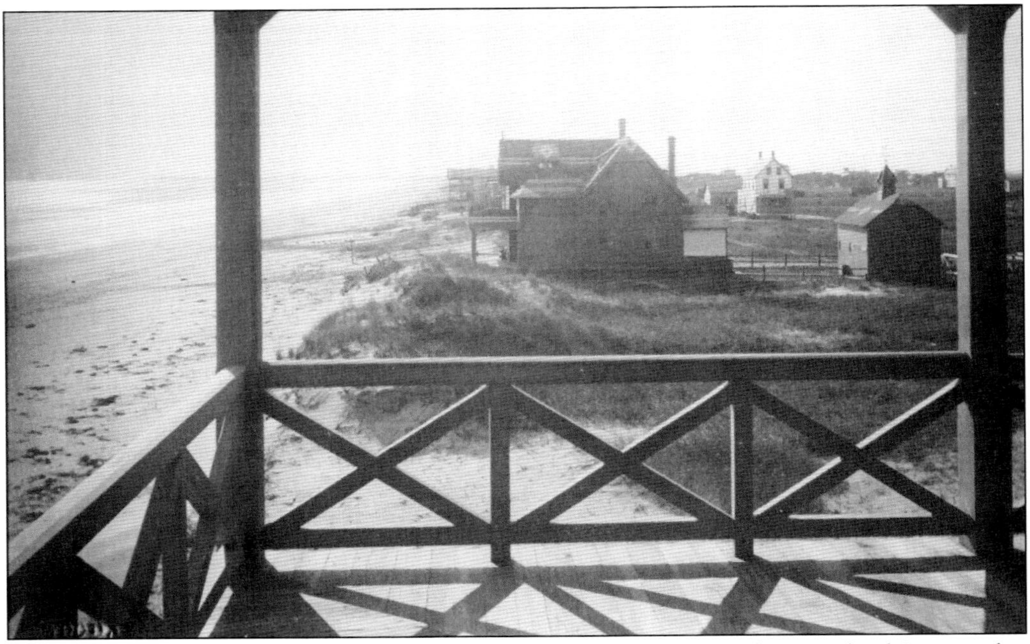

Taken before the boardwalk was built in 1907 between Twentieth and Sixty-Third Streets, this photographic view shows Sea Isle City in its infancy, with vacant oceanfront and ocean block lots still plentiful. The streets are unpaved. The view is identified as looking south, but the photographer's exact location has not been determined. (CMCHGS.)

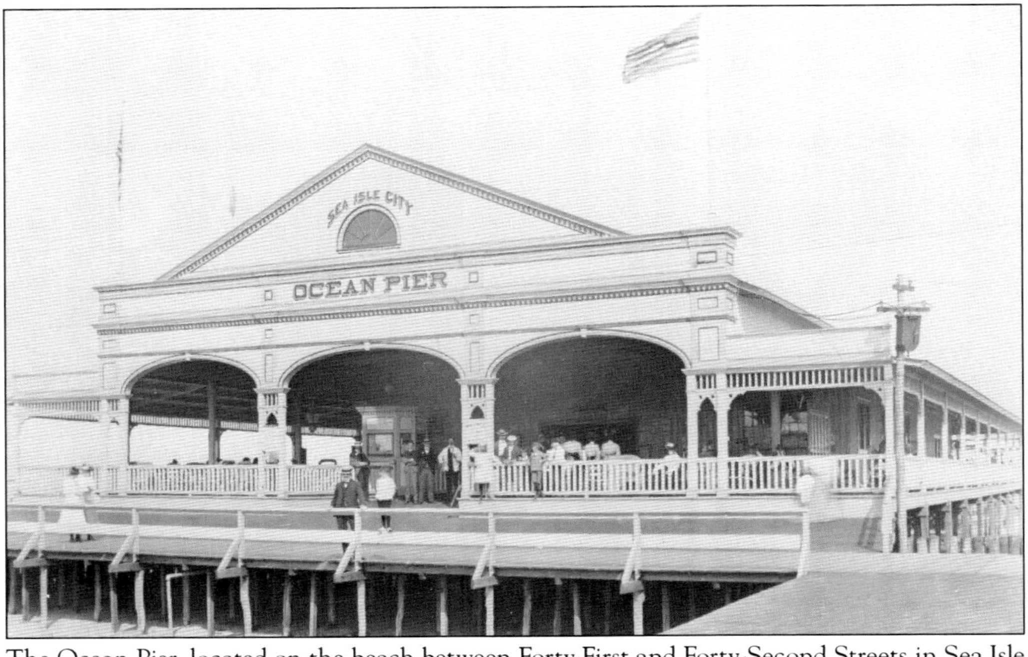

The Ocean Pier, located on the beach between Forty-First and Forty-Second Streets in Sea Isle City, opened in 1906 and offered an entertainment "casino" and a fishing pier. Matinees were held daily at 2:00 p.m., and a children's carnival was held every Wednesday night. The pier was washed away in the Great Atlantic Storm of 1962. (CMCHGS.)

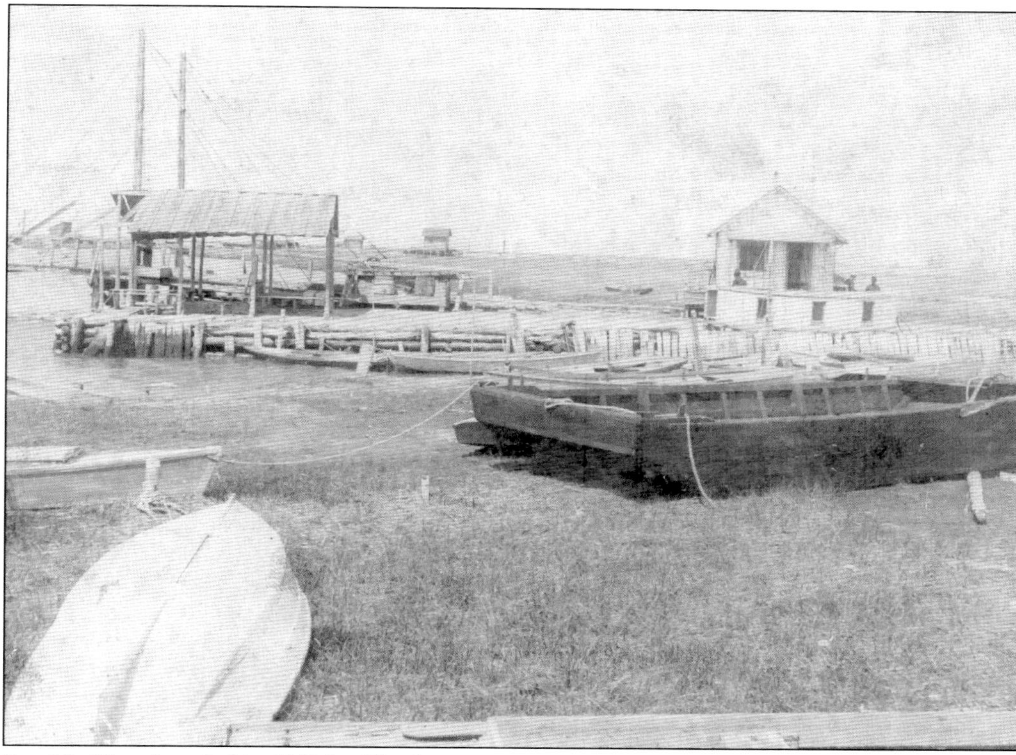

Sea Isle City, founded in 1882 by Charles Landis, was accessible by both railroad and a turnpike. The turnpike bridge, seen here at the far left, crossed Ludlam's Thoroughfare at Forty-Fourth Street. Crawford Buck, a Sea Isle City resident, was its first bridgetender. Around 1908, a new drawbridge was built. (CMCHGS.)

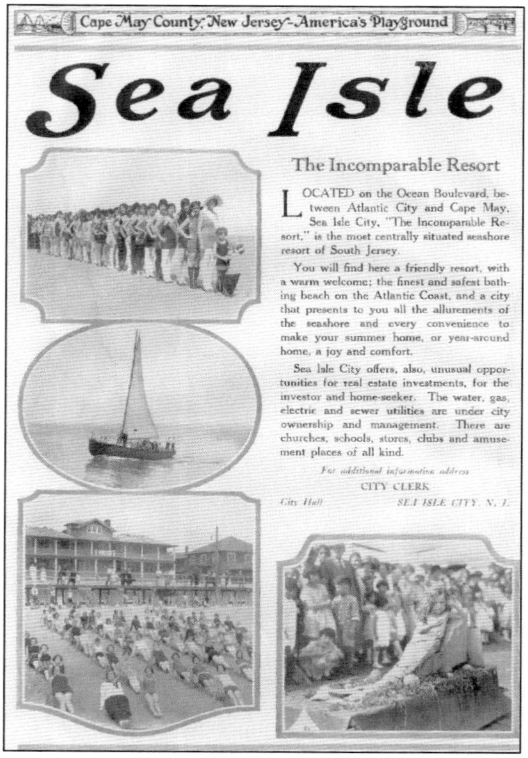

Cape May County, New Jersey—America's Playground

Sea Isle

The Incomparable Resort

LOCATED on the Ocean Boulevard, between Atlantic City and Cape May, Sea Isle City, "The Incomparable Resort," is the most centrally situated seashore resort of South Jersey.

You will find here a friendly resort, with a warm welcome; the finest and safest bathing beach on the Atlantic Coast, and a city that presents to you all the allurements of the seashore and every convenience to make your summer home, or year-around home, a joy and comfort.

Sea Isle City offers, also, unusual opportunities for real estate investments, for the investor and home-seeker. The water, gas, electric and sewer utilities are under city ownership and management. There are churches, schools, stores, clubs and amusement places of all kind.

For additional information address

CITY CLERK

City Hall *SEA ISLE CITY, N. J.*

A 1926 travel brochure called Cape May County "America's Playground" and Sea Isle City, the "Incomparable Resort." The photographs show popular attractions the vacationer would find in Sea Isle City, including a line of bathing beauties, a pleasure yacht, group exercises on the beach, and a parade on the boardwalk. (CMCHGS.)

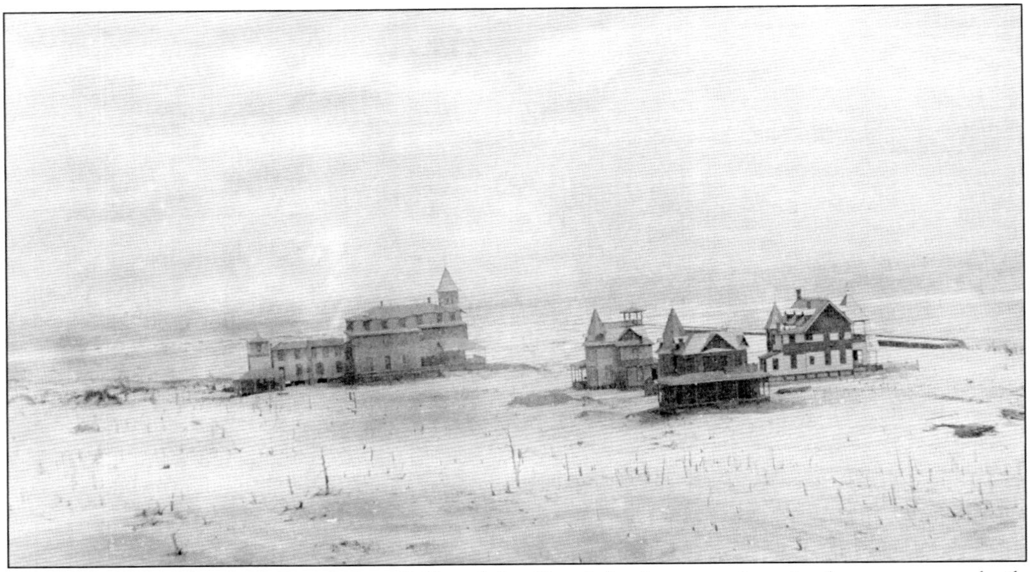

The resort of Avalon was founded in 1887 and the Hotel Avalon, seen here in the center, was built the following year on Seventh Street. It was erected by Joseph Wells and a syndicate of investors who sought to develop one of last undeveloped beaches in the county. To lure guests, the hotel advertised its "braided wire torsion spring mattresses," a fairly recent invention. (CMCHGS.)

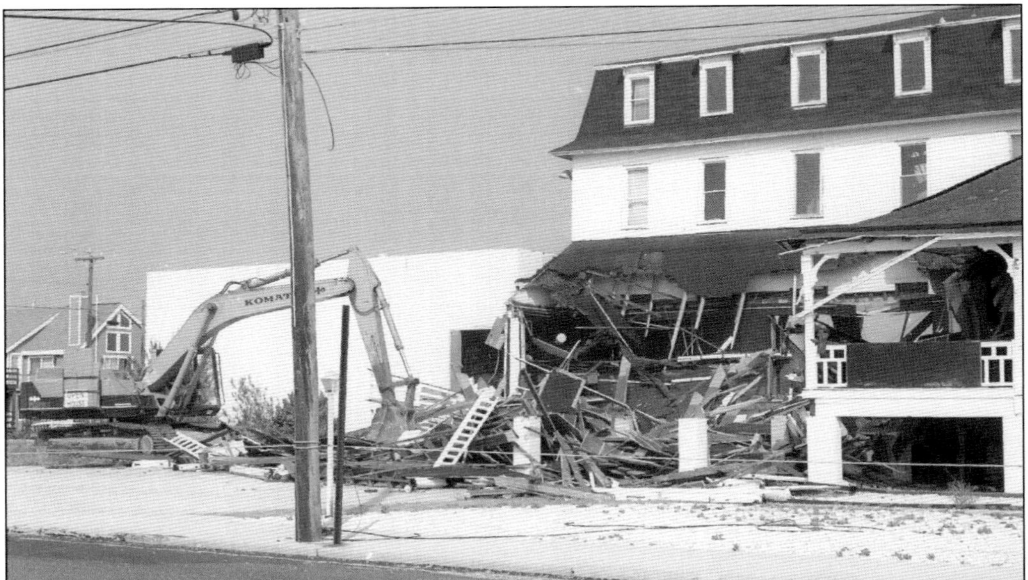

The four-story, green and white clapboard-covered Hotel Avalon survived numerous hurricanes and storms, but at 99 years old, it was demolished in 1987 to make way for a modern condominium complex. By the late 1960s, the hotel had been remodeled into a rock 'n' roll club first called the Catacombs, then later Phil's Bongo Room. (AHC.)

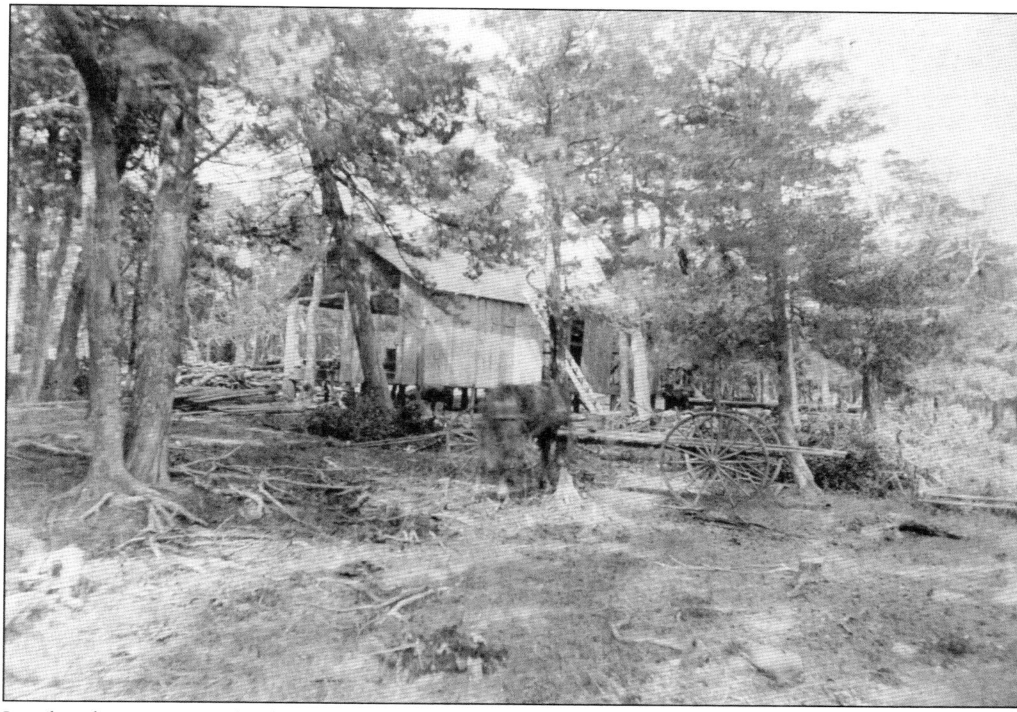

It is hard to imagine Avalon covered with trees, but they needed to be cleared to make way for the houses and other buildings that would be erected there. This photograph, taken in 1888 just after Avalon was founded, shows a sawmill that had been erected to process fallen trees into building materials. (CMCHGS.)

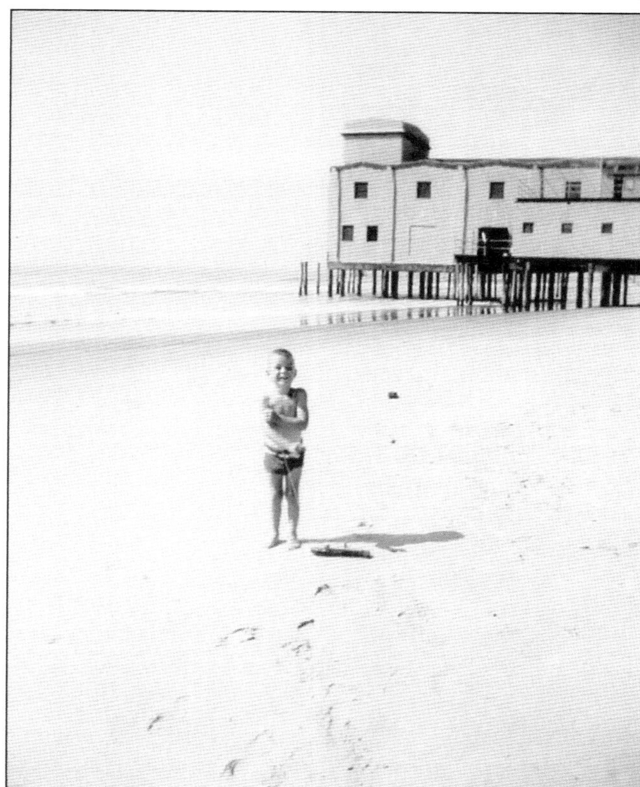

This 1945 photograph shows a young child playing on the Thirtieth Street beach in Avalon. The building in the background is the Avalon Pier, an entertainment complex that was the hub of Avalon's social life from 1929 until 1980. Among other things, it included a movie theater and dance hall. (AHC.)

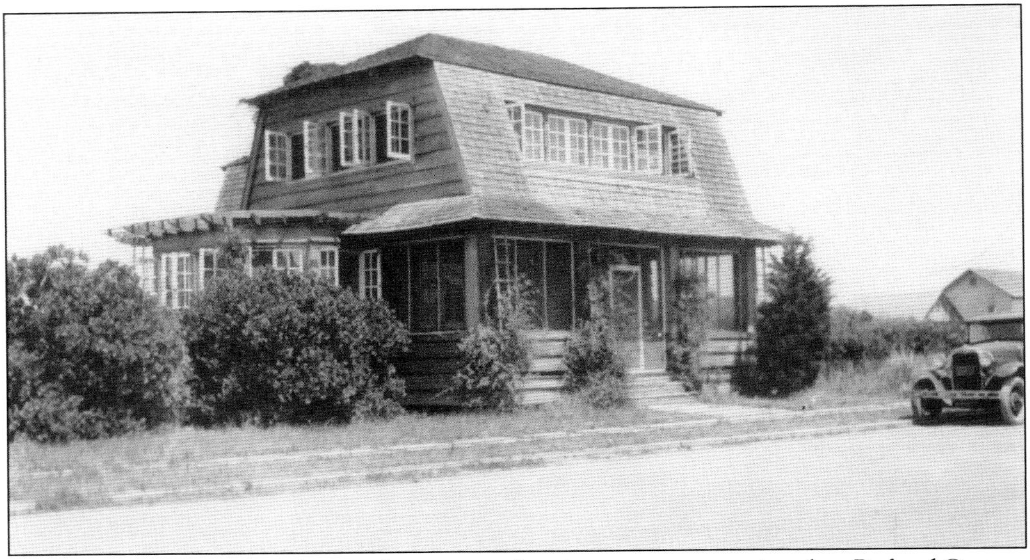

Founded in 1907, Stone Harbor was becoming a thriving resort community when Rufwud Cottage was built in 1917 at 394 Ninety-Third Street, where it still stands. The house was designed in the Craftsman style by well-known Philadelphia architect Oscar Hokanson as his personal summer home. It retains many original features, including rough-sawn wood sheathing (hence its name), grouped casement windows, a fireplace, and exposed beams on the interior. (Chris Brown.)

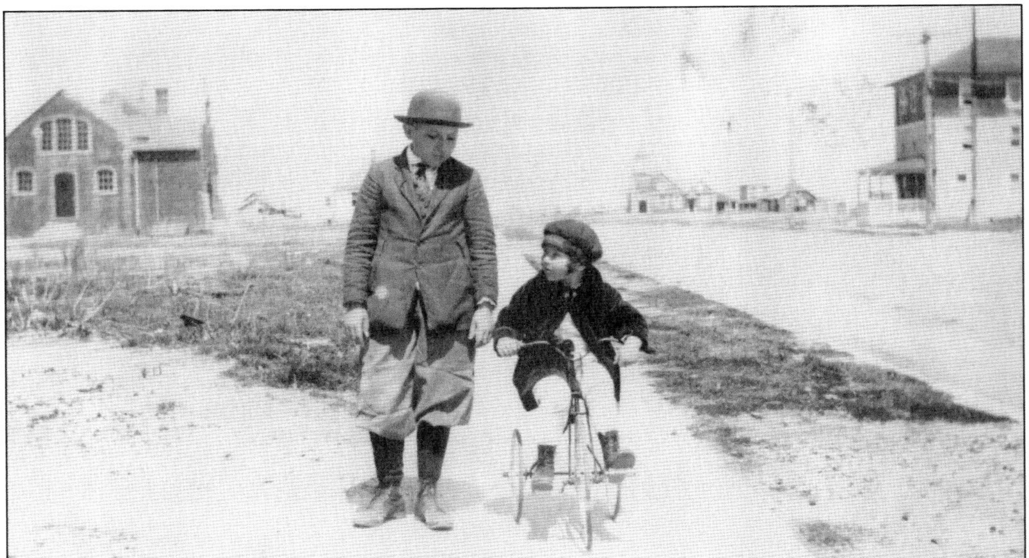

Two children pose about 1918 at the corner of Third Avenue and Ninety-Fifth Street in Stone Harbor. Seen at the left is St. Mary's Episcopal Church, built in 1911, and in the far distance at center right is Our Savior Lutheran Church, built in 1917. Both still stand. The three-story building at the right was a boardinghouse and later a hotel; it now serves as Springer's Ice Cream. (SHM.)

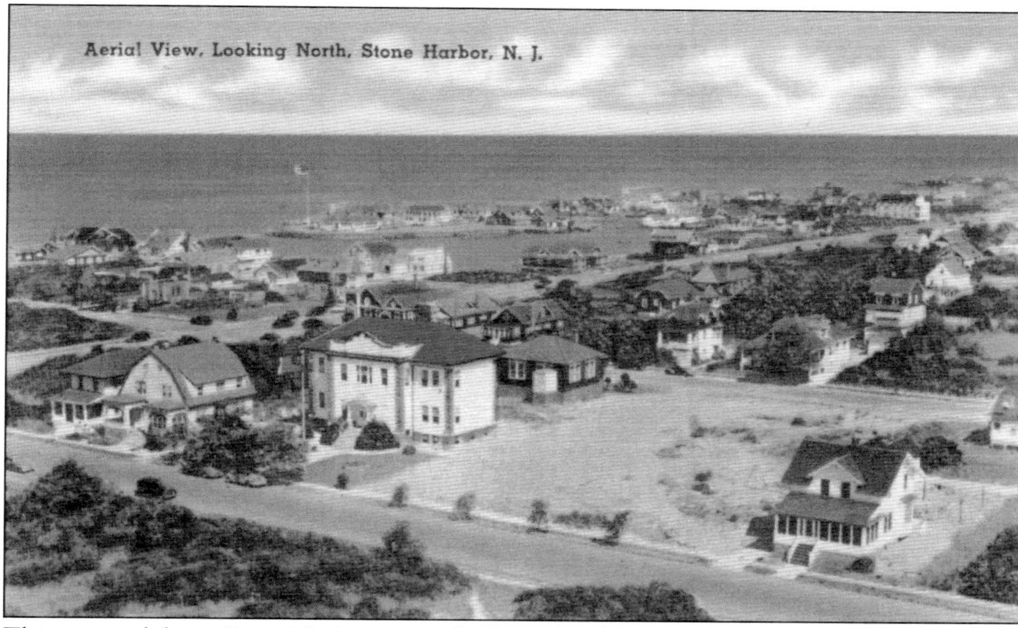

This postcard shows Stone Harbor's second public school, built in 1915 on Ninety-Fourth Street. The first school, built in 1913 and seen behind the new school, then became borough hall. In the background, with the flag flying, is the Stone Harbor Yacht Club. The two houses on the block seen at the far right are the only two buildings still standing. (SHM.)

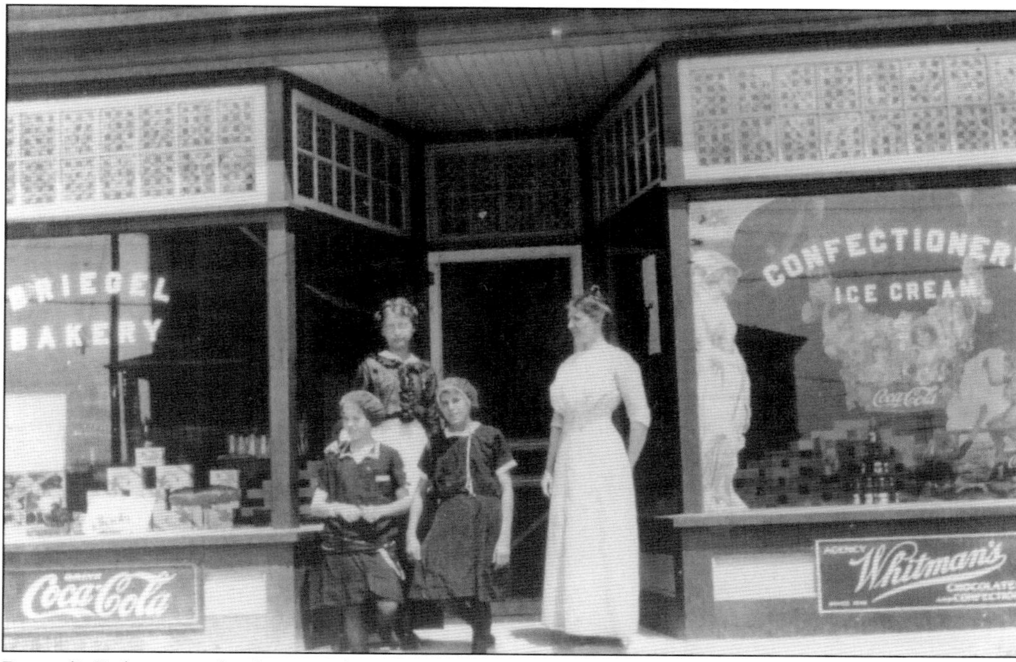

Briegel's Bakery was built around 1908 in Stone Harbor on the north side of Ninety-Sixth Street at the Third Avenue intersection. It later became American Stores, then was divided, adding Leon's Meats. Today, the Green Cuisine Restaurant is located in the building, which still stands but has been highly altered from its appearance in this c. 1915 photograph. (SHM.)

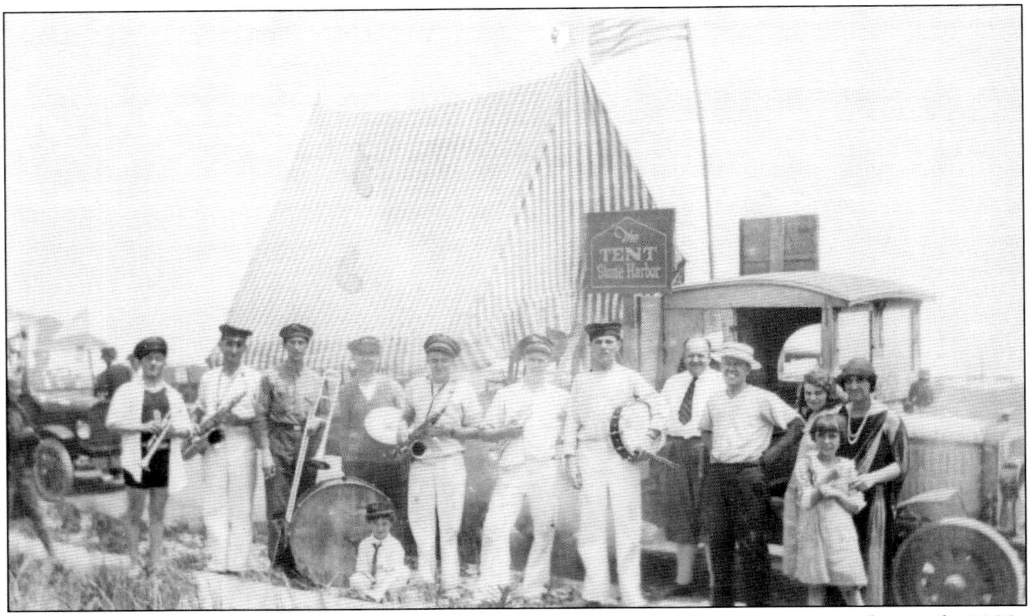

Members of an unidentified band pose with their various musical instruments in front of a 1920s Ford truck that appears to be towing a striped tent. The occasion was Stone Harbor's Fourth of July parade in 1925. Their names and the exact location where the event was photographed are not known. (SHM.)

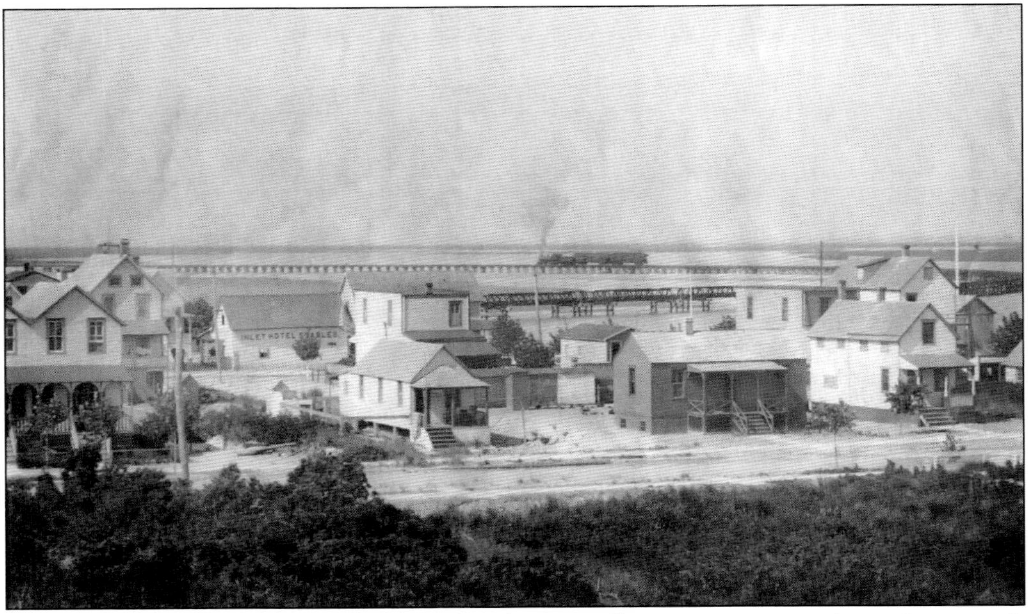
This c. 1920 photograph shows Townsend's Inlet, a small resort community located just south of Sea Isle City and overlooking Townsend's Inlet. Seen in the background is the West Jersey & Seashore Railroad's second bridge across the inlet; this line connected the mainland with the resorts of Avalon and Stone Harbor via Sea Isle City. The bridge had been relocated due to exposure and continual damage from frequent storms. (SHM.)

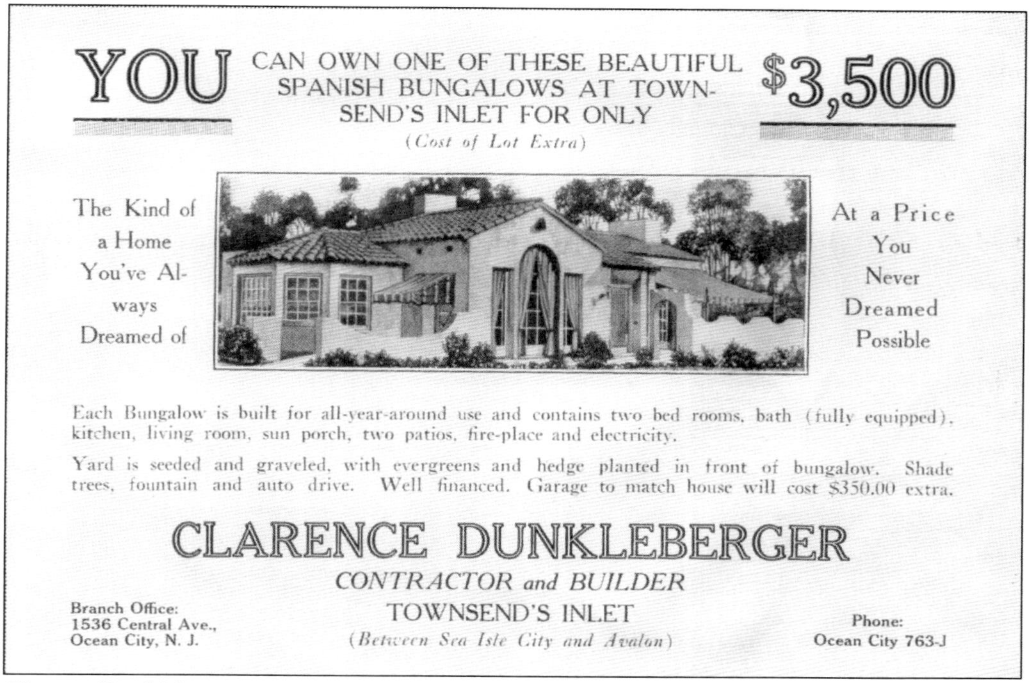

Clarence Dunkleberger, a contractor and builder from Camden, advertises this Spanish Revival–style bungalow that he would build on a prospective buyer's lot in Townsend's Inlet. Although the resort was occupied mostly by summer vacationers, Dunkleberger touts in this 1926 ad that the house could be lived in year-round. He offered a garage for an additional cost of $350. (CMCHGS.)

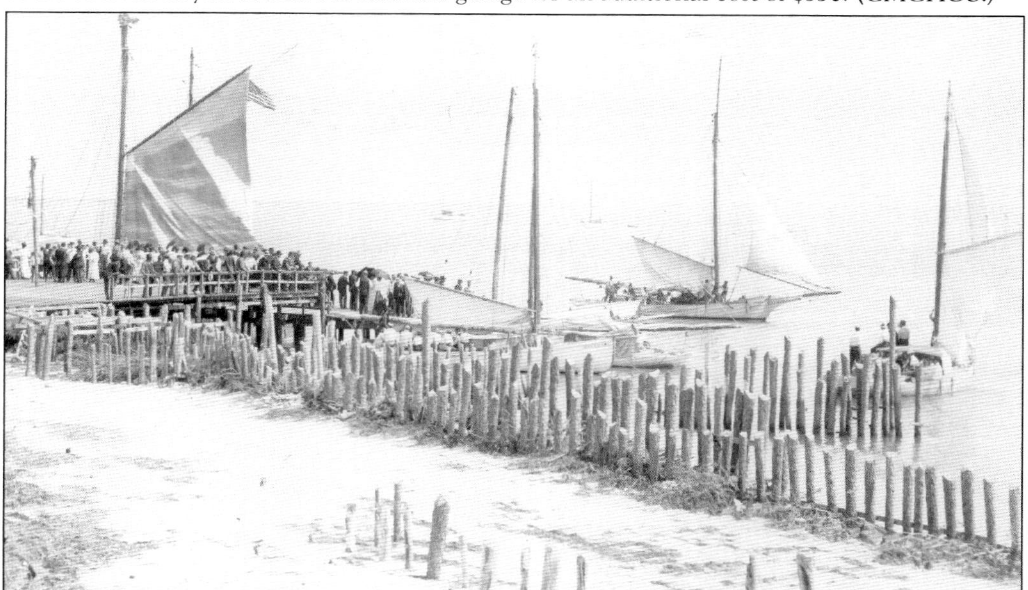

Mace's Landing at the north end of Anglesea (now North Wildwood), seen here about 1900, was a popular place where sportfishing charters and party boats could be hired. Commercial fishermen, living in shacks along the water, also operated their vessels from the landing, bringing in catches of fluke, weakfish, and black sea bass. (CMCHGS.)

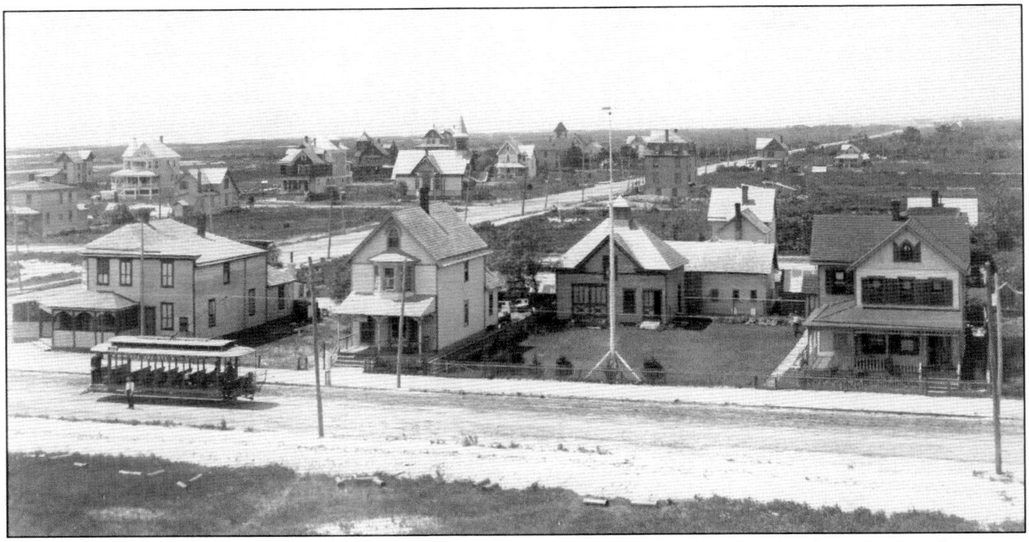

Taken from atop the 1874 Hereford Inlet Lighthouse in North Wildwood about 1910, this view looks southeast and shows the junction of First Avenue (in the foreground) with Pennsylvania (now Atlantic) Avenue. Seen roughly in the center is the North Wildwood Baptist Church, built in 1898. It has been replaced by a modern church structure. (CMCHGS.)

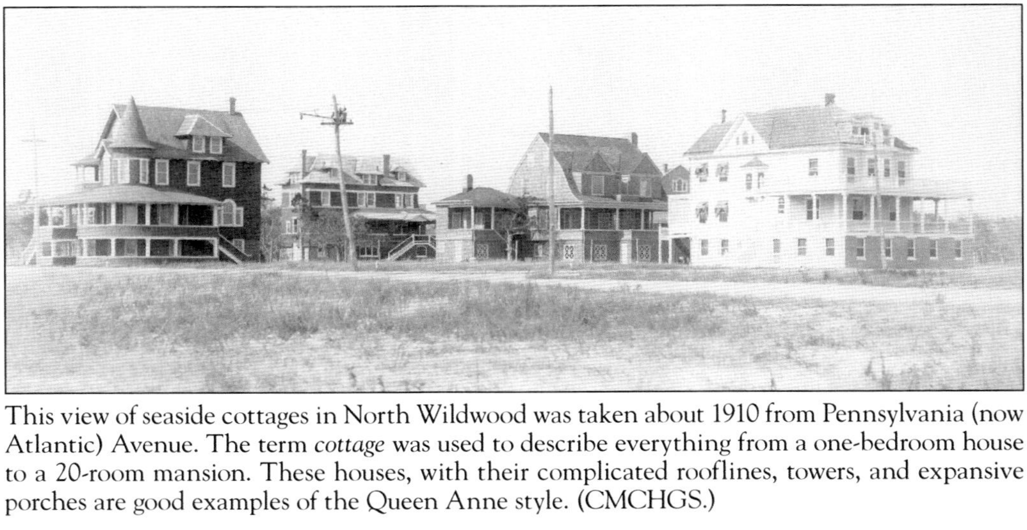

This view of seaside cottages in North Wildwood was taken about 1910 from Pennsylvania (now Atlantic) Avenue. The term *cottage* was used to describe everything from a one-bedroom house to a 20-room mansion. These houses, with their complicated rooflines, towers, and expansive porches are good examples of the Queen Anne style. (CMCHGS.)

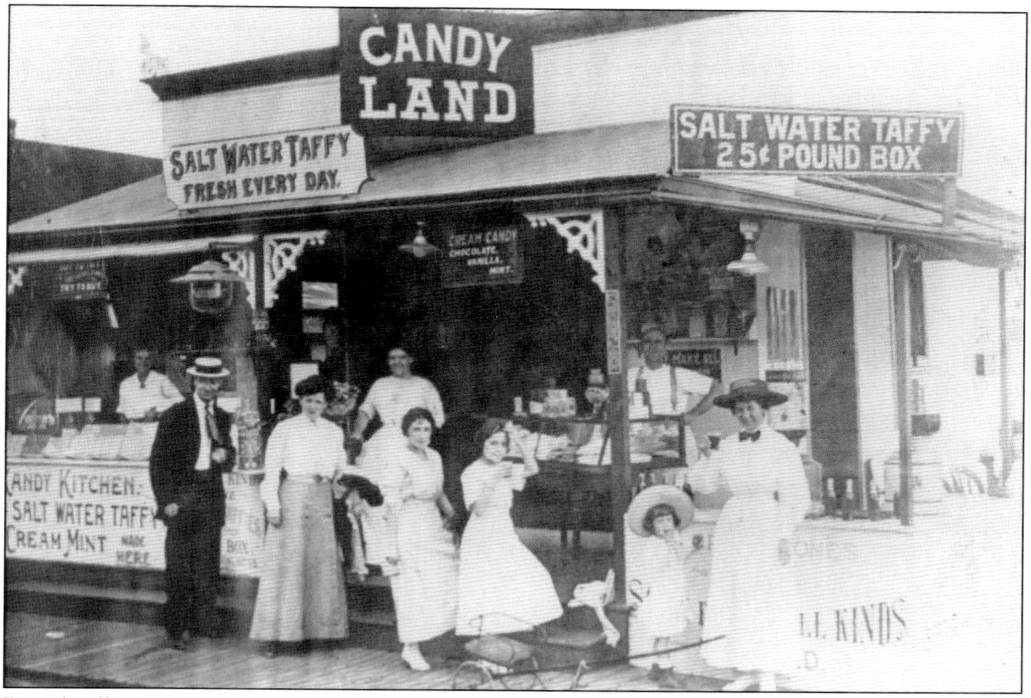

Boardwalk entrepreneurs quickly learned that candy, ice cream, and other sweet treats were a sure hit with vacationers. The Candy Land candy shop (above) was located in Anglesea (now North Wildwood) and appears to have specialized in saltwater taffy. This confection was originally produced and marketed in Atlantic City starting in the 1880s and is made from sugar, cornstarch, corn syrup, water, butter, and salt with added color and flavorings. The name "salt water taffy" reportedly arose when an Atlantic City boardwalk merchant's stock of taffy got dampened by the sea-foam from an unusually high tide. Douglass Candy (right), a Wildwood confectioner still in business since 1919, advertised a variety of sweets including saltwater taffy in a 1926 ad. (Both, CMCHGS.)

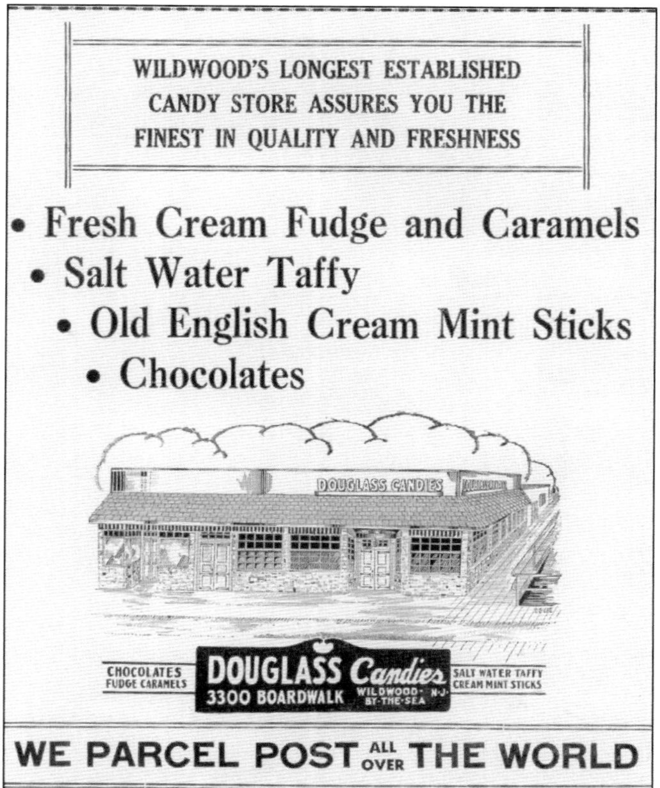

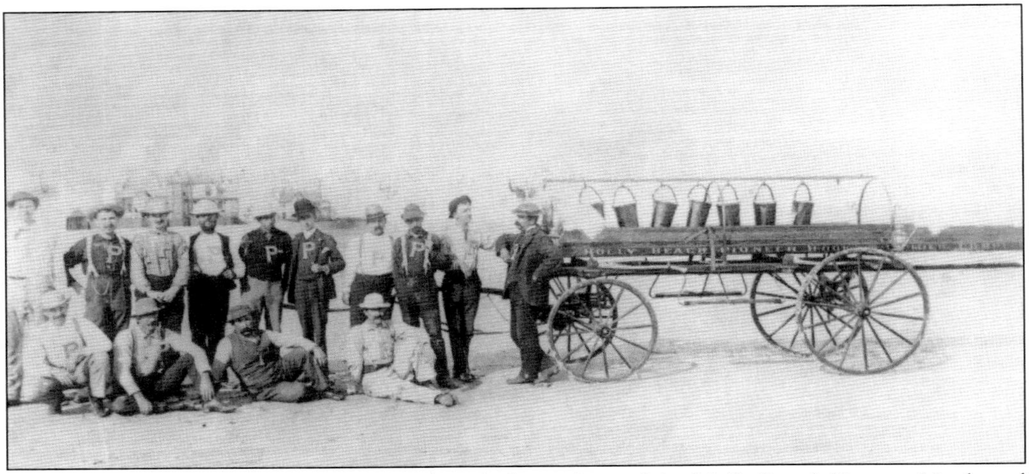

This c. 1890 photograph shows the unidentified members of the Holly Beach Pioneer Hook and Ladder Company No. 1, a bucket brigade. The company was founded in 1884, and its wagon (seen here) arrived in 1885. Behind the firemen are several of the wooden cottages they were charged with protecting. Founded in the 1870s, Holly Beach was a separate borough until it merged with Wildwood in 1912. (CMCHGS.)

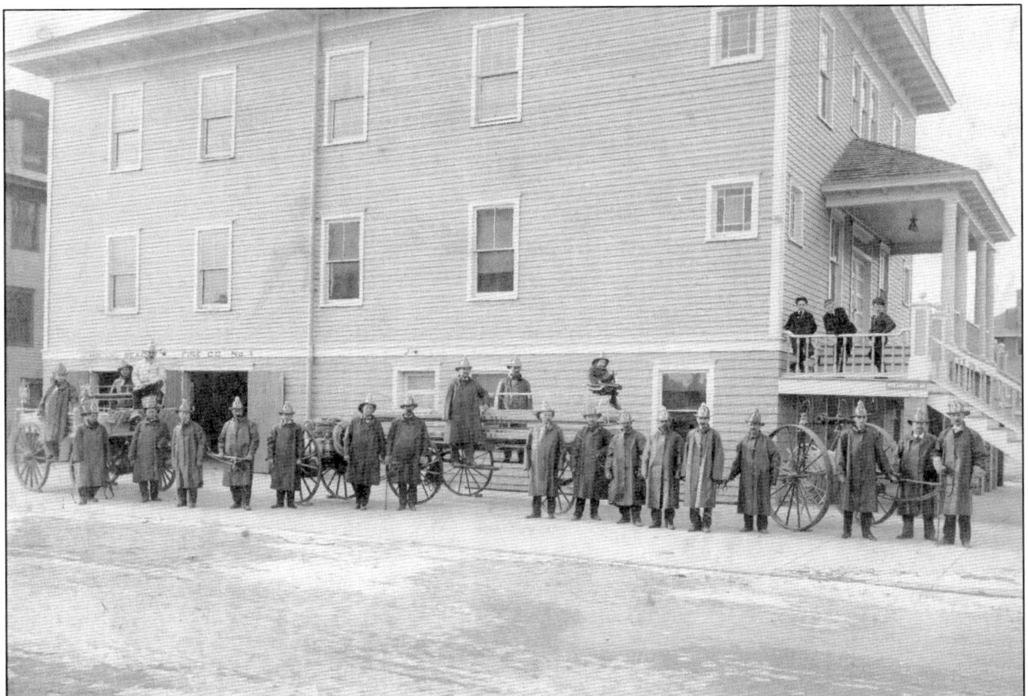

Later known as Holly Beach Fire Company No. 1, the firefighters moved into the ground floor of the Wildwood City Hall at Pacific and Montgomery Avenues. The horse-drawn apparatus seen in this 1903 photograph was used until around 1915, when it was replaced by a 65-foot ladder truck that the fire company still owns. (CMCHGS.)

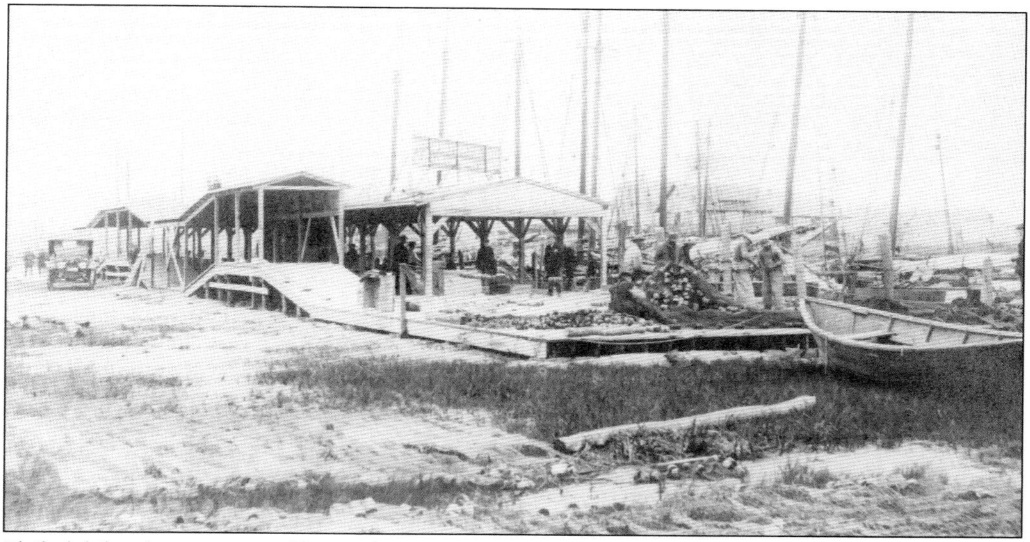

Philadelphia businessman Henry Ottens came to Wildwood in 1898 and established a bayside port, seen here about 1925, for commercial fisherman around 1920. The man-made harbor still bears his name. A railroad spur run to the fishing wharf in July 1922 allowed catches to reach the market faster than by wagon. At the time, Wildwood was considered to be the greatest seafood shipping port south of Gloucester, Massachusetts. (CMCHGS.)

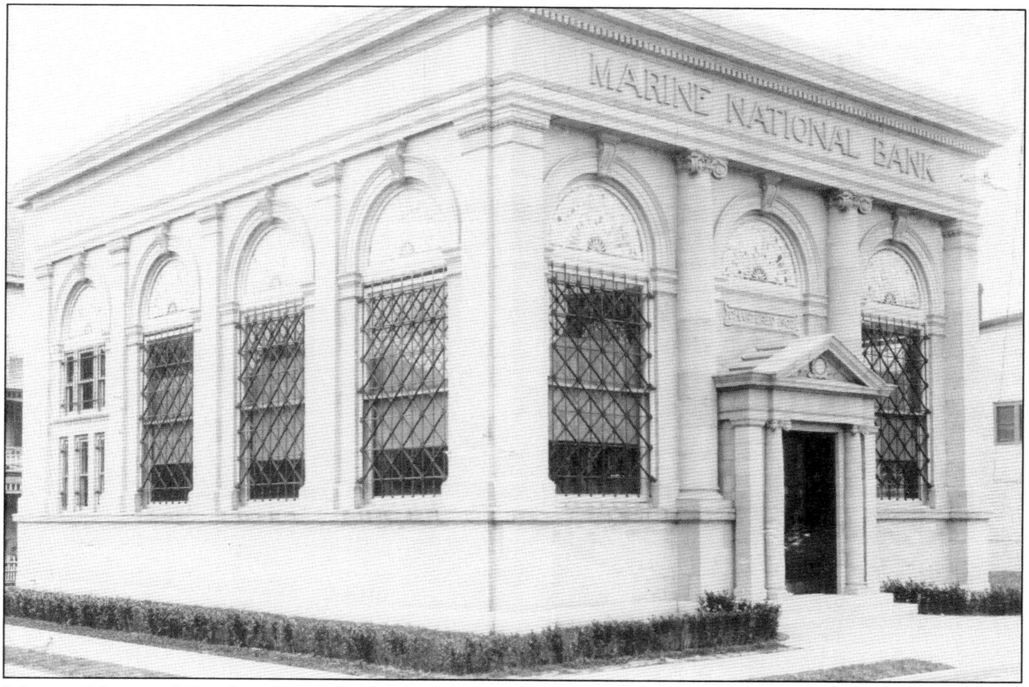

Marine National Bank opened its doors at 3410 Pacific Avenue in Wildwood in 1908. Modern for the time, it featured a two-story banking hall in the front with a rear mezzanine level. Chartered in 1902, this was the first financial institution established in the Wildwoods and originally operated out of a rented office. Part of this building was reused when the present bank was built in 1927. (CMCHGS.)

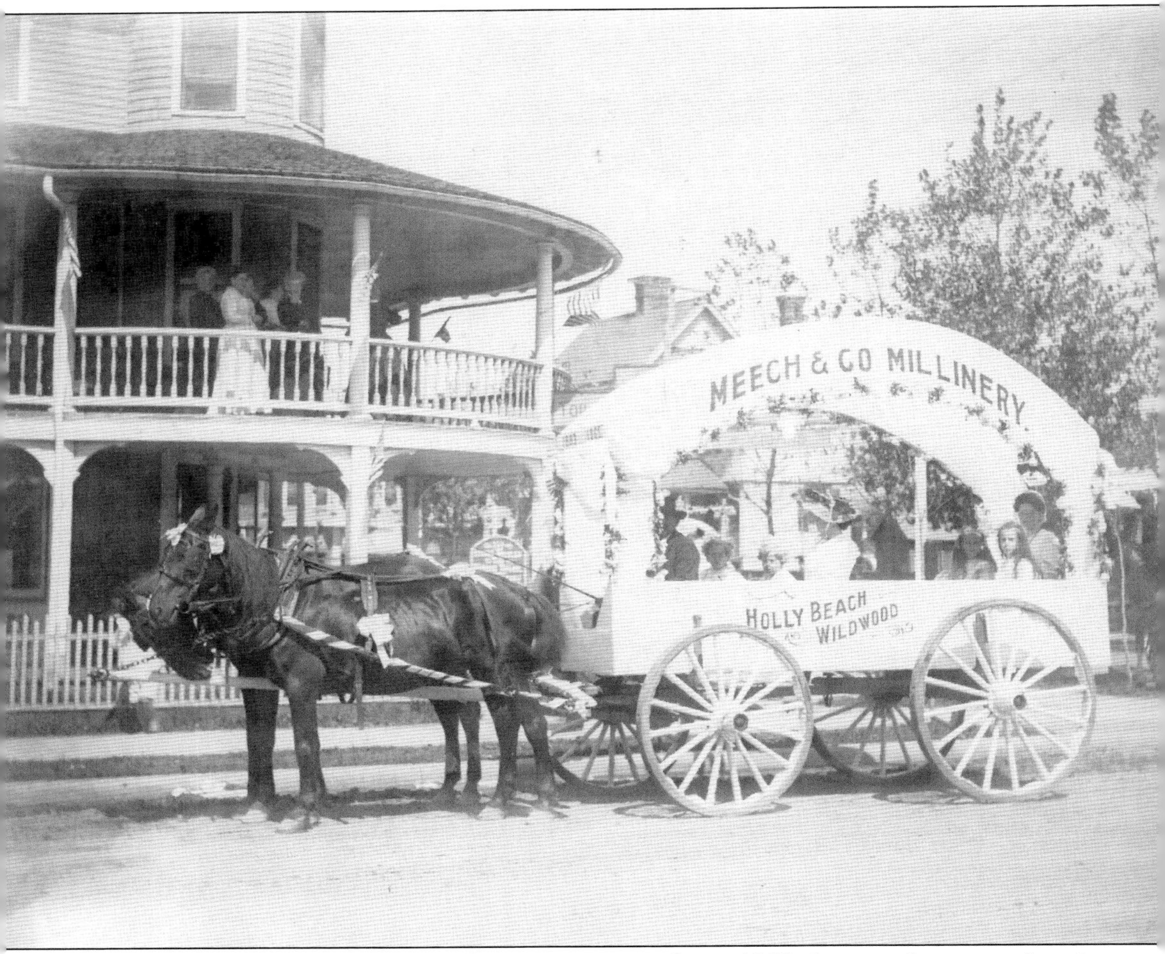

Meech's Millinery, seen advertised on a carriage in this c. 1905 photograph, occupied various locations in both Holly Beach and Wildwood. The company's founder, Jeanette DuBois Meech, came from Vineland to Holly Beach with her husband, the Reverend W.W. Meech, in 1884 and opened a dry goods store in a space they rented. They then built a store on cedar pilings over the water at Taylor and Beach Avenues, relocating several times whenever larger space was needed. When the Baker brothers began developing Wildwood in the 1880s, Philip Baker offered Jeanette the first store in the borough, but she refused. Recognizing the need for a local paper, Jeanette convinced the editor of the *Vineland Journal* to publish a Holly Beach edition, which she wrote—thus establishing the first local newspaper, the *Holly Beach Herald*, in 1885. Her daughter, Lydia Meech, assumed the business after her mother's death in 1911 but was forced to close during the Depression. (CMCHGS.)

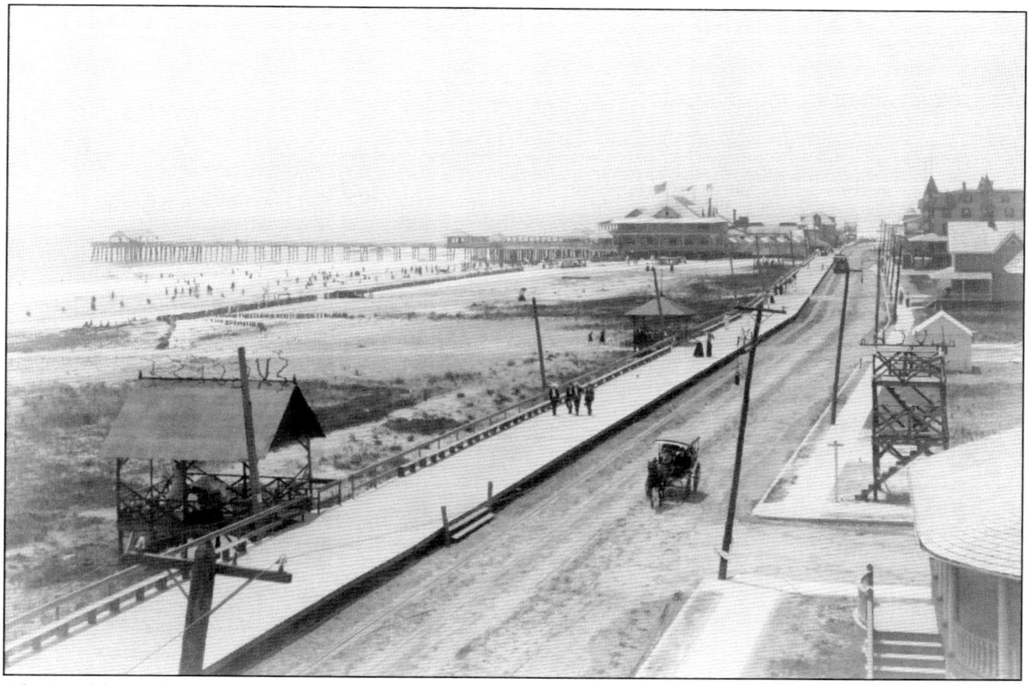

The Wildwood Casino, built in 1897 between Oak and Cedar Avenues, is seen in the distance in this c. 1920 view taken from the Sheldon Hotel a few blocks to the north. The casino offered a skating rink, poolroom, bowling alleys, bathhouses, and two carousels in addition to a fishing pier. (CMCHGS.)

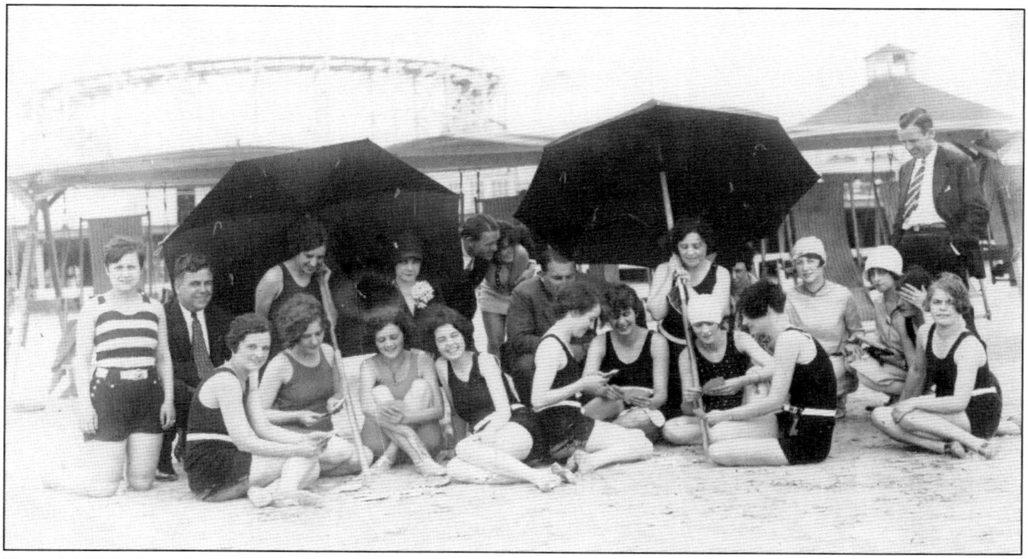

Dated 1927, this photograph shows an unidentified group of bathers playing cards on the Wildwood beach. Seen behind them is a roller coaster built in 1919 as part of the amusement center at East Cedar and East Schellenger Avenues. The roller coaster, which was named Jack Rabbit, a carousel, and another ride called Ye Old Mill were all part of the center that was torn down in October 1984. (CMCHGS.)

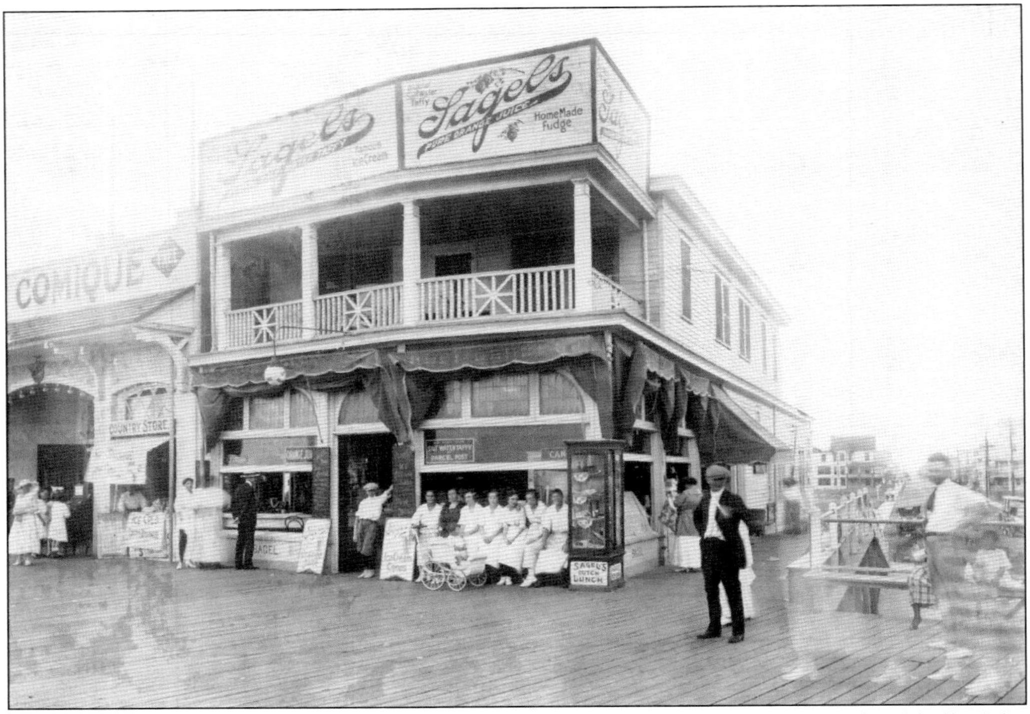

Sagel's, located at the corner of Poplar Avenue and the Boardwalk in Wildwood, sold all of the popular summer treats, including saltwater taffy, ice cream, and ice-cream soda. The business began in 1918 in a storefront on Lincoln Street. The store seen here was lost in the Christmas Day fire of 1943. (CMCHGS.)

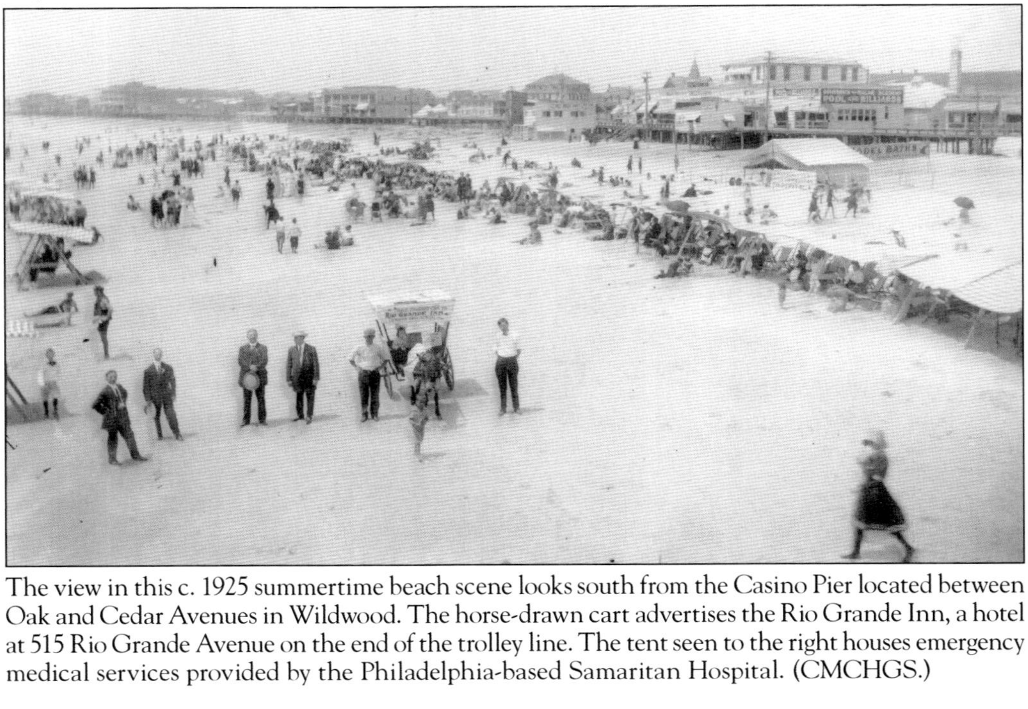

The view in this c. 1925 summertime beach scene looks south from the Casino Pier located between Oak and Cedar Avenues in Wildwood. The horse-drawn cart advertises the Rio Grande Inn, a hotel at 515 Rio Grande Avenue on the end of the trolley line. The tent seen to the right houses emergency medical services provided by the Philadelphia-based Samaritan Hospital. (CMCHGS.)

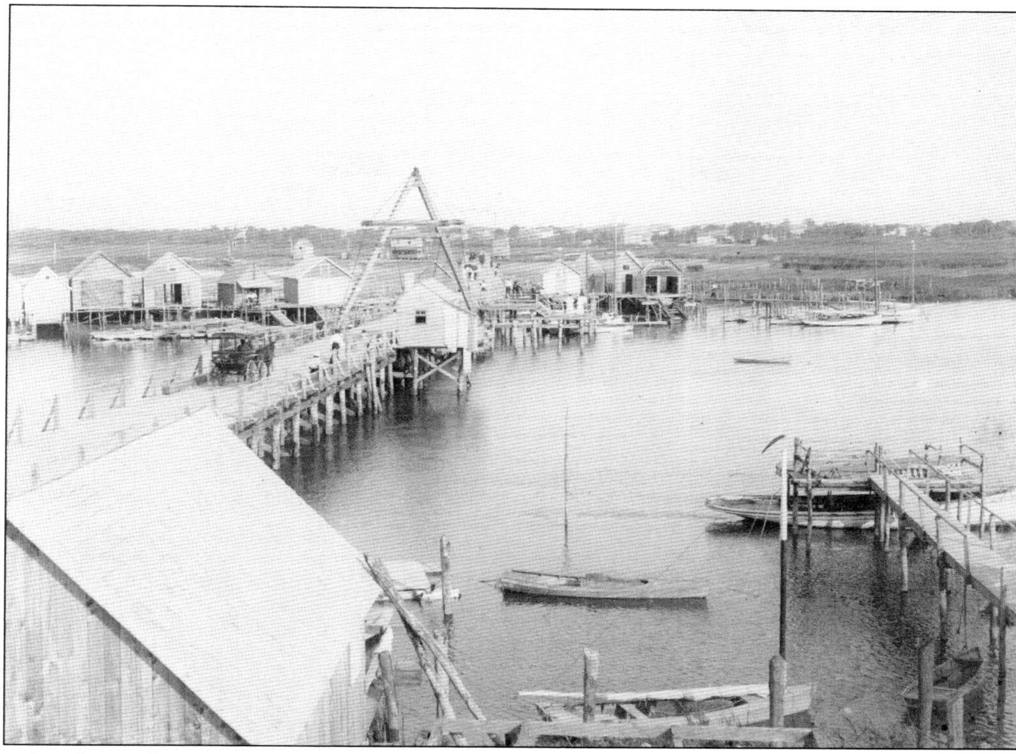

Vehicular traffic coming into Wildwood on what is now State Route 47 traveled over this wooden bridge, connecting the resort with the mainland at the south end of Middle Township in Rio Grande. The drawbridge seen here arches over the Atlantic Intracoastal Waterway. Fishing shanties like these were familiar sights along Cape May County's many back bays and creeks. (CMCHGS.)

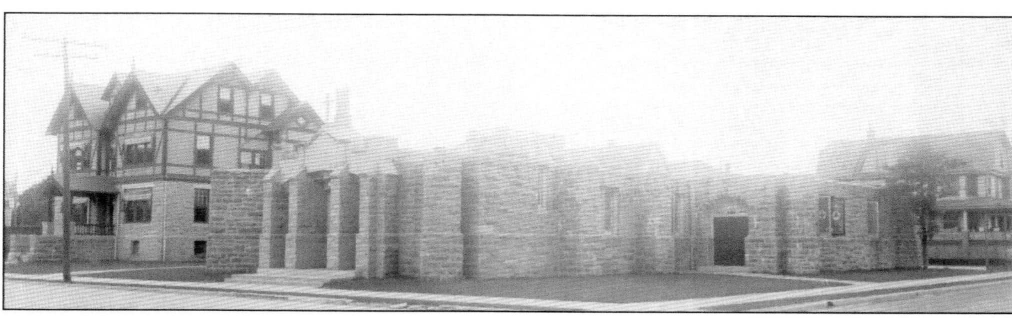

St. Ann's Catholic Church was built about 1916 at the corner of Glenwood and Pacific Avenues in Wildwood. Its architect, George Lovatt, also designed St. Mary's Church in Cape May City. A second story containing classrooms was added in 1926. Immediately adjacent to the church is the Tudor–style parish house. The church no longer remains, but the parish house still stands and has had few alterations. (CMCHGS.)

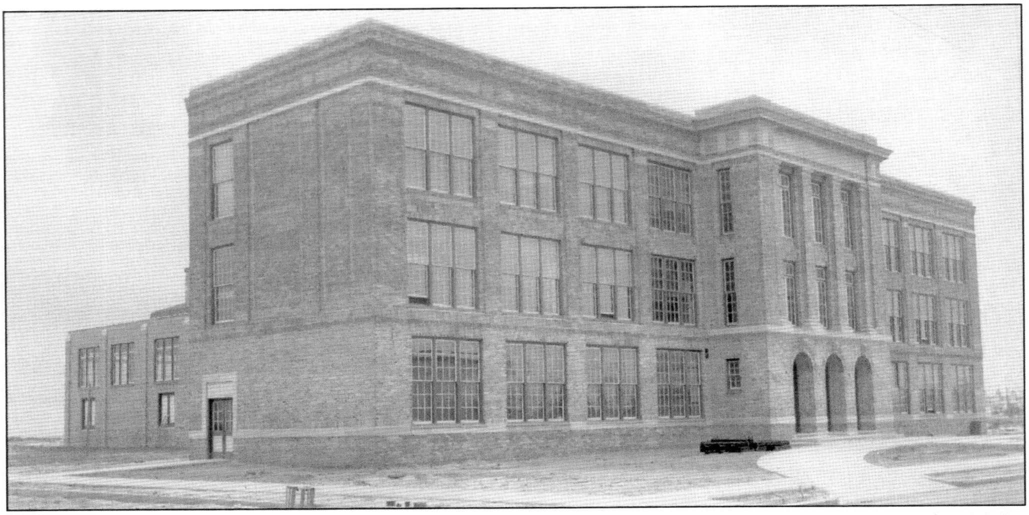

This two-story school was built in North Wildwood at 1201 North Atlantic Avenue around 1920. In 1929, its name was changed to the Margaret Mace School in recognition of Dr. Mace's 25 years as a practicing physician in that town. She founded a hospital at 2410 Atlantic Avenue and was much-loved for her kindness and generosity. The building has been highly altered. (CMCHGS.)

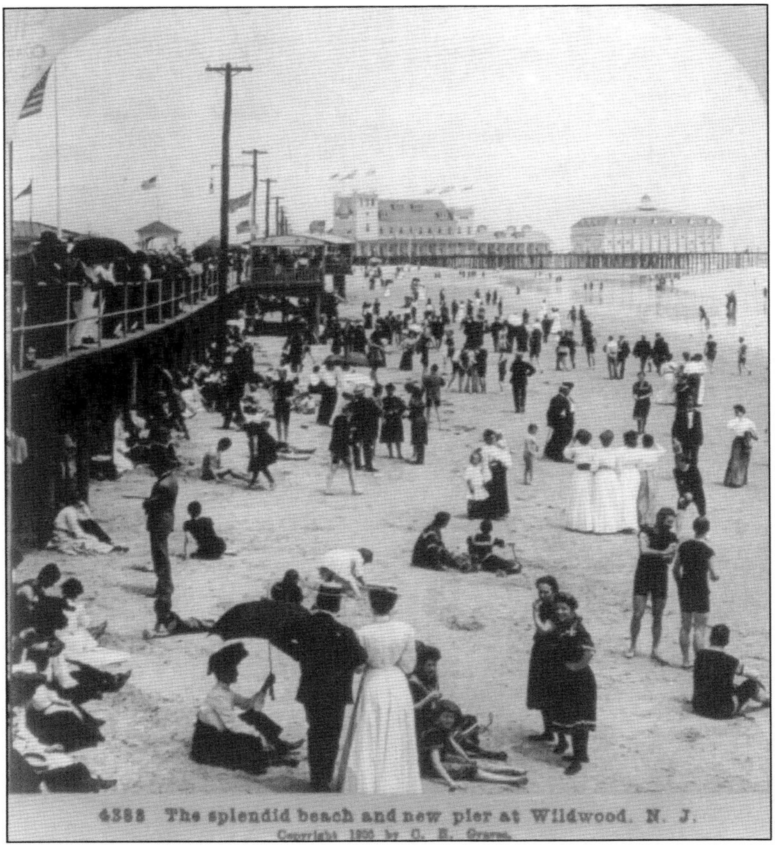

This stereoscopic view of the Wildwood beach, taken about 1905, shows the boardwalk to the left and Ocean Pier with its distinctive four-story towers in the distance. Located between Poplar and Juniper Avenues and built in 1905, Ocean Pier featured a theater, skating rink, game room, casino, carousel, and bathhouses. It later became Hunt's Pier. (LOC.)

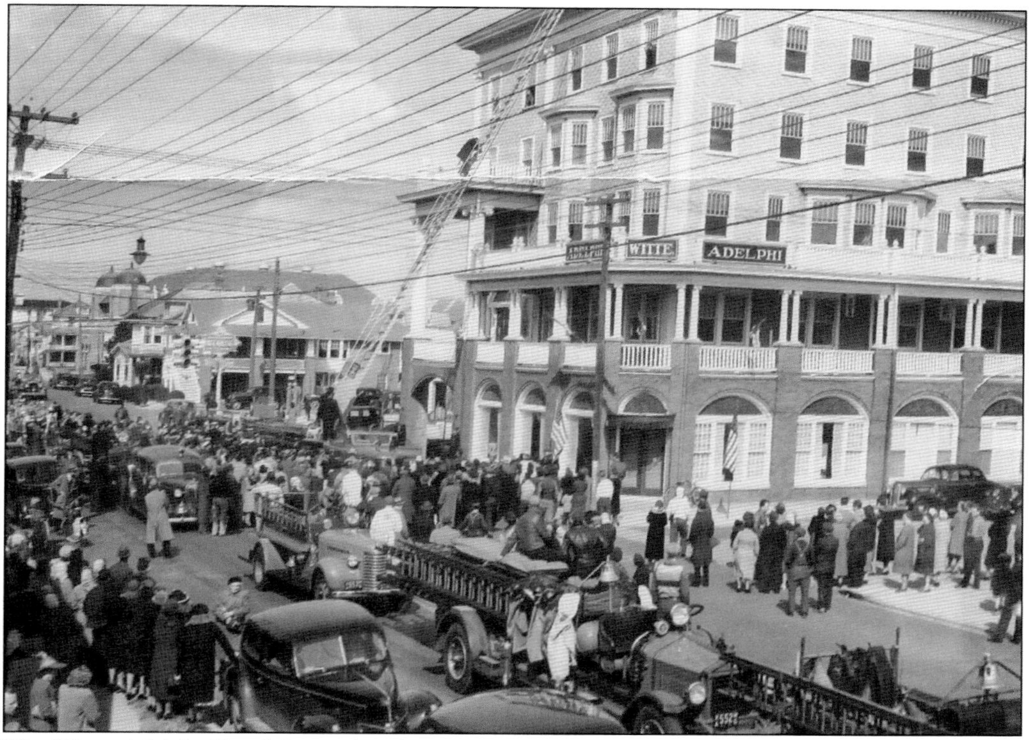

The Witte Adelphi Hotel, located at the intersection of Atlantic and Pine Avenues in Wildwood, suffered a small fire in the 1940s that drew a crowd of onlookers as the fire department responded to the emergency. The hotel opened in the 1910s, and by 1920 was charging four dollars per day. It no longer stands. (WHS.)

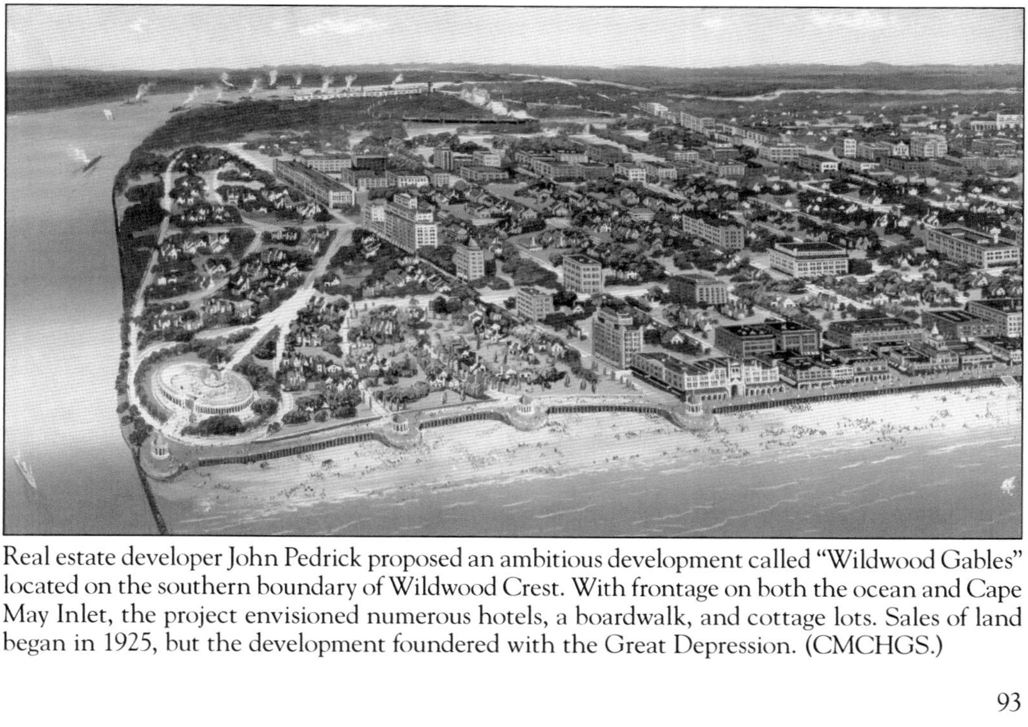

Real estate developer John Pedrick proposed an ambitious development called "Wildwood Gables" located on the southern boundary of Wildwood Crest. With frontage on both the ocean and Cape May Inlet, the project envisioned numerous hotels, a boardwalk, and cottage lots. Sales of land began in 1925, but the development foundered with the Great Depression. (CMCHGS.)

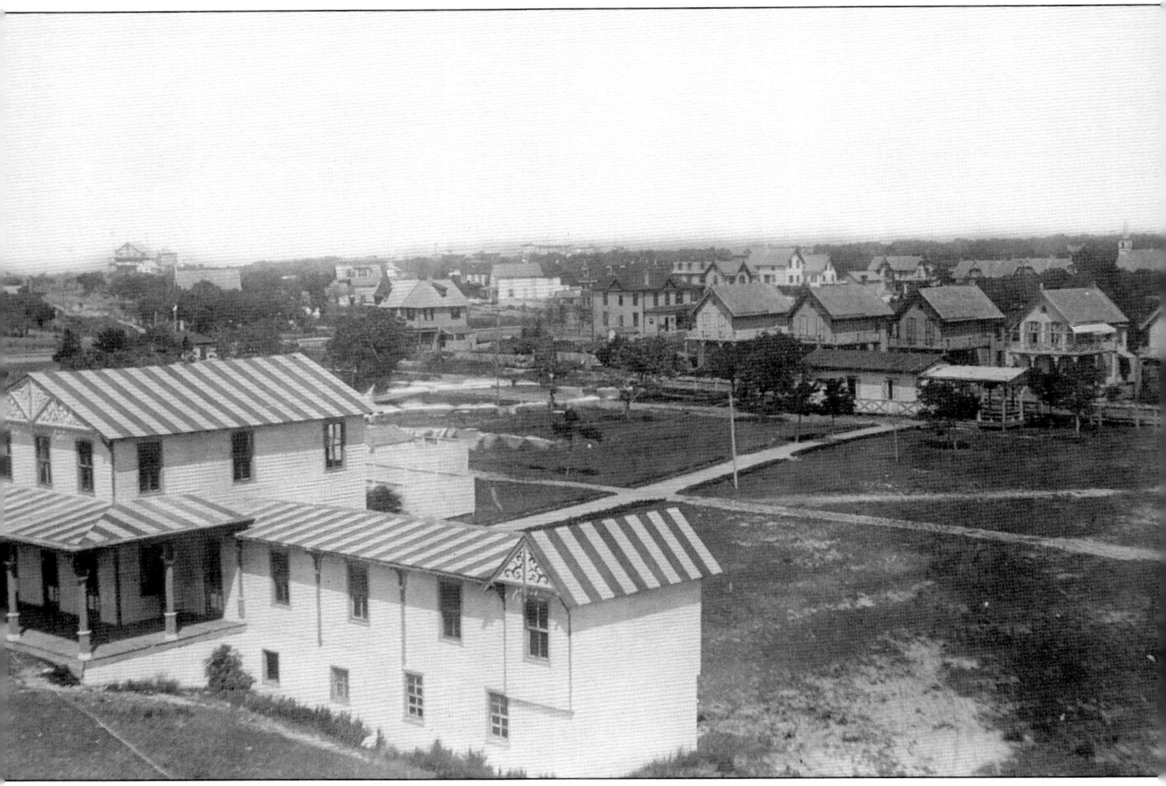

Cape May Point, seen here about 1900, was founded as a Presbyterian resort community in 1875 at the southwestern end of the Cape May peninsula in Lower Township. Originally called Sea Grove, the community changed its name because of its similarity to Ocean Grove, another New Jersey seaside resort. The resort was developed by the Sea Grove Association, which banned the sale of "spirituous or intoxicating liquors" and dictated the style and character of the houses built. Other Christian denominations—Episcopalians, Lutherans, and Methodists among them—were also welcome. This view was taken around 1900 from the Carleton Hotel and looks northwest. The building in the foreground with a striped roof houses a drugstore in addition to hot and cold saltwater baths. The one-story building in the center right with an open-air shelter next to it is the station for a train that ran from Steamboat Landing to Cape May City via Cape May Point along Lincoln Avenue. (CMCHGS.)

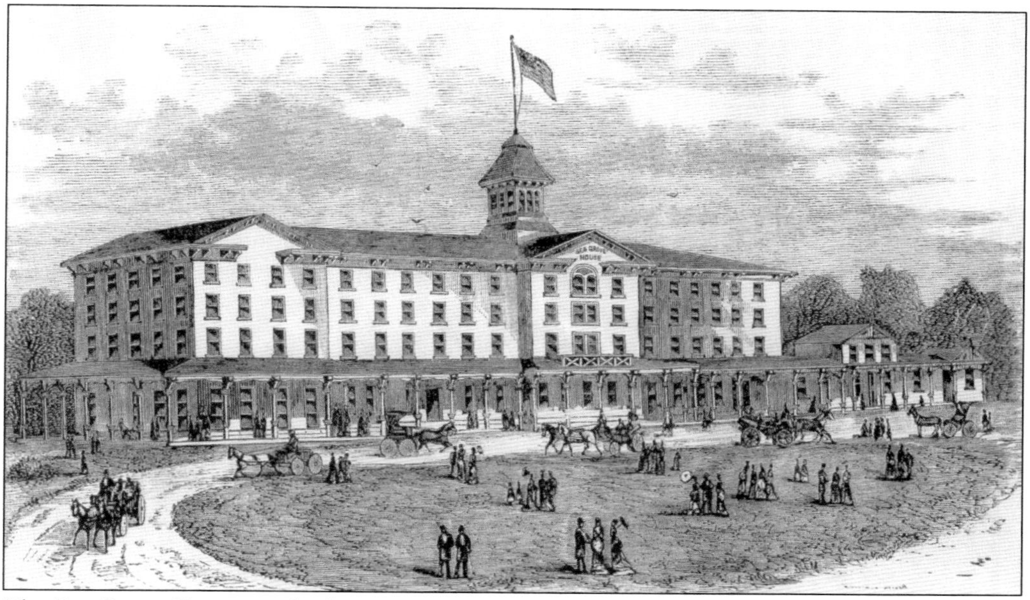

The Sea Grove House was built in 1875 to accommodate visitors to Cape May Point; it was one of three hotels erected in the resort, all under the same management. The other two were the Centennial and the Cape May Point. From 1881 to 1910, this was called the Carleton and offered 126 bedrooms, a 250-seat dining room, music pavilion, two billiards rooms, and four bowling alleys. The etching above shows the 1875 appearance of its waterfront facade. The Sisters of the Immaculate Heart of Mary bought the hotel as a summer retreat in 1914, calling it the Villa Maria by the Sea. The photograph below was taken in August 1928 and shows the facade had changed little since it was built. By 1937, the ocean was almost at its doorstep and the building was abandoned. It no longer stands. (Above, NASW; below, CMCHGS.)

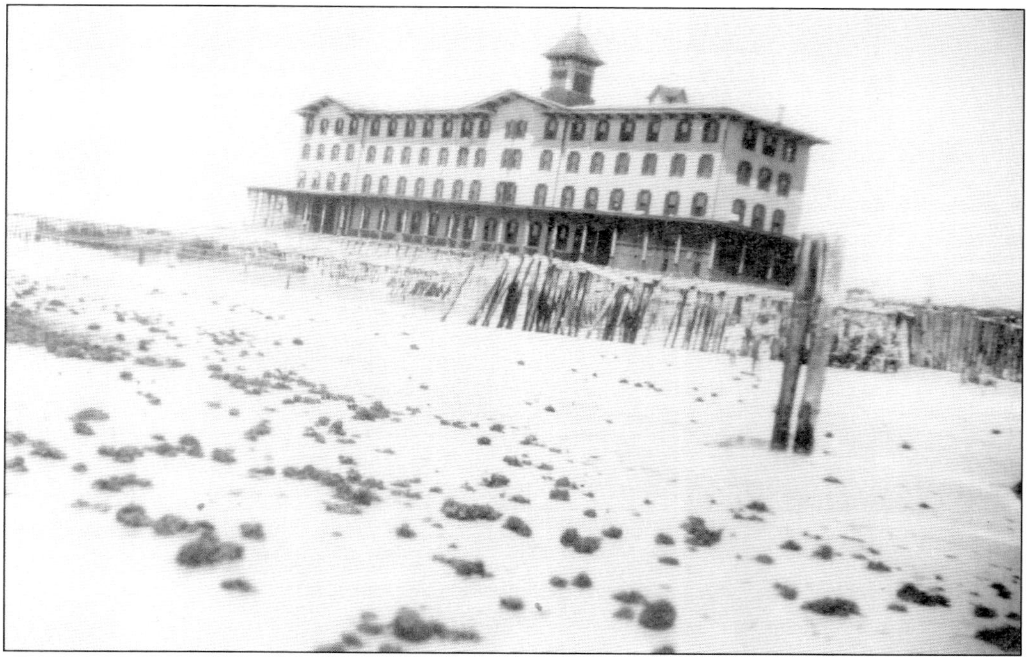

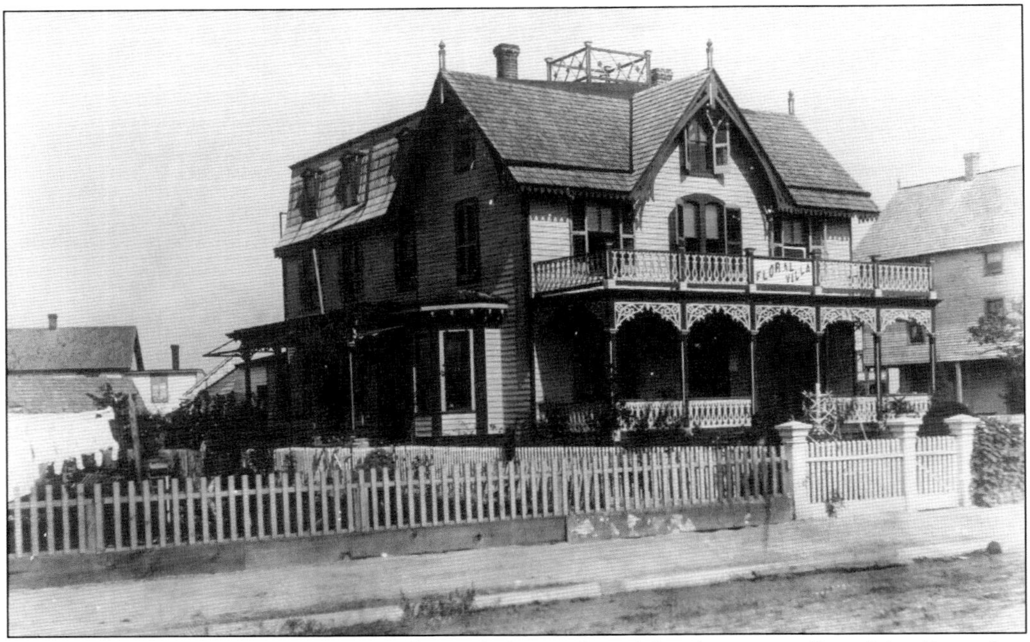

The Floral Villa, built before 1890, still stands facing Cape May Avenue in Cape May Point, but its appearance has been somewhat modified. In the late 1890s and early 1900s, it was managed by Mary E. Springer, who touted its moderate rates, airy rooms, proximity to the beach, and "home comforts" in Philadelphia newspaper advertisements. (CMCHGS.)

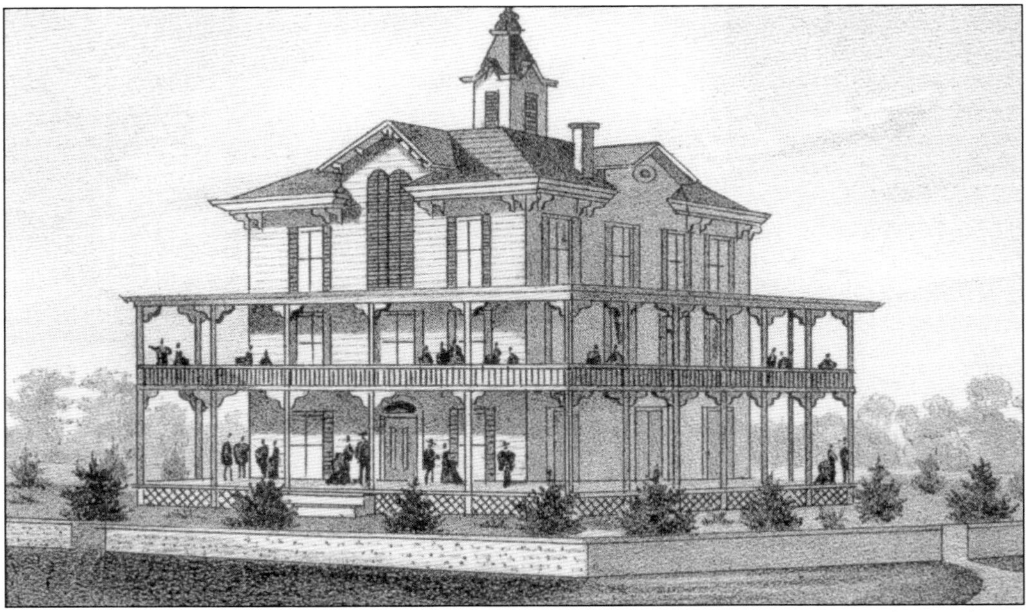

Around 1876, Philadelphia department store owner John Wanamaker built this handsome three-story cottage on Yale Avenue in Cape May Point, where it still stands. Reportedly, Pres. Benjamin Harrison and his first wife, Caroline, were entertained by then postmaster general Wanamaker in this house around 1889. The Harrisons enjoyed their stay so much that they built a 20-room mansion there also, using it the summers of 1890 and 1891. (CMCHGS.)

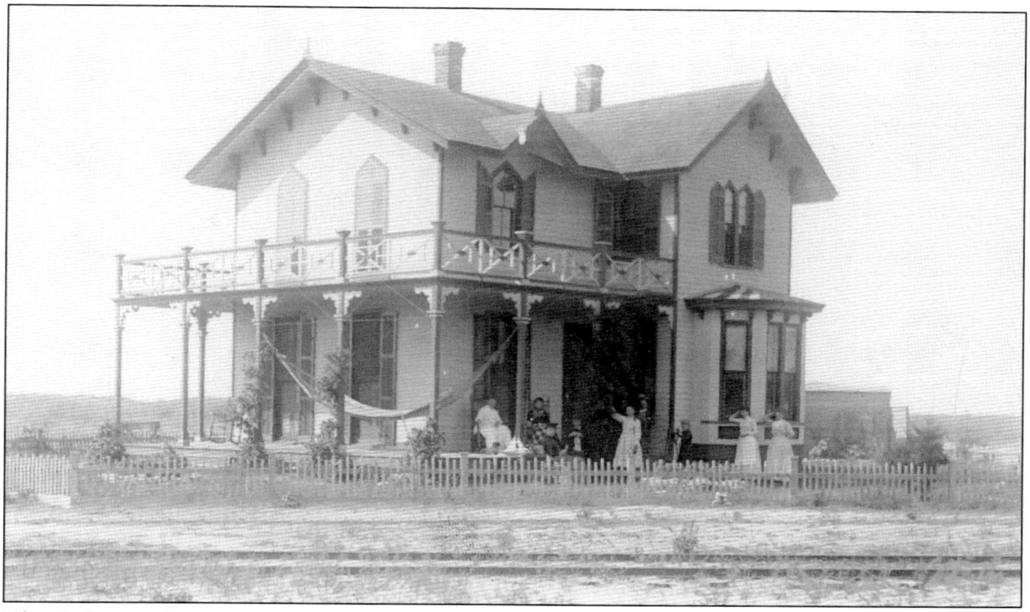

The Delaware Bay & Cape May Railroad tracks run past this house, which still stands at the corner of Ocean and Lincoln Avenues in Cape May Point. This short line was organized around 1882 by Jonathan Cone, owner of the steamship *Republic*, which operated out of Steamboat Landing. Cone sought an easier way than by carriage or wagon to transport his customers into Cape May City. (CMCHGS.)

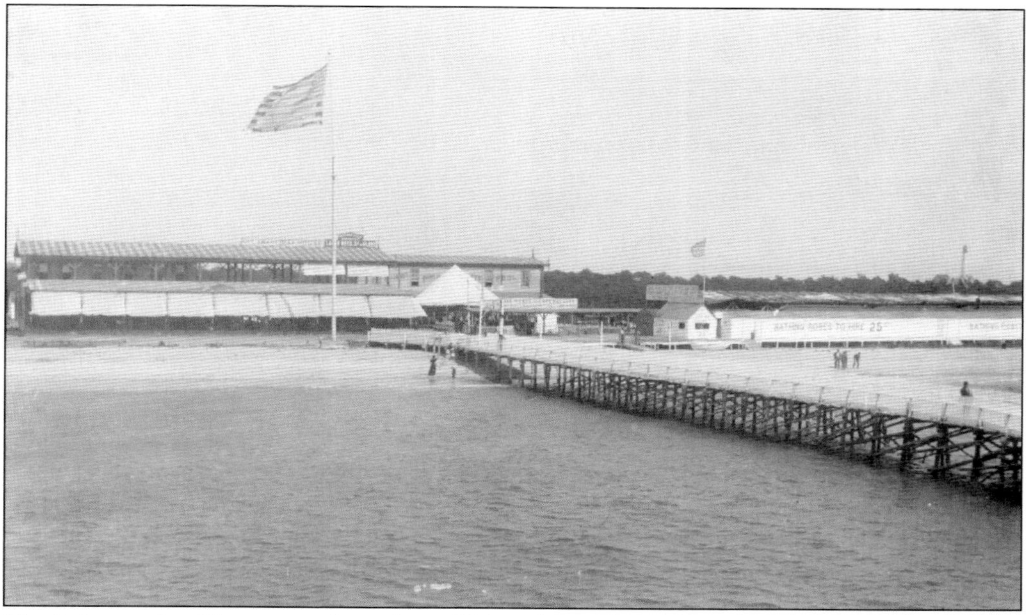

The Delaware Bay House, seen here about 1900, welcomed visitors to Cape May who disembarked at Steamboat Landing, located at the western terminus of Sunset Boulevard. Tourists could enjoy a meal of fish, clams, or oysters, play billiards or go bowling, or even rent a bathing suit for 25¢. The train left here every eight minutes for Cape May via Cape May Point. Note the lighthouse in the distance. (CMCHGS.)

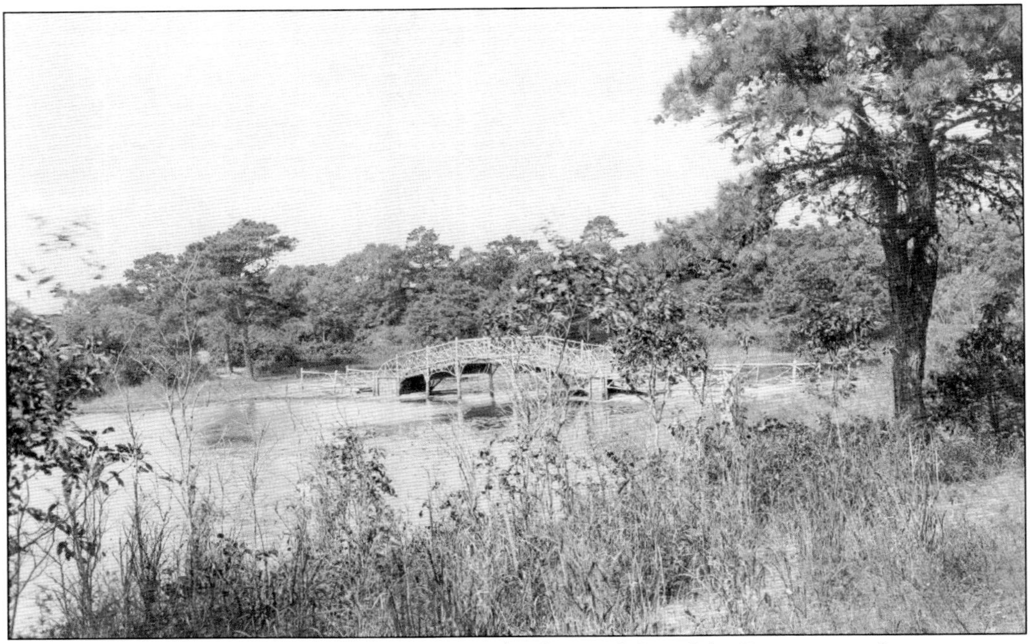

J.C. Sydney, the architect/landscape architect who designed Cape May Point, created a picturesque bridge over Lake Lily, a natural freshwater pond located in the borough's northeast quarter. The shores of the lake were graded to create a level road dotted with boat houses, making the lake a focal point of the resort. (CMCHGS.)

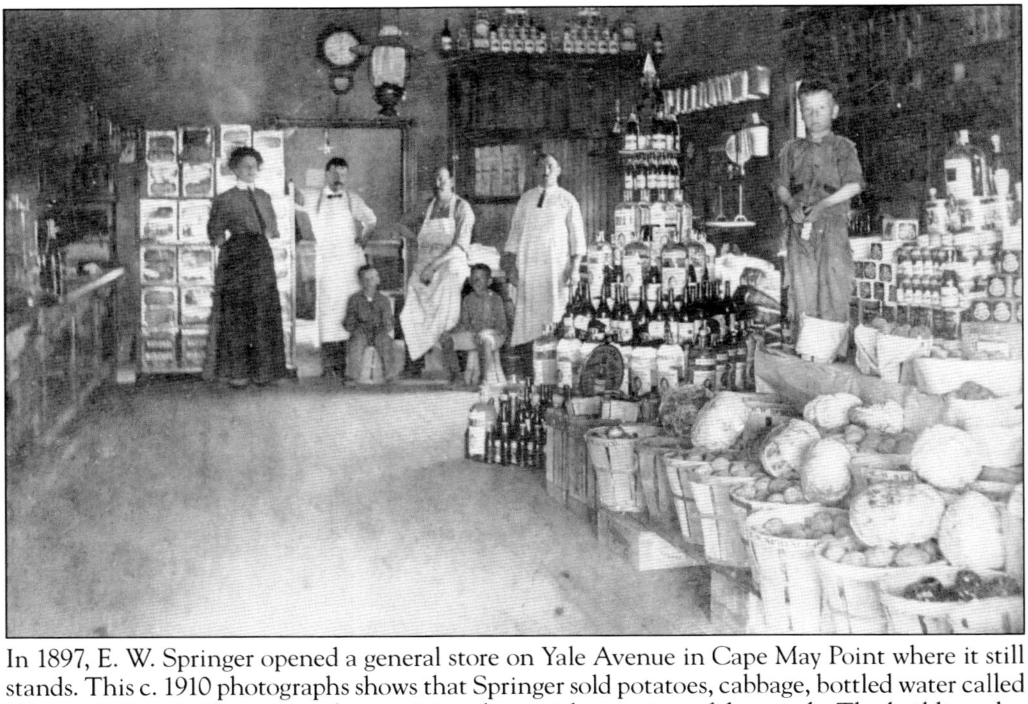

In 1897, E. W. Springer opened a general store on Yale Avenue in Cape May Point where it still stands. This c. 1910 photographs shows that Springer sold potatoes, cabbage, bottled water called "Hyoxia," Campbell's soup, and grape juice along with a variety of dry goods. The building also housed the post office. (CMCHGS.)

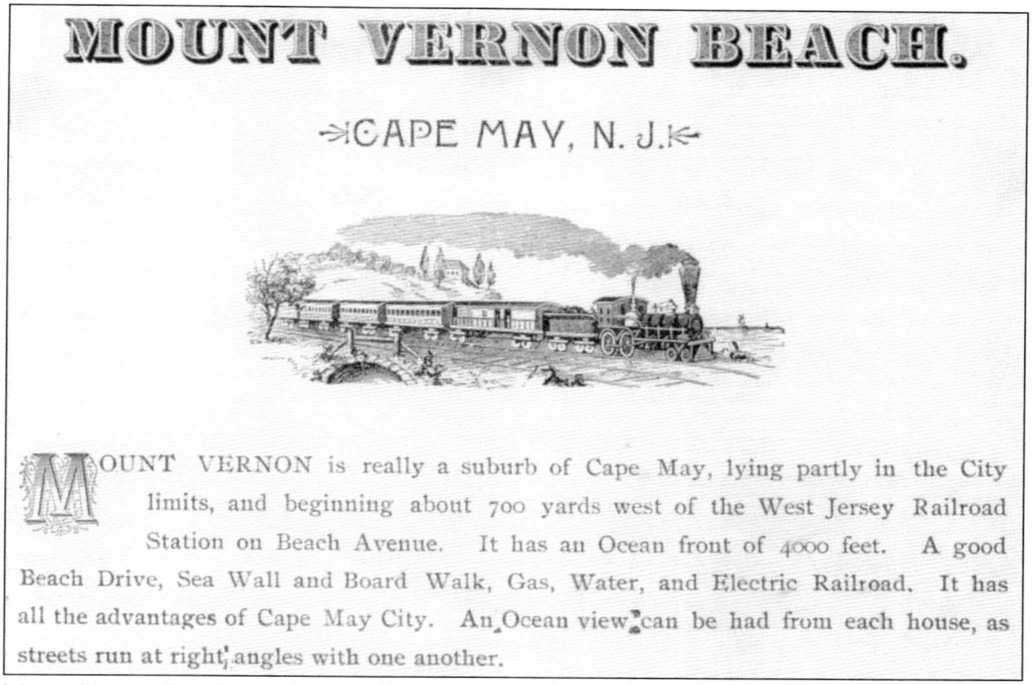

MOUNT VERNON BEACH.

CAPE MAY, N. J.

MOUNT VERNON is really a suburb of Cape May, lying partly in the City limits, and beginning about 700 yards west of the West Jersey Railroad Station on Beach Avenue. It has an Ocean front of 4000 feet. A good Beach Drive, Sea Wall and Board Walk, Gas, Water, and Electric Railroad. It has all the advantages of Cape May City. An Ocean view can be had from each house, as streets run at right angles with one another.

Mount Vernon Beach was a late-1800s development located just west of Cape May City on the site where the massive Mount Vernon hotel stood before it burned to the ground in 1856. According to this advertising brochure (above), the new community began 700 feet west of the West Jersey & Seashore Railroad station on Beach Avenue, which places it near present-day Grant Street. Slowly, waterfront cottages were built (below), and Mount Vernon Beach was incorporated as the borough of South Cape May in 1894. Erosion and storms had obliterated the borough by 1945, but many of the houses were moved to other locations, several to West Cape May, to save them. (Both, CMCHGS.)

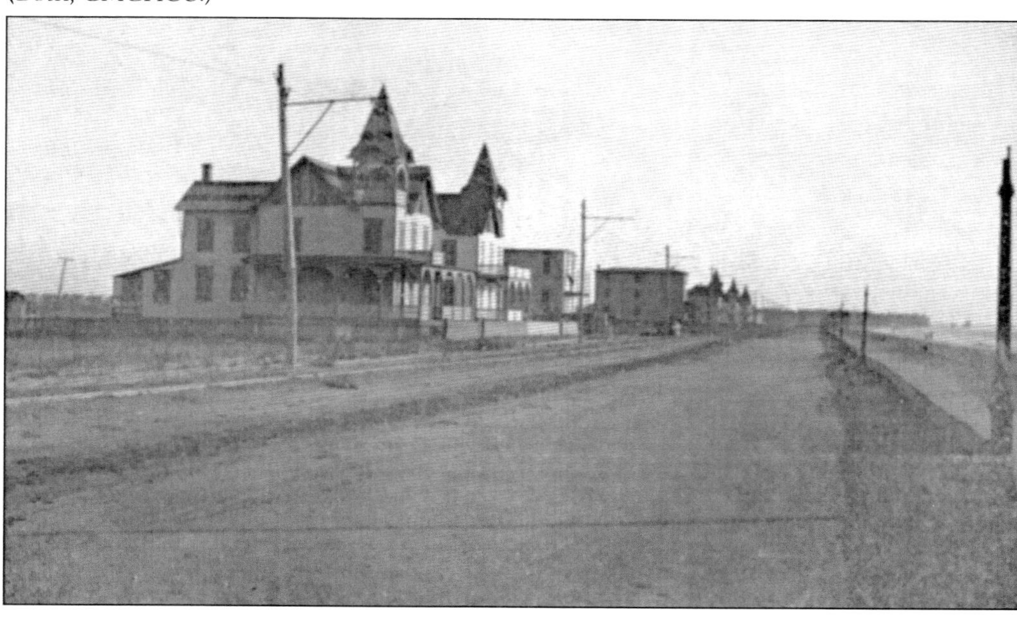

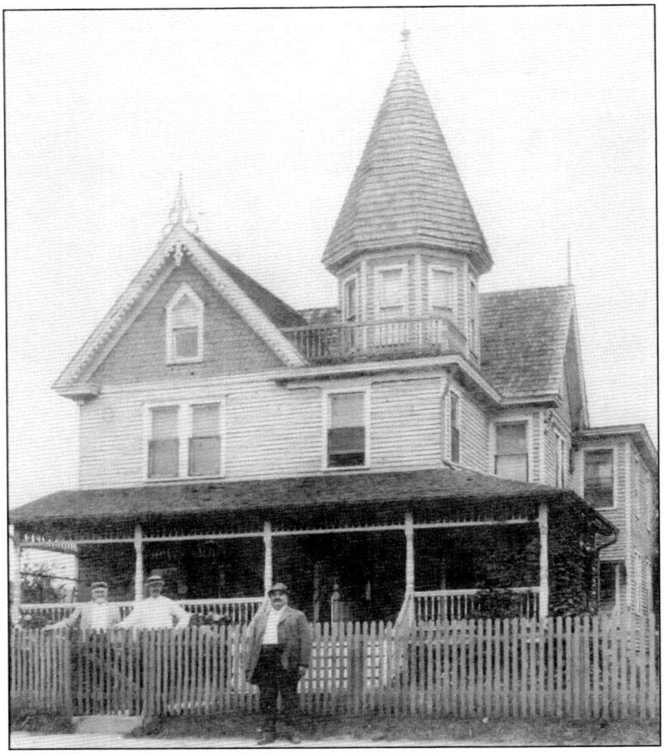

Dr. Albert G. Stevens built this Queen Anne house in 1900, purportedly as a wedding present for his wife. It overlooks Wilbraham Park in West Cape May, where it stills stands on Myrtle Avenue. The house remained in the Stevens family until 1944; it is currently a bed-and-breakfast. (Marie Iaconangelo.)

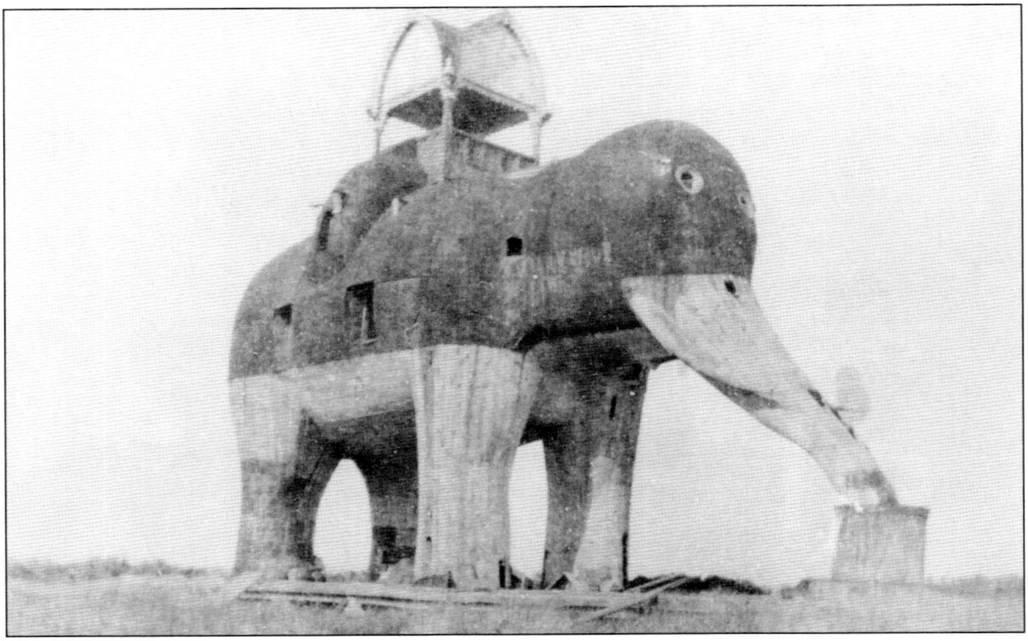

A wooden elephant called the Light of Asia was built in 1884 as a way to lure potential buyers to inspect building lots for sale on the large Mount Vernon tract between Cape May City and West Cape May. The elephant stood almost 41 feet tall; spiral stairs in the legs led to the second story, where more stairs led to the "howdah" observatory on the animal's back. (CMCHGS.)

Five

Leisure Time

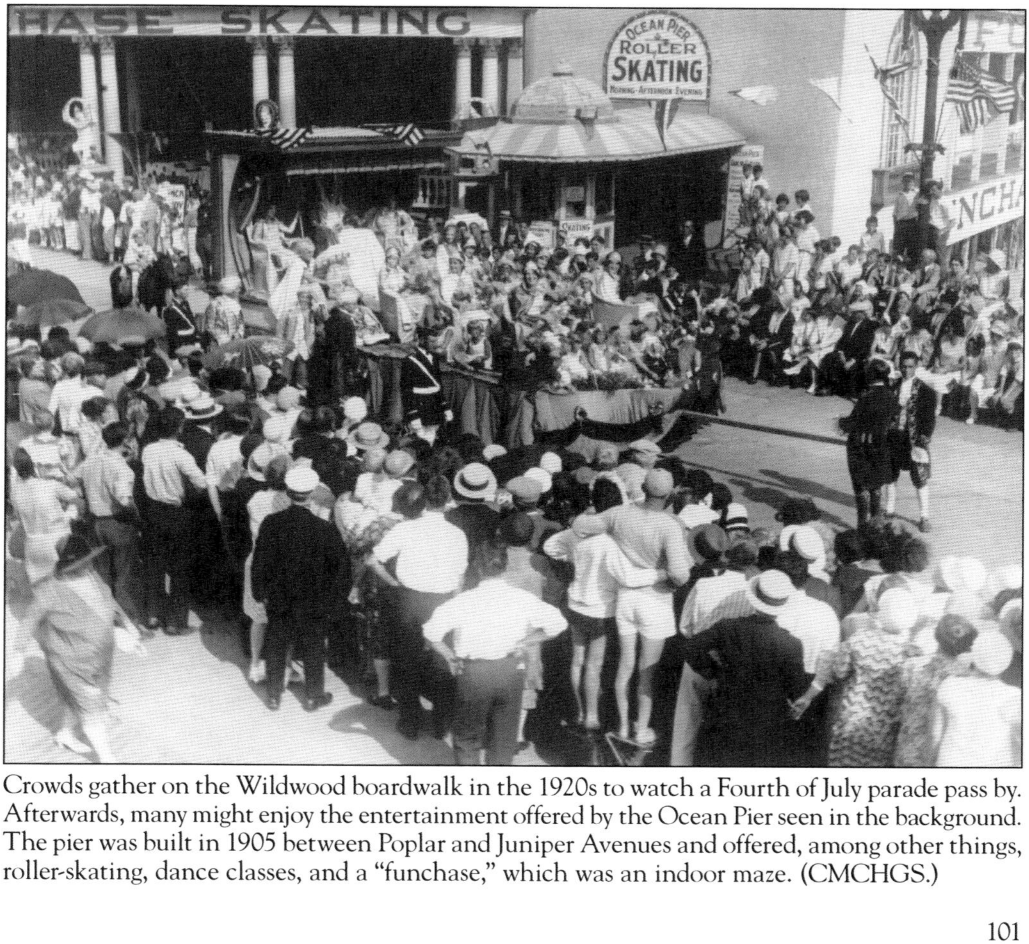

Crowds gather on the Wildwood boardwalk in the 1920s to watch a Fourth of July parade pass by. Afterwards, many might enjoy the entertainment offered by the Ocean Pier seen in the background. The pier was built in 1905 between Poplar and Juniper Avenues and offered, among other things, roller-skating, dance classes, and a "funchase," which was an indoor maze. (CMCHGS.)

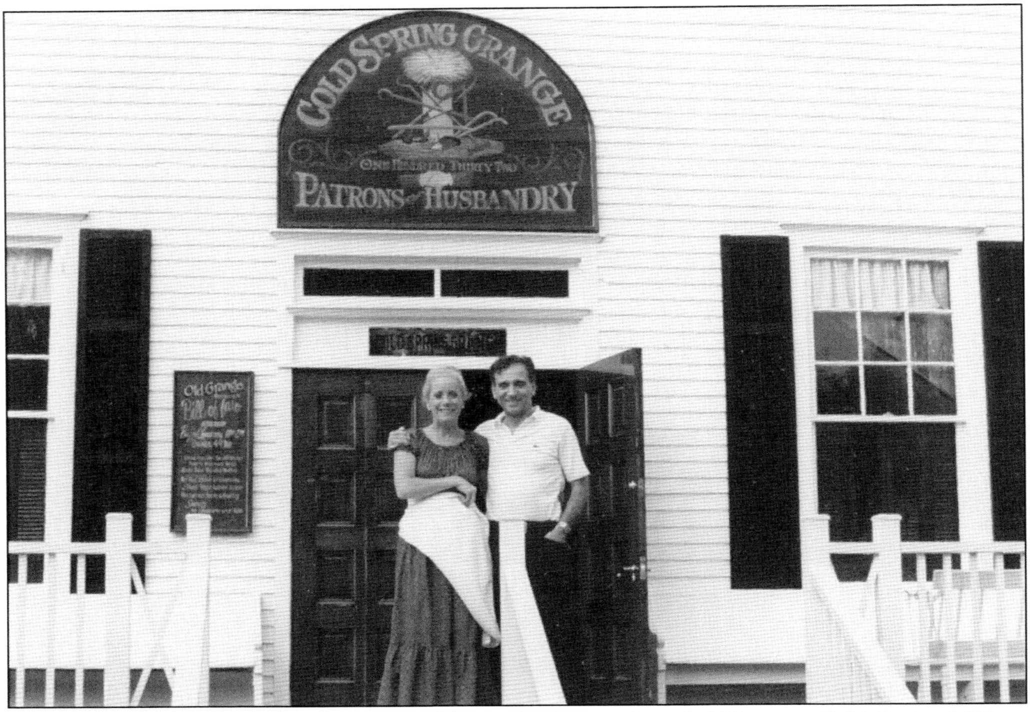

Pictured above, Dr. Joseph Salvatore and his wife, Annie, founded Historic Cold Spring Village in 1973. The open-air living history museum village contains 29 historic buildings that range in date from around 1691 to about 1957. The Cold Spring Grange, built in 1912 and seen above in 1981, stands at its original location. All but one of the remaining buildings were moved from other sites in Cape May County. Open six days a week during the summer, the village offers visitors an authentic experience of early-1800s life through demonstrations of hearth cooking, weaving, printing, bookbinding, carpentry, blacksmithing, basketry, and carpentry in the historic buildings. Visitors can also tour an 1836 inn, a c. 1850 school, several barns (one of them housing a craft brewery), and a general store. The village is also a popular place for weddings, as seen below. (Above, NASW; below, CMCHGS.)

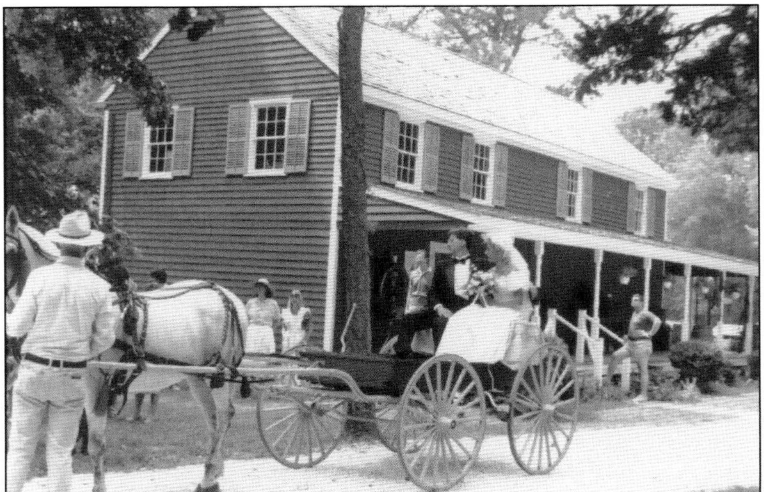

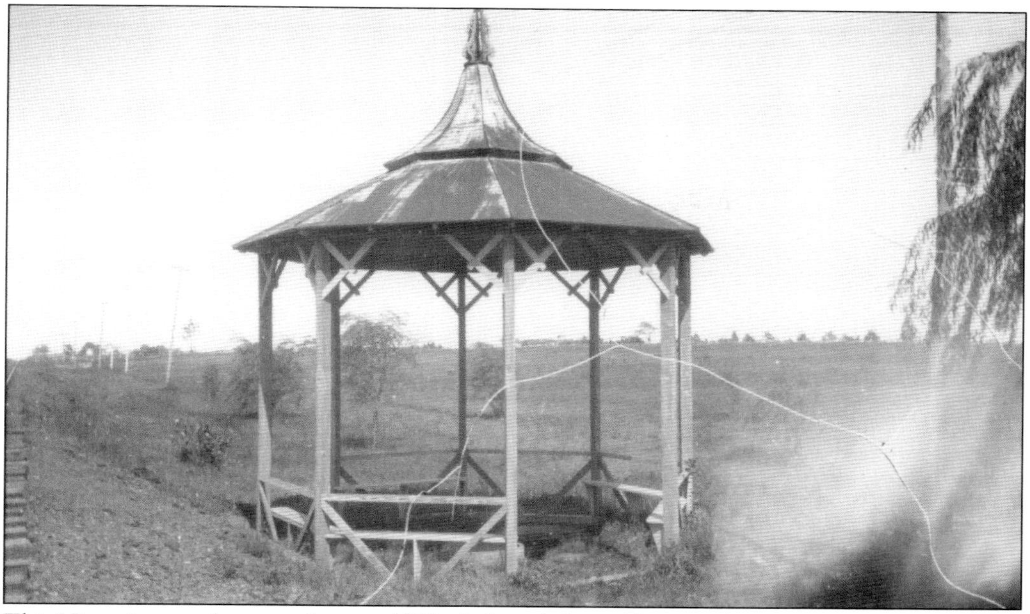

This Victorian gazebo, seen here in 1899, sheltered the cold spring for which this area of Lower Township was named. The spring was a tourist attraction, drawing vacationers from Cape May City, who arrived by carriage or wagon to sit under the copper roof and drink the fresh water. Note the railroad tracks for the West Jersey line, which brought visitors from Philadelphia to Cape May. (CMCHGS.)

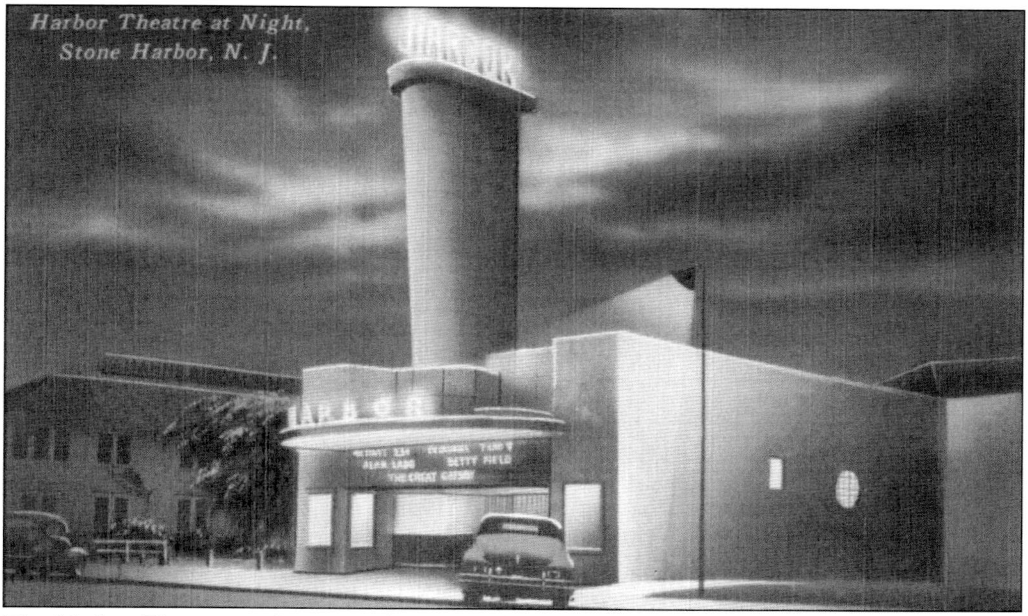

The Harbor Theatre in Stone Harbor opened its doors in June 1949 under the ownership of Philadelphian Jack Greenberg. An 800-seat theater located on Ninety-Sixth Street, it ran year-round. It was later sold to Hunt Theatres and to the Frank Theatre chain, which created a fiveplex in 1986. New owners in 2016 renovated the theater, adding luxury amenities like a burger bar and private balcony suites. (SHM.)

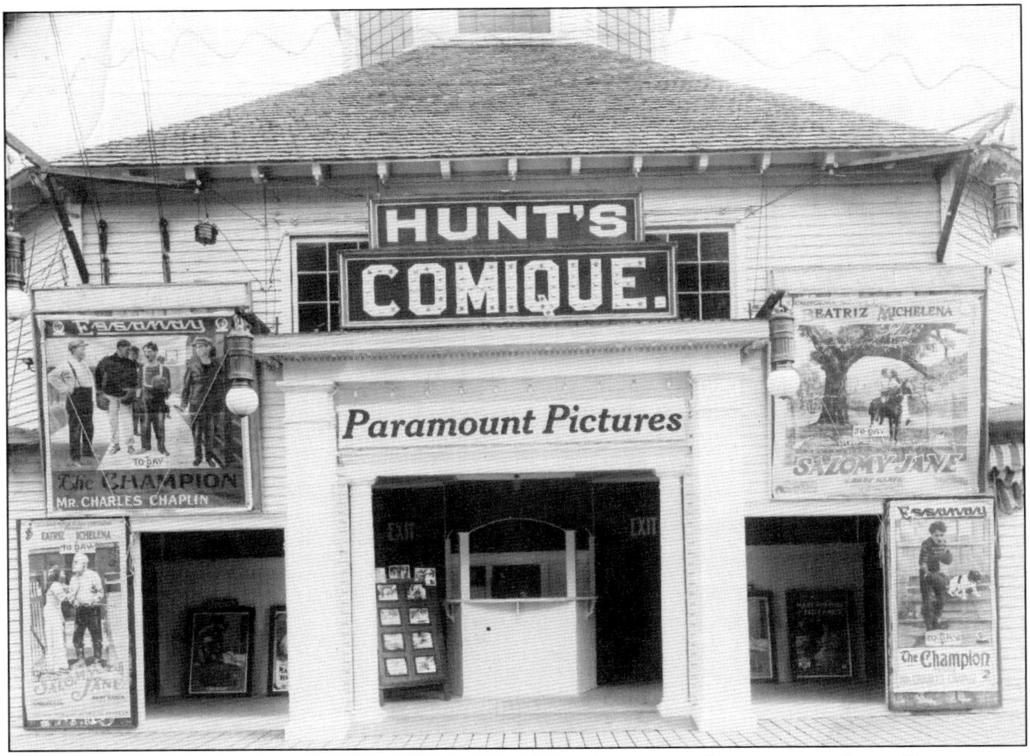

The Comique Theatre, seen here about 1915, was one of several Wildwood theaters operated by entrepreneur and entertainer William C. Hunt in the early 1900s. The Comique opened in 1906 on the boardwalk, charging adults 10¢ and children 5¢. Posters advertise the silent movies *Salomy Jane* and *The Champion*. (CMCHGS.)

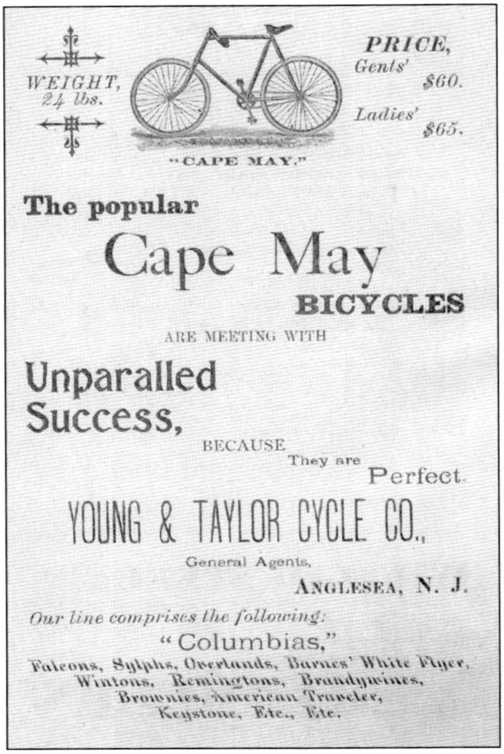

Bicycle riding was a popular leisure time activity in the late 1800s and early 1900s. Major newspapers often published scenic bike routes from city to the shore and many resorts held bicycle races to attract tourists. The Cape May County Bicycle Road Improvement Association spent thousands of dollars creating paths from Millville to Cape May in the 1890s. (CMCHGS.)

Watching or participating in yacht races was another popular activity for shore visitors. Spectators in this c. 1905 stereoscopic view watch anxiously while several sailboats navigate along Wildwood's coastline. That year, over 30 sailboats and motorboats were part of a Fourth of July race sponsored by the borough, with prizes. (LOC.)

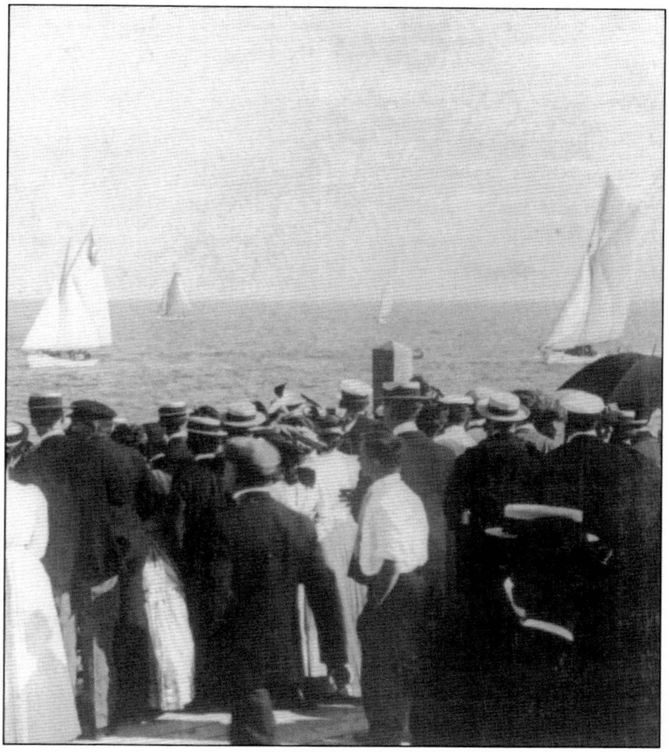

Spectators in this 1928 photograph stand on what is probably the dock of the Ocean City Yacht Club on Sixth Street as they watch four Chris-Craft Runabouts race each other in the Great Egg Harbor Bay behind the yacht club. Other spectators watch the event from their boats. The occasion for the race is not identified. (CMCHGS.)

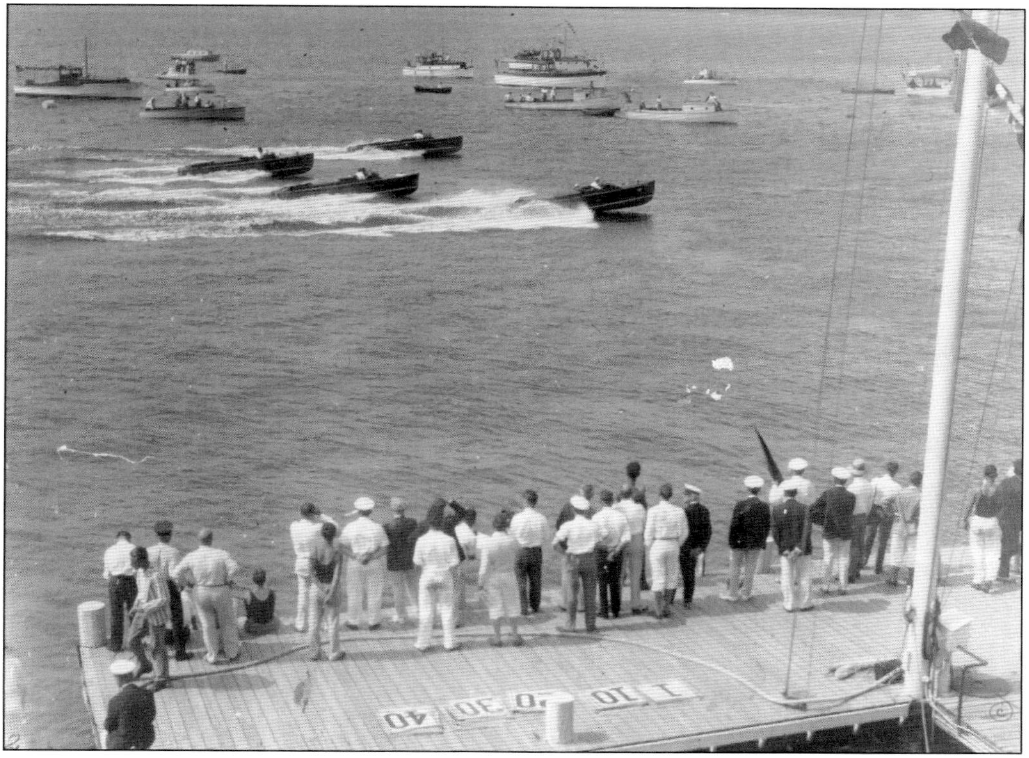

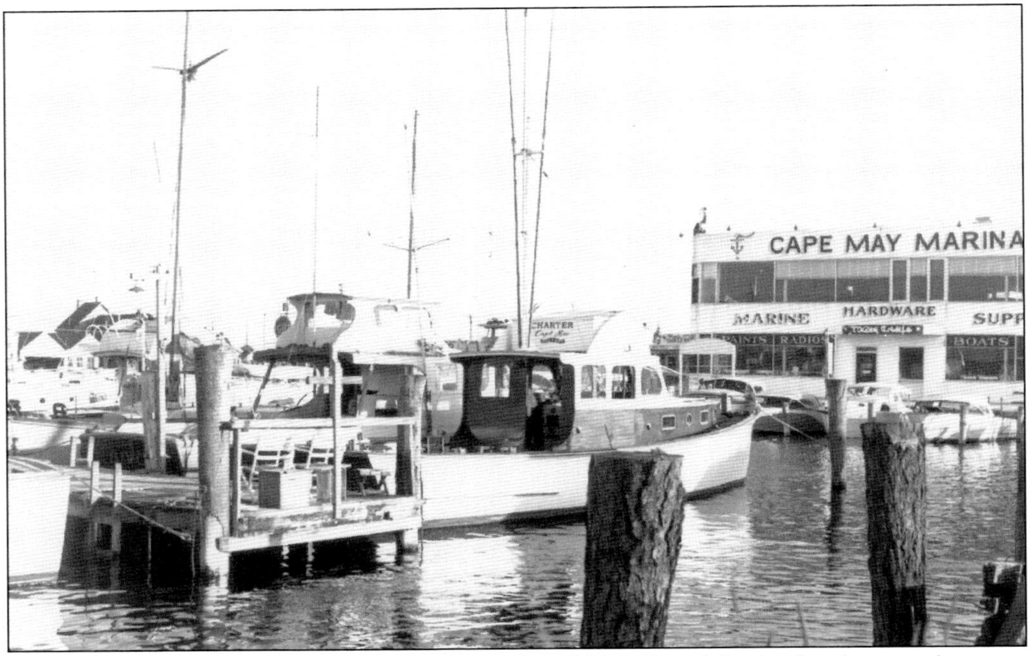

As sportfishing grew increasingly popular in the 1900s, Cape May harbor became home to numerous charter boats that could be hired by the half and whole day for local fishing around the peninsula or deep-sea fishing in the Atlantic Ocean. This mid-1950s view shows Cape May Marina in Cape May City, where several charter boats are docked. (CMCHGS.)

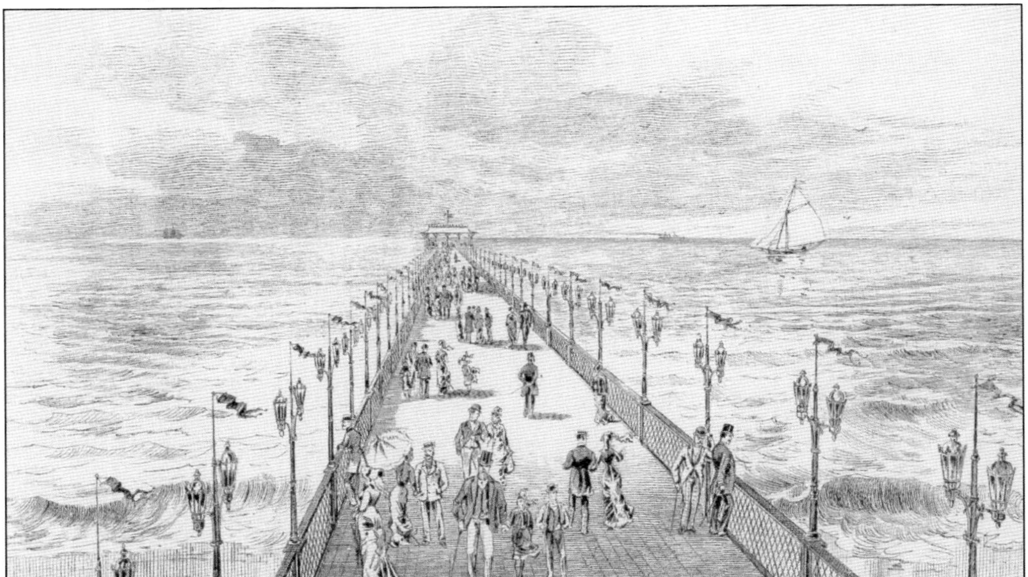

The 1,000-foot-long Iron Pier was built in Cape May City in 1884. Designed by the Pennsylvania-based Phoenix Iron Company, it was located opposite the Lafayette Hotel at the foot of Decatur Street. Accessible only with a paid admission, it offered shops, a bathing pavilion, and a music pavilion that hosted concerts and dancing. The pier and its buildings were demolished in the 20th century. (CMCHGS.)

It is not known when the first fishing contest was sponsored, but they continue to this day. This 1954 advertisement is for a six-month-long fishing contest sponsored by the County of Cape May. It was open to the public, and the fact that no fees are charged is emphasized because many contests rely on fees to fund the prizes. (CMCHGS.)

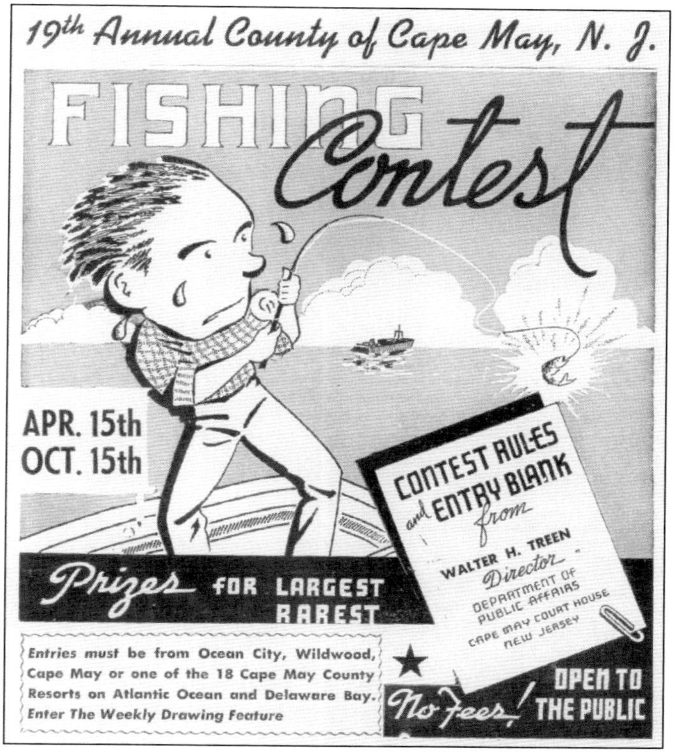

In addition to sportfishing, hunting was another popular pastime in Cape May County. The region's abundance of wildfowl like ducks, rail birds, and pheasants lured out-of-state hunters, as did plentiful herds of deer on the mainland. Seen here are unidentified members of the Lower Township Gun Club around 1930. (HGM.)

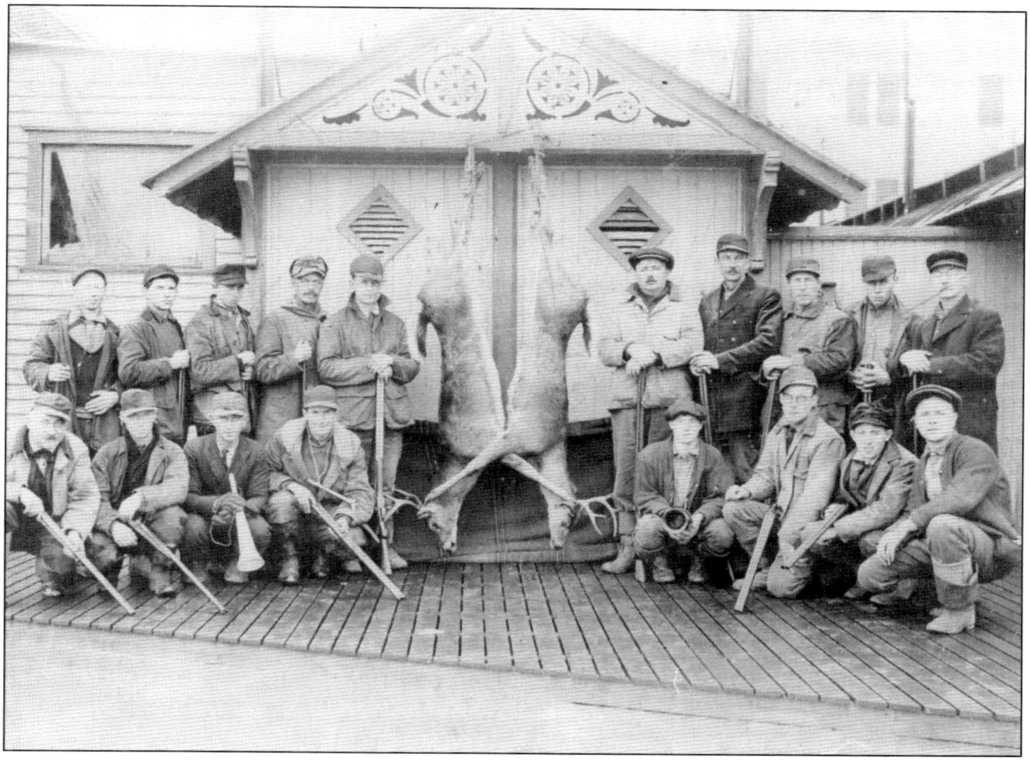

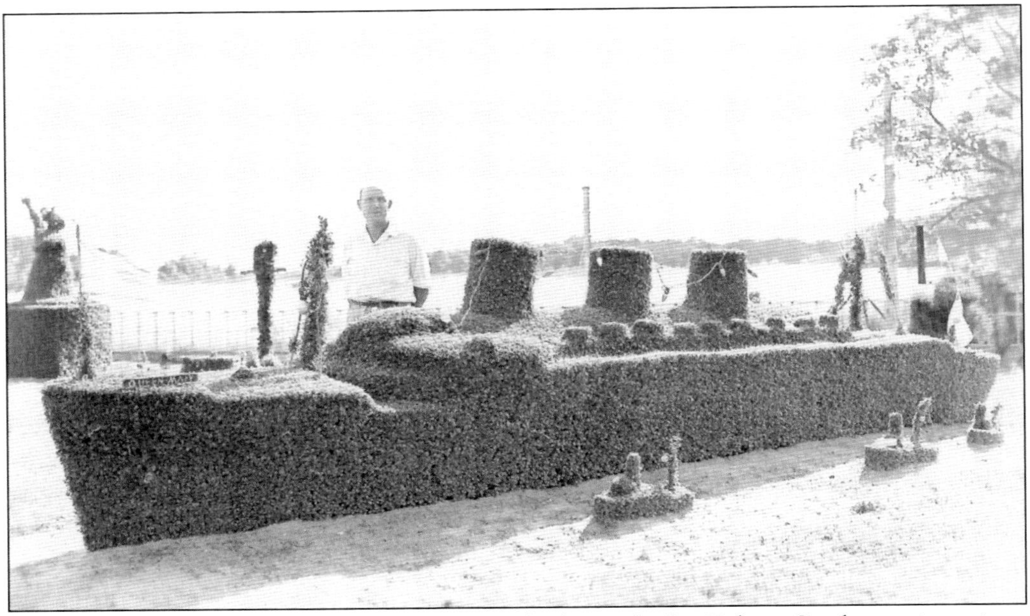

Lower Township resident Gus Yearicks created a "hedge garden" in Fishing Creek, pruning privets into topiary forms of boats, the Statue of Liberty, a miniature village, the Liberty Bell, various animals, and even Santa and his reindeer. The one-acre garden drew thousands of visitors from across the United States. Yearkicks did not charge admission; rather, he placed a box on-site for voluntary donations. (Philippa Campbell.)

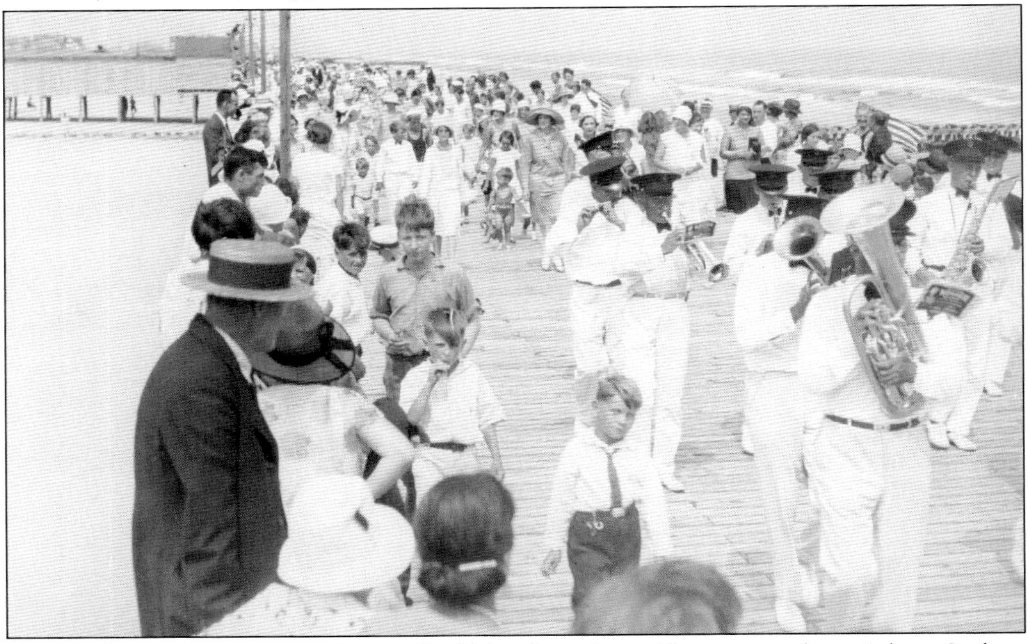

Boardwalk parades were popular in all of New Jersey's seaside resorts—from Asbury Park to Atlantic City to Cape May City. This photograph, probably taken in the 1920s or 1930s, shows a group of unidentified band members playing their instruments as they march down the Stone Harbor boardwalk, possibly celebrating the Fourth of July. (CMCHGS.)

Six

Coastal Protection

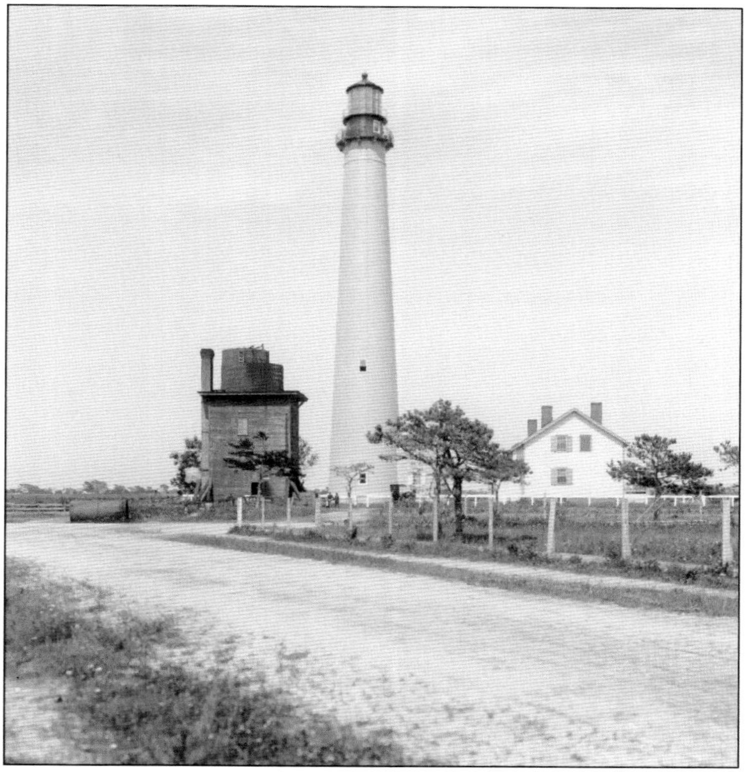

Erected in 1859, the 157-foot-tall Cape May Lighthouse, seen here about 1915, is at least the third navigational aid built at this location. The 1847 lighthouse was dismantled because of the encroaching sea, and its bricks were reused in this building. The first lighthouse marking the entrance to the Delaware Bay from the Atlantic Ocean at Cape May Point was built sometime before 1795. (LOC.)

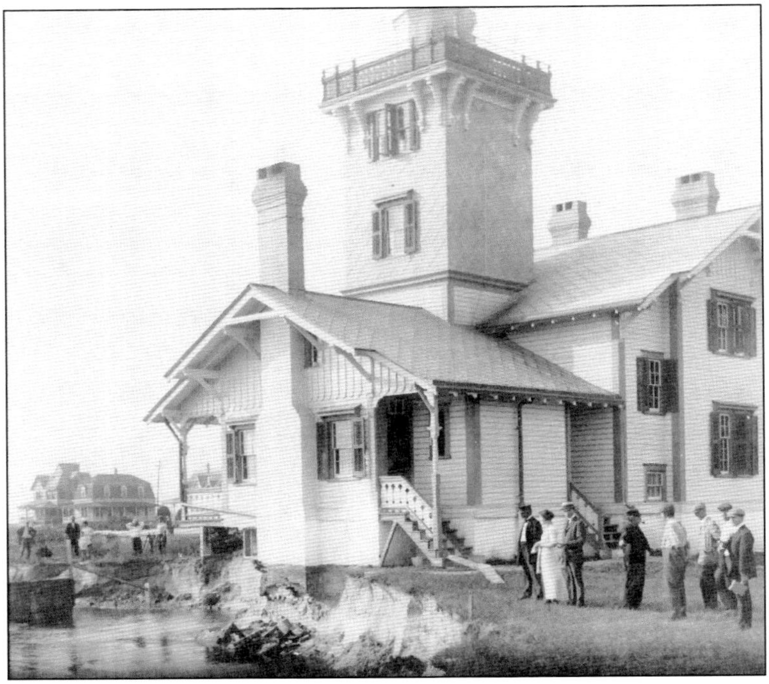

Encroaching water was also a problem for the Anglesea (now North Wildwood) lighthouse, built overlooking the Hereford Inlet in 1872 when the island was still uninhabited. As seen in this photograph, a severe storm in August 1913 significantly damaged the lighthouse's foundation, so the building was moved 150 feet to the west, where it stands today. It has been restored and is open to the public. (CMCHGS.)

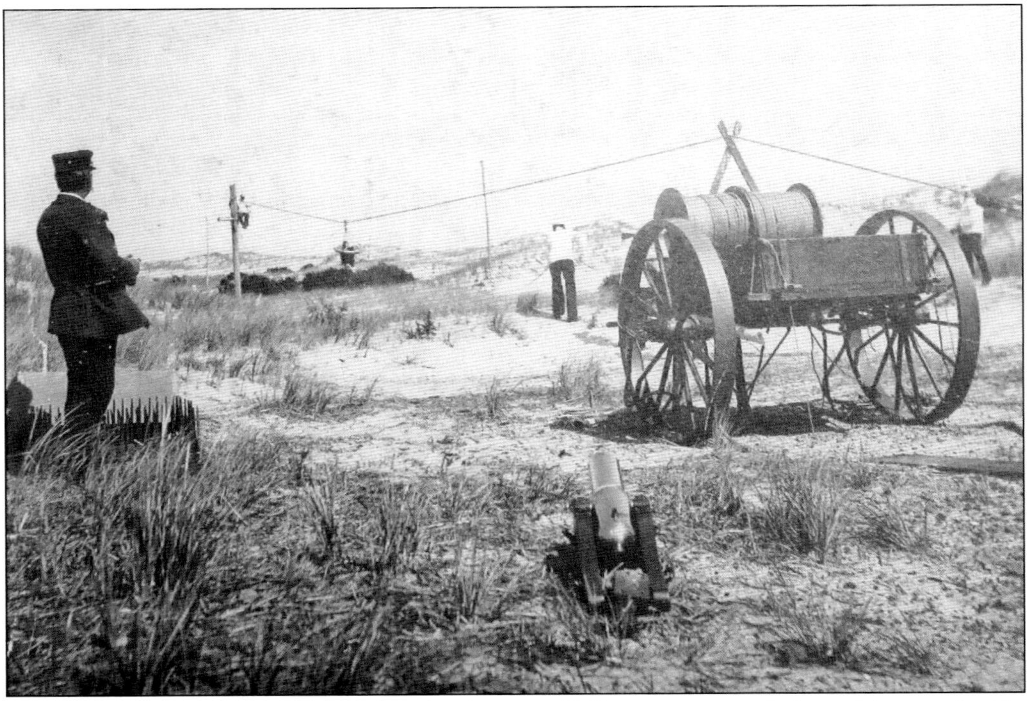

A lifesaving station was established in Anglesea in 1849 to rescue people from ships wrecked in Hereford Inlet. A larger station replaced it in 1871 when the US Life-Saving Service was created. Seen here in 1890, station members practice with a cannon-like Lyle gun that was used to shoot a lifeline to a crippled ship when seas were too rough for rescue by surfboats. (WHS.)

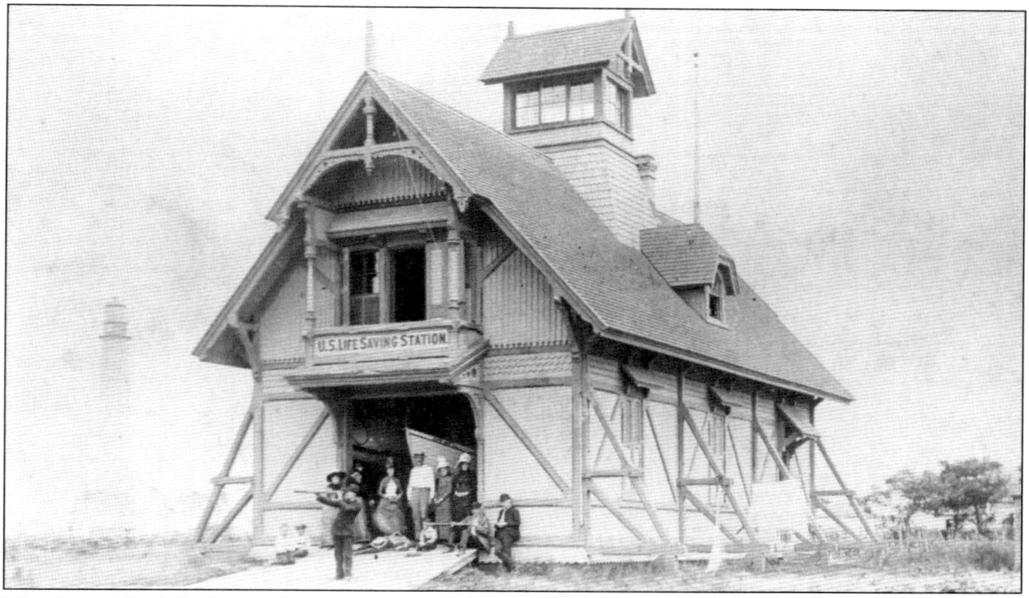

The Cape May Life-Saving Station was erected in 1876 for the Centennial Exhibition in Philadelphia and was then moved to Cape May Point. The station was destroyed by a storm in the 1950s, but the Cape May Maritime Museum and Education Center plans to rebuild it according to the original plans near its original site. (CMCHGS.)

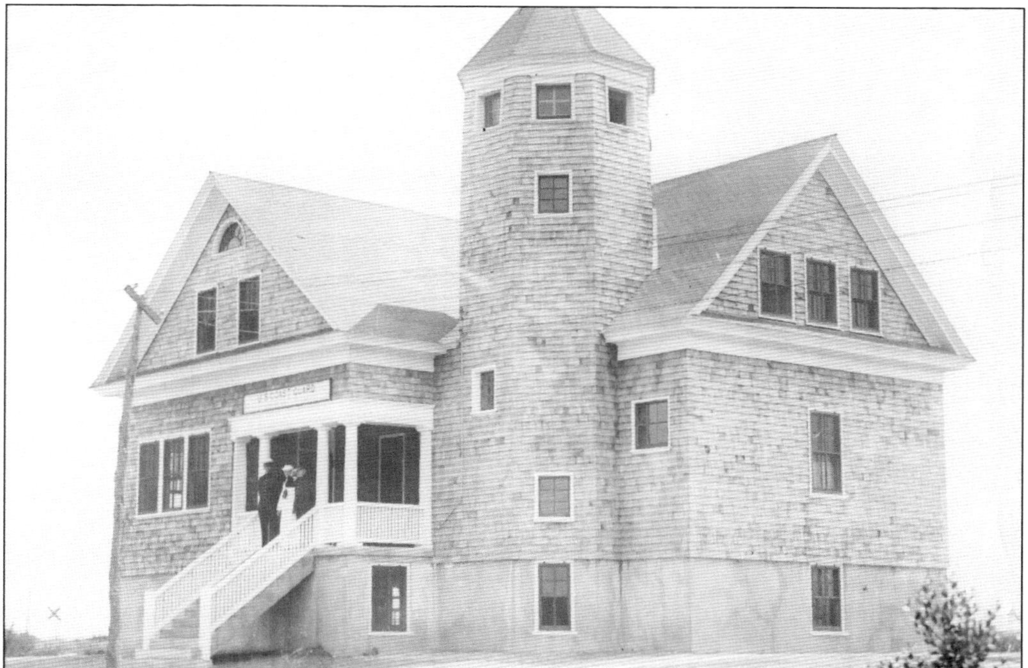

The Corson's Inlet Life-Saving Station once stood on the beach at Fifty-Eighth Street in Ocean City. This c. 1925 photograph shows it after it was enlarged in 1899. After a damaging storm in 1924, the building was dismantled, moved, and rebuilt in Strathmere. It ceased being used as a station in 1964 and is now a private house. (CMCHGS.)

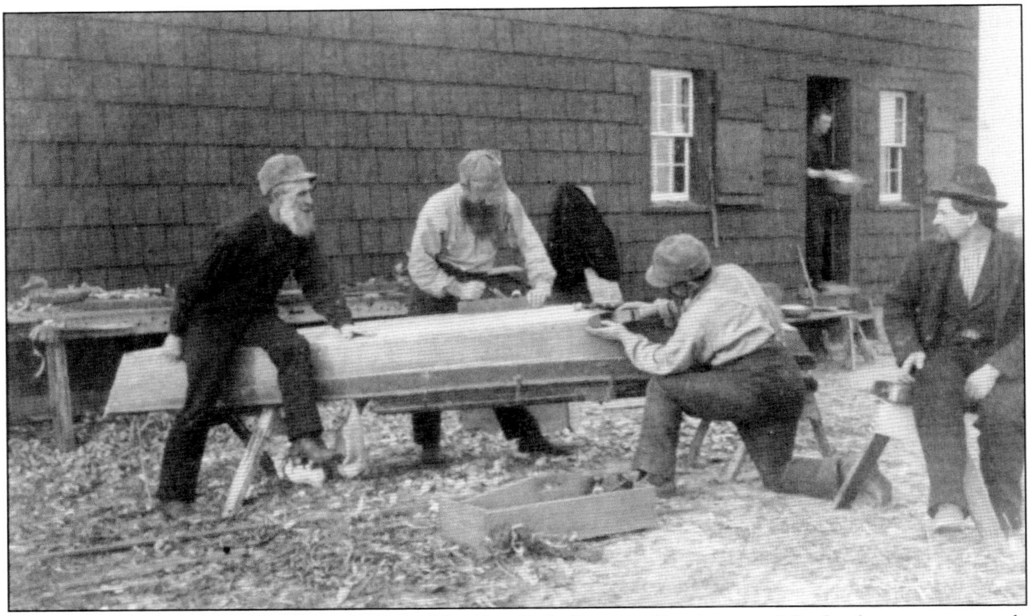

Unidentified crew members at the Sea Isle City Life-Saving Station use block planes to smooth the bow of a wooden boat constructed in their spare time. The station, built around 1885, was manned by a captain and seven surfmen who worked eight months (September to May) and were paid $50 to $90 per month at the time. They worked mostly at night, taking turns patrolling the beach for shipwrecks. (CMCHGS.)

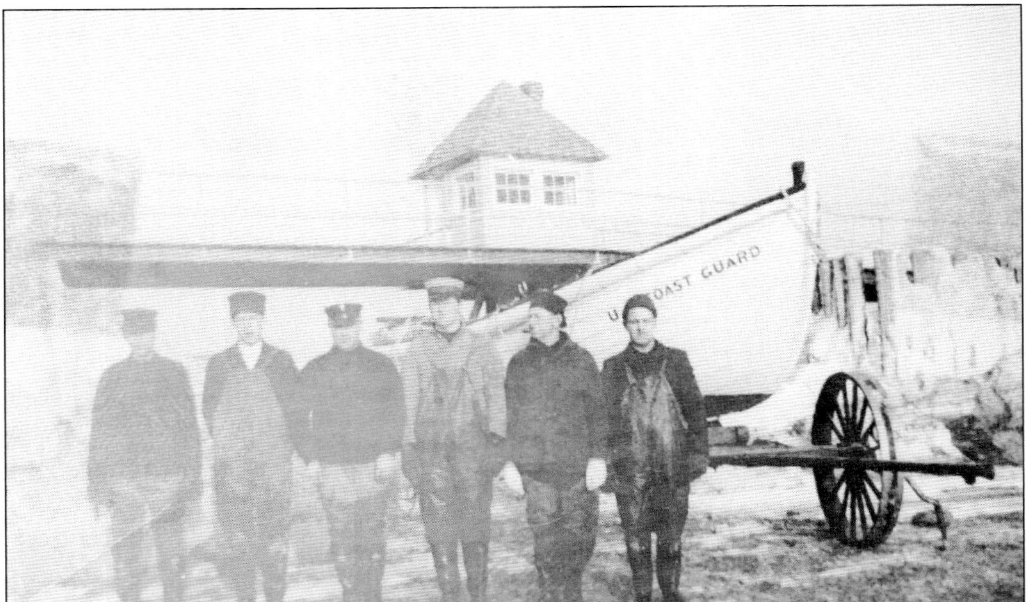

Members of the Sea Isle City Life-Saving Station pose on a cold January day in 1918 in front of a US Coast Guard lifesaving boat. They are, from left to right, Allison Ludlam, Frank Endicott, Richard Sutton, Evans Robinson, Frank Clark, and Albert Adams. This station was located at the north end of the city; it no longer stands. (CMCHGS.)

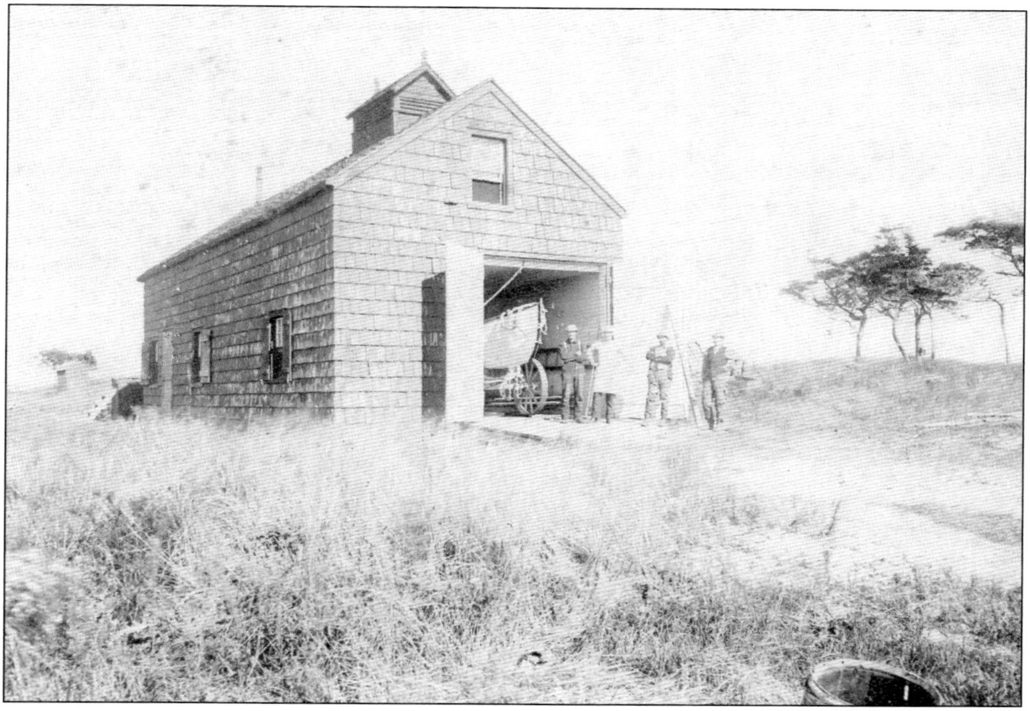

The Stone Harbor Life-Saving Station was built in 1872 and was used until a new, larger station was built in 1895. This c. 1890 photograph shows the 1872 building at its original location near Eightieth Street and First Avenue, the area surrounding it completely devoid of development. The names of the men posing out front are not known. (CMCHGS.)

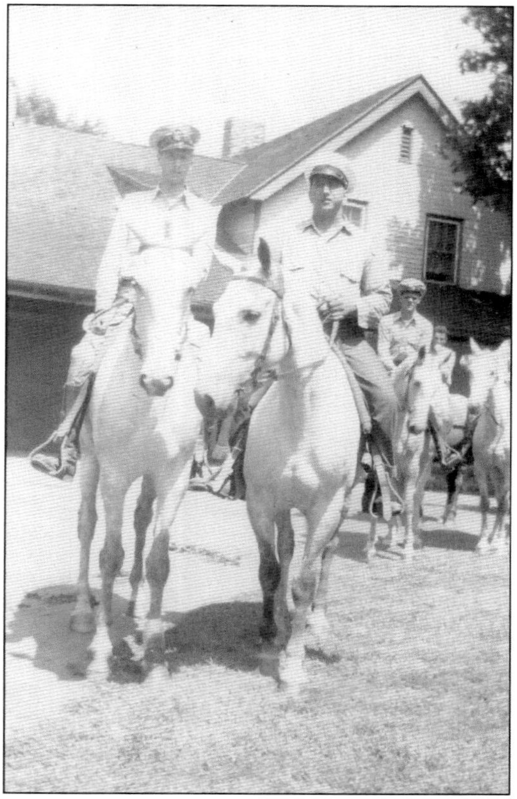

During World War II, the US Coast Guard used mounted patrols to monitor activity along the beaches in southern New Jersey where U-boats had been seen. This photograph, taken in 1942 or 1943 in Avalon, shows a group of Coast Guardsmen led by Chief Sortino (left) and Spencer L. Windle (right). (AHC.)

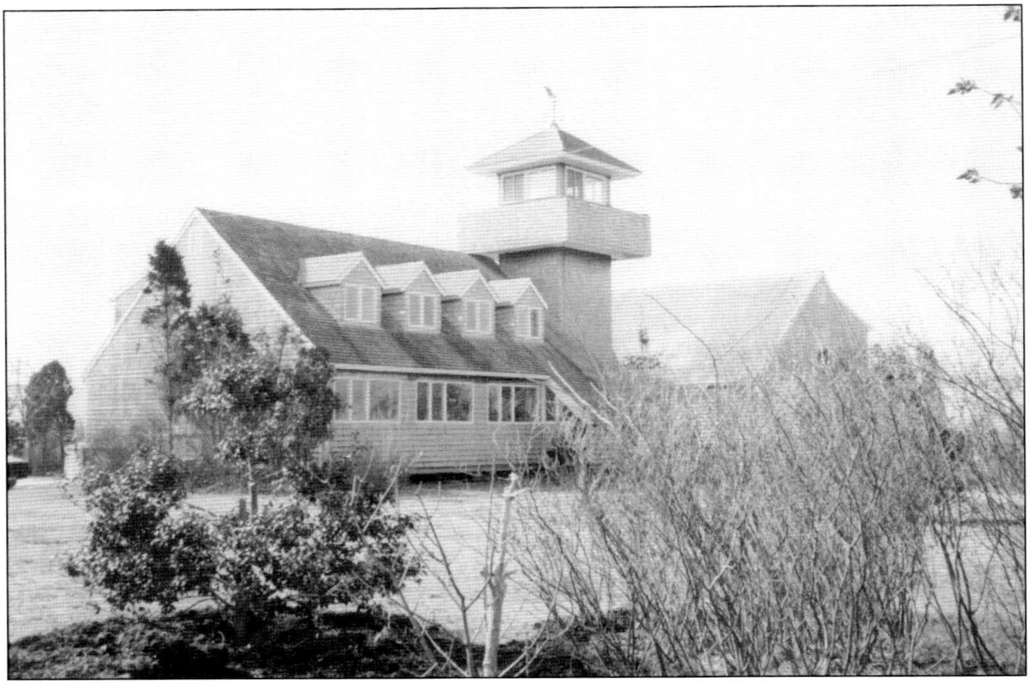

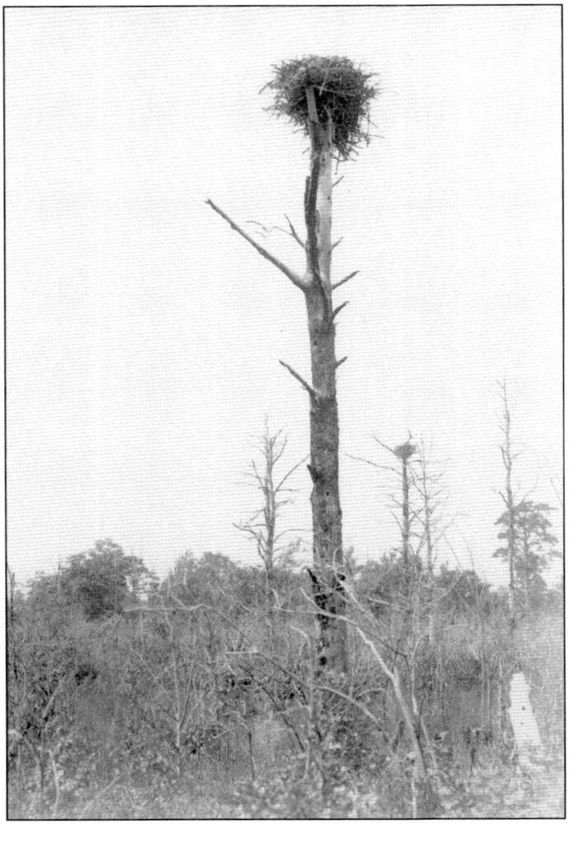

The Wetlands Institute, shown above shortly after it was built in 1972, stands on a 34-acre tract fronting Stone Harbor Boulevard. The institute was founded by Herbert Mills in the late 1960s, fulfilling his vision of creating a world-class research, education, and conservation center at the Jersey Shore. Mills strove to inspire everyone to conserve, sustain, and protect coastal ecosystems and the natural environment. The institute also educates about the importance of nesting and migratory birds for which Cape May County is nationally famous. Ospreys, also known as fish hawks, arrive every spring to nest near the county's marshlands. They have been popular photography subjects since the late 1800s but became a threatened species in the 20th century. Seen at left are two osprey nests pictured around 1900; they were located in a woodland about two miles northwest of North Wildwood not far from the railroad line. The nest in the foreground is about 30 feet off the ground and about 3½ feet in diameter. (Both, CMCHGS.)

Seven

MILITARY SITES

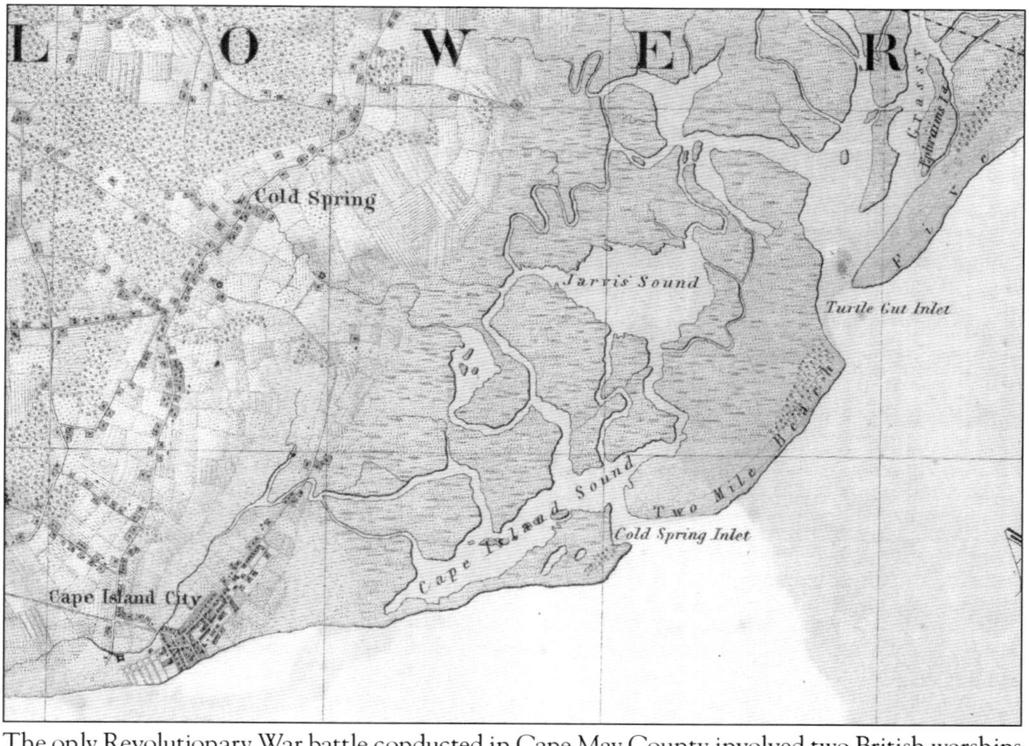

The only Revolutionary War battle conducted in Cape May County involved two British warships chasing the American brig *Nancy*. Loaded with war supplies for the government in Philadelphia, she took refuge in Turtle Gut Inlet, where she was quickly off-loaded before being blown up by the British. The inlet, seen to the right in this 1856 map, was infilled in 1922 and the site is now part of Wildwood Crest. (NASW.)

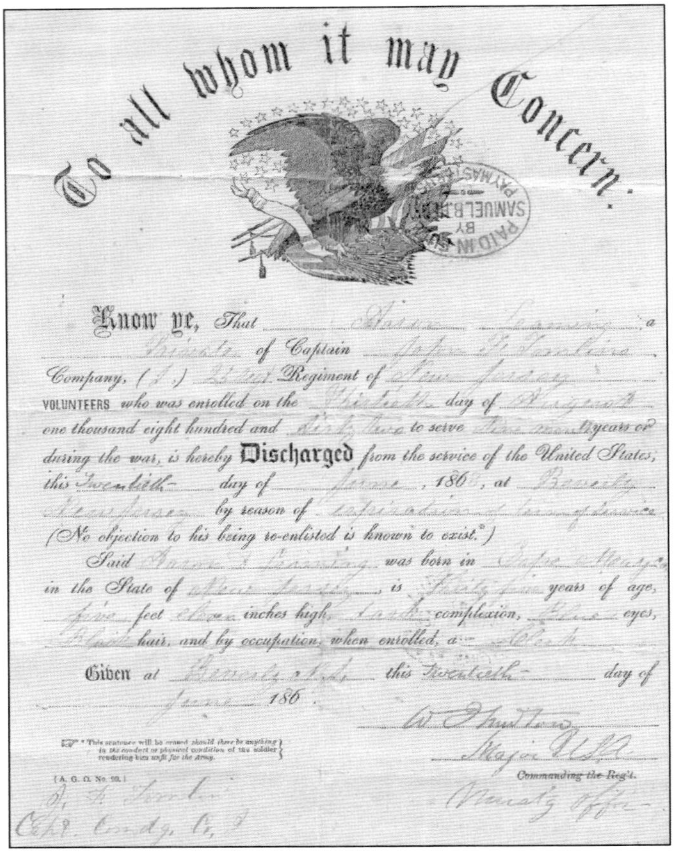

To all whom it may Concern.

PAID IN FULL BY SAMUEL B. [illegible] PAYMASTER

Know ye, That Aaron Leaming a Private of Captain John F. Tomlin's Company, (I) 25th Regiment of New Jersey VOLUNTEERS who was enrolled on the [illegible] day of August one thousand eight hundred and sixty two to serve nine months years or during the war, is hereby **Discharged** from the service of the United States, this twentieth day of June, 1863, at Beverly New Jersey by reason of expiration of term of service (No objection to his being re-enlisted is known to exist.*)

Said Aaron Leaming was born in Cape May in the State of New Jersey, is [illegible] years of age, five feet [illegible] inches high, [illegible] complexion, Blue eyes, [illegible] hair, and by occupation, when enrolled, a Clerk

Given at Beverly N.J. this twentieth day of June 1863.

W. [illegible]
Major U.S.A.
Commanding the Reg't.

* This sentence will be erased should there be anything in the conduct or physical condition of the soldier rendering him unfit for the Army.

[A. G. O. No. 99.]

J. F. Tomlin
Capt. Cmdg. Co. I

Mustering Offr.

No Civil War battle was fought on Cape May County soil, but over 360 Cape May County men joined the Union forces. Of these, 32 died during the war, four of them on the battlefield. This paper documents the honorable discharge of Aaron Leaming, a Middle Township resident who served nine months in 1862–1863. (CMCHGS.)

Civil War reenactors dressed in period uniforms march during Civil War Weekend, held every September at Historic Cold Spring Village in Lower Township. As one of the village's most popular living history presentations, it includes military encampments, demonstrations of infantry and artillery drills, camp life, and weaponry. A special battle reenactment is held both days. (Historic Cold Spring Village.)

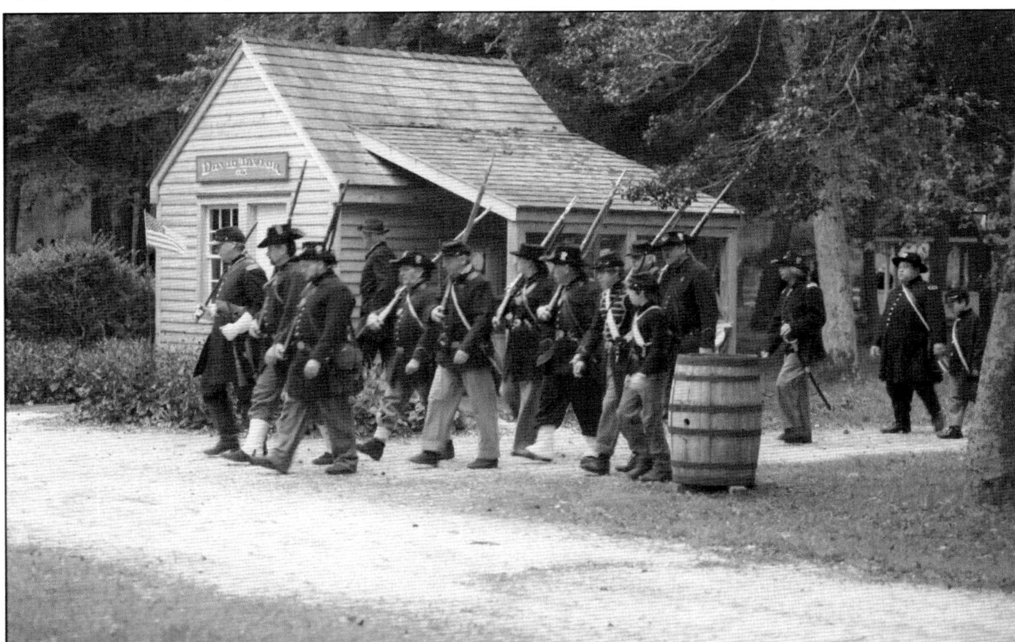

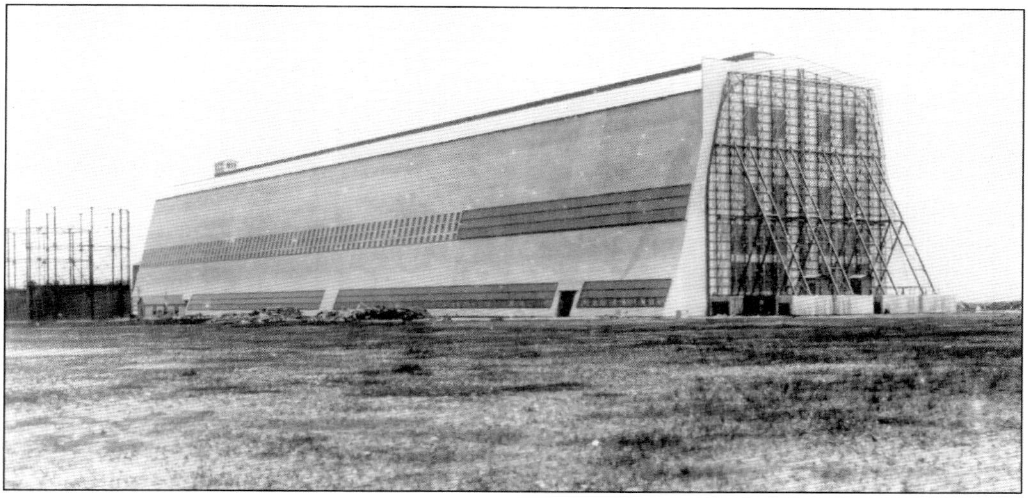

A 708-foot-long dirigible hangar, seen here in 1929, was part of US Navy Section Base Nine established in 1917 on the site of the present US Coast Guard Training Center at Cape May. When built, the hangar was the largest in the world at the time. The hangar was torn down in July 1941. (NASW.)

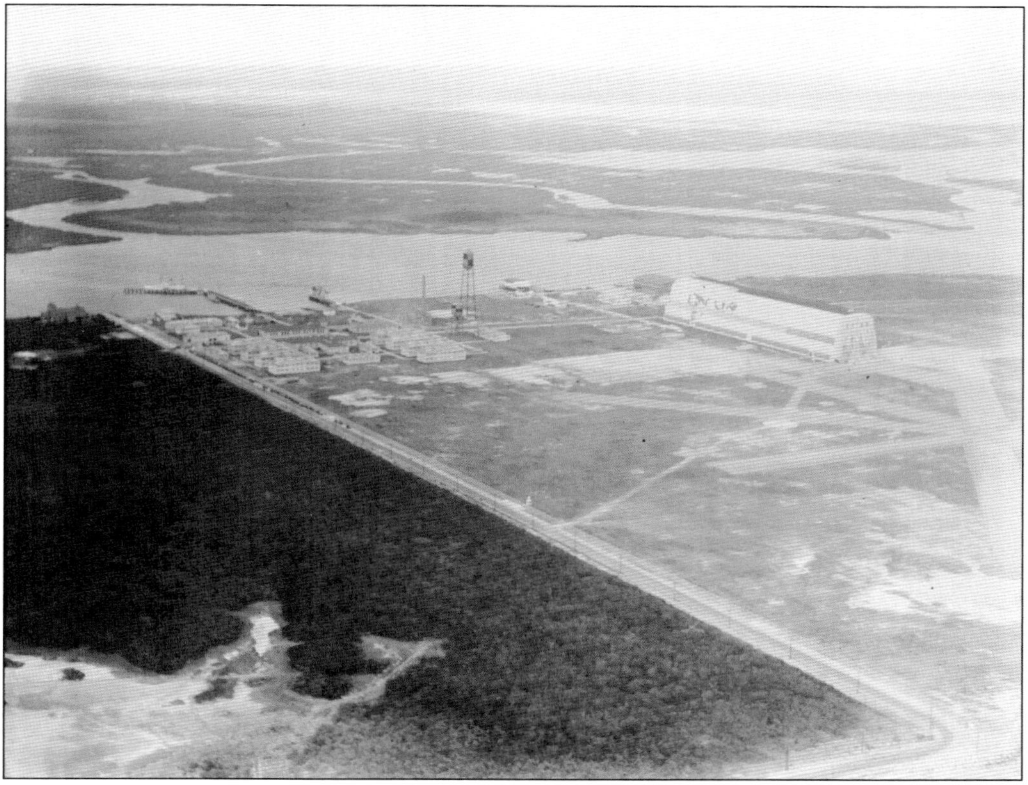

This aerial photograph of US Navy Section Base Nine, taken December 1936, shows the enormity of the dirigible hangar. Behind it are four runways that served the base. Some of the buildings seen to the left of the hangar still stand and are part of the US Coast Guard Training Center. The view looks north over Cape May Harbor. (LOC.)

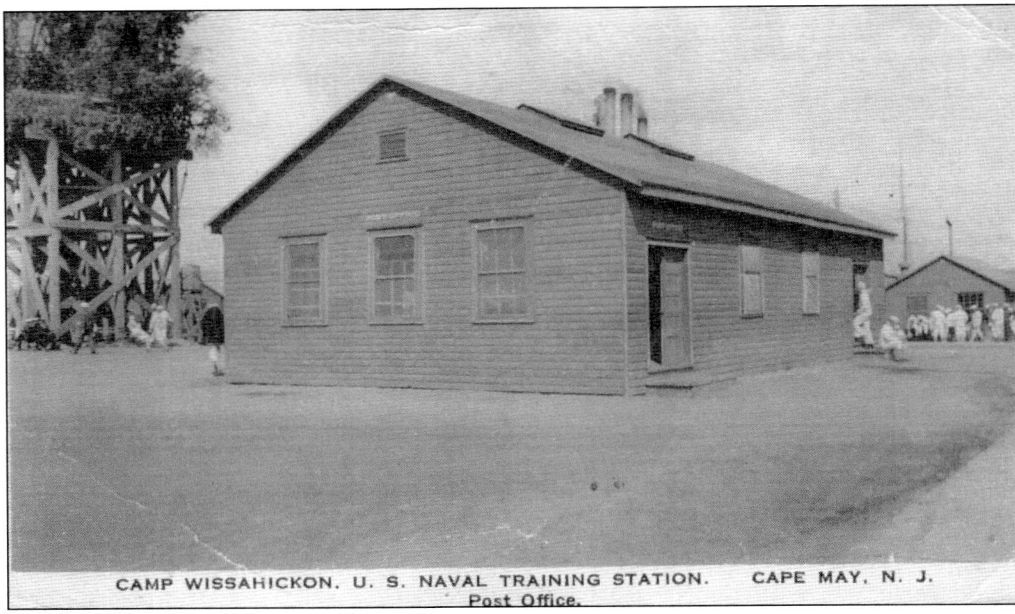

Camp Wissahickon was built in 1917 across from Sewell's Point as a Navy Reserve training center for 3,000 men. The camp, located near the southernmost end of the Garden State Parkway, cost $1.5 million to build, with the City of Cape May furnishing water and sewer lines without charge. The camp was abandoned after World War I and demolished in 1919. (HGM.)

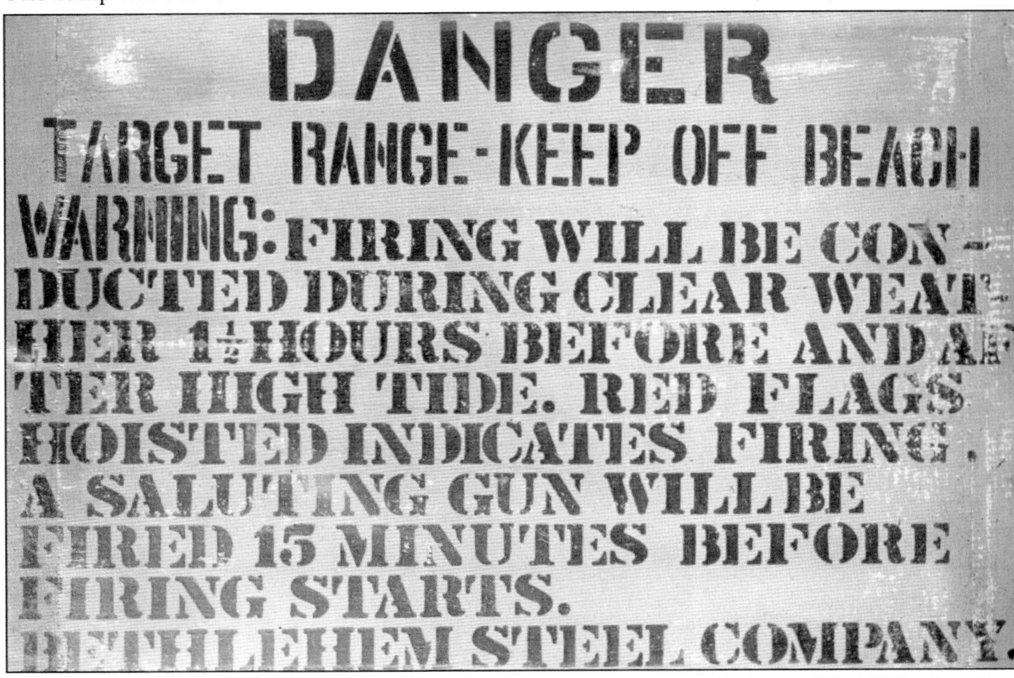

Bethlehem Steel Company established several ordnance testing grounds during World War I in Cape May County. This sign was used to warn visitors from using Higbee's Beach in Lower Township on the Delaware Bay when target practice was being conducted. Artillery shells manufactured at the company's munitions factory in nearby Atlantic County were probably used. (CMCHGS.)

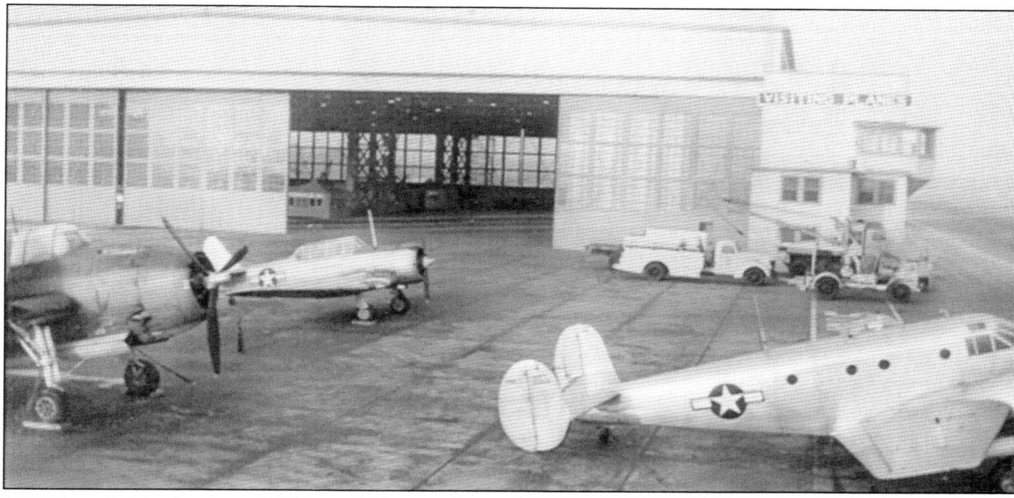

US Naval Air Station Wildwood, located southwest of Rio Grande in Lower Township, was commissioned in 1943 to train fighter-bomber squadrons for World War II. Hangar No. 1, seen here in 1944, was the largest building there. Three training aircraft—a Grumman Avenger, a North American Texan, and a Beechcraft Kansan—are parked out front. The restored hangar now houses Naval Air Station Wildwood Aviation Museum. (NASW.)

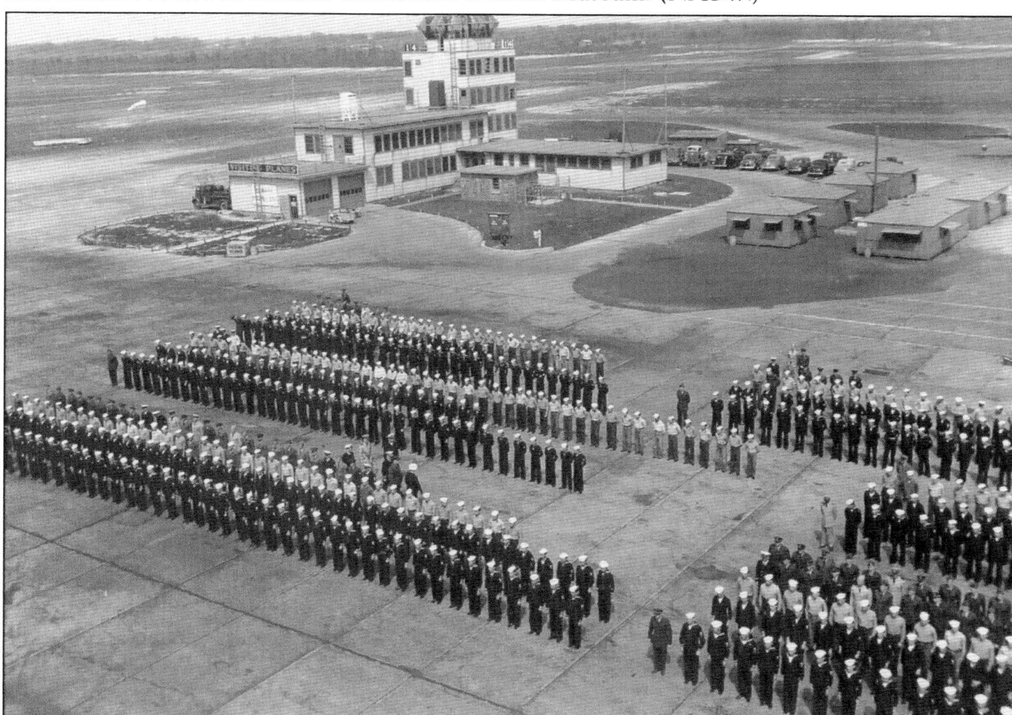

Medal ceremonies and personnel inspections at US Naval Air Station Wildwood were often conducted on the apron between Hangar No. 1 and the operations building. The operations building, seen here in the background, was one of the first buildings to be erected when construction began in 1943. The building still stands, but the all-glass observation room at the top was blown off in a 1962 storm and never replaced. (NASW.)

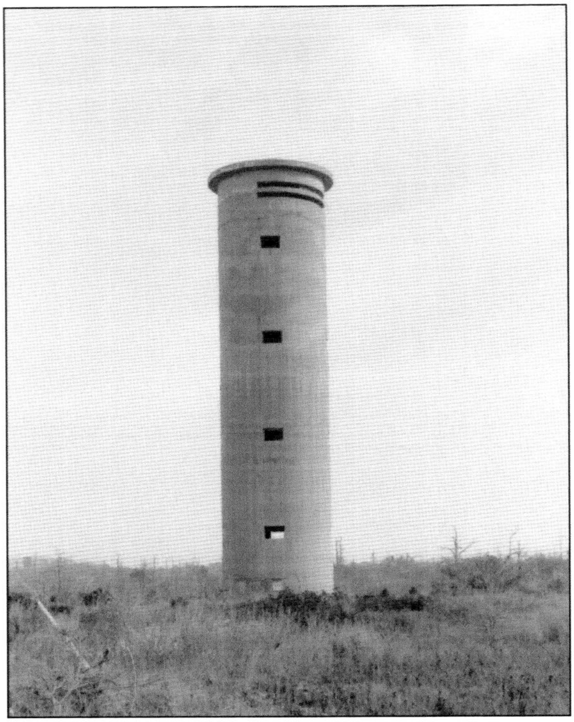

Fire Control Tower No. 23, built in 1942 on Sunset Boulevard in Lower Township, was one of 15 World War II towers that helped aim batteries of coastal artillery to protect the entrance to the Delaware Bay and River. The tower, seen here in 1964, was fully restored by the Mi`d-Atlantic Center for the Arts and Humanities and is open to the public, its upper floor offering spectacular views. (CMCHGS.)

In 1946, the US Coast Guard established a base at the site of the US Navy Section Base Nine; and in 1948, a recruit training center was begun here. In 1982, the Cape May facility became the sole recruit training center in the country. This photograph, taken in March 1951, shows four active piers and the many buildings comprising the center. (NASW.)

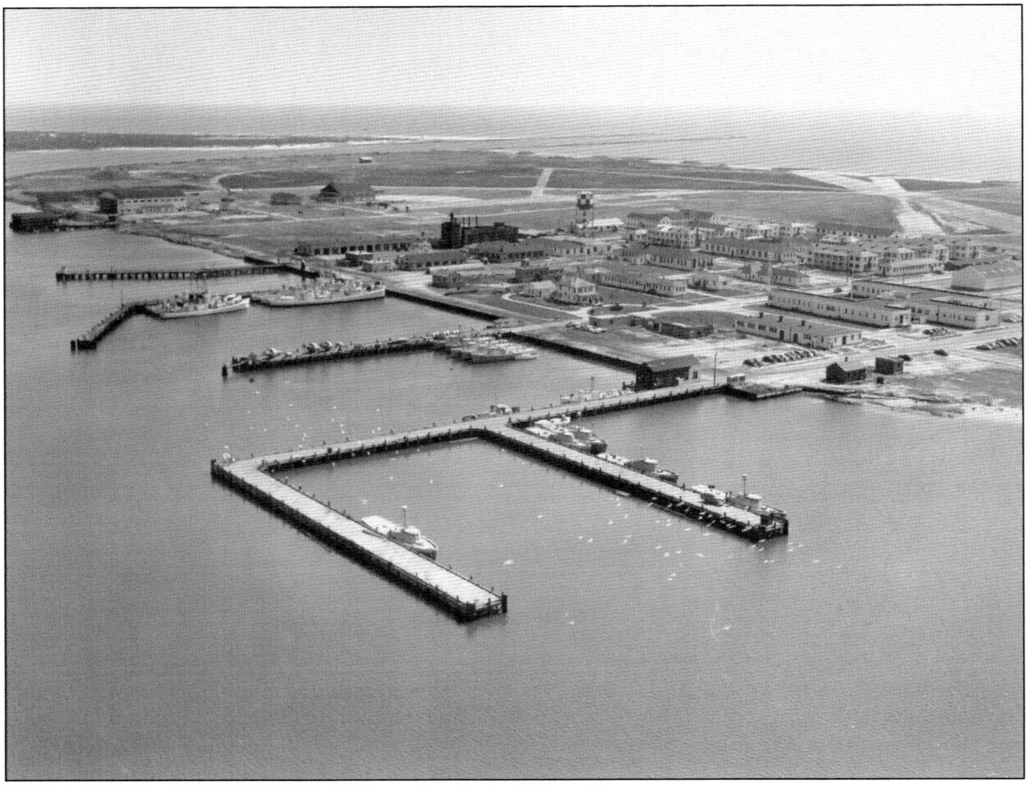

Eight

DISASTERS

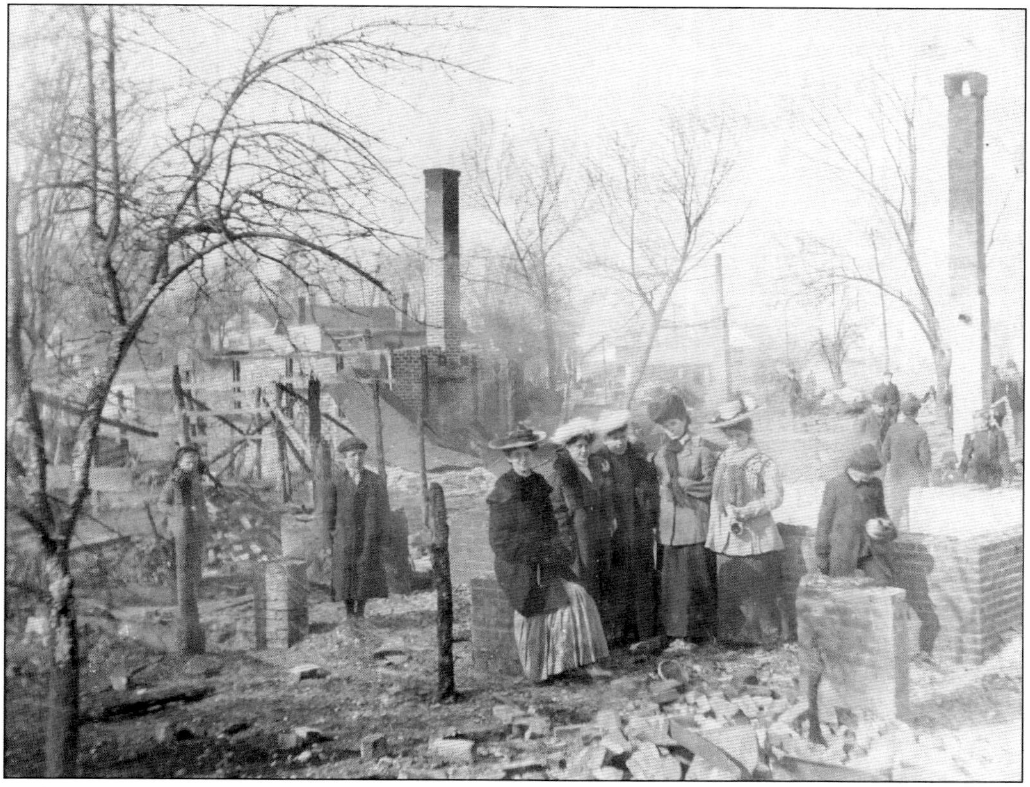

A devastating fire destroyed 23 buildings in the heart of Cape May Court House in February 1905. The fire began in a hardware store where a dozen kegs of gunpowder exploded, spreading the flames to nearby businesses. Among those destroyed were the offices of the *Cape May County Gazette* and the Bellevue Hotel, both of which were rebuilt. (CMCHGS.)

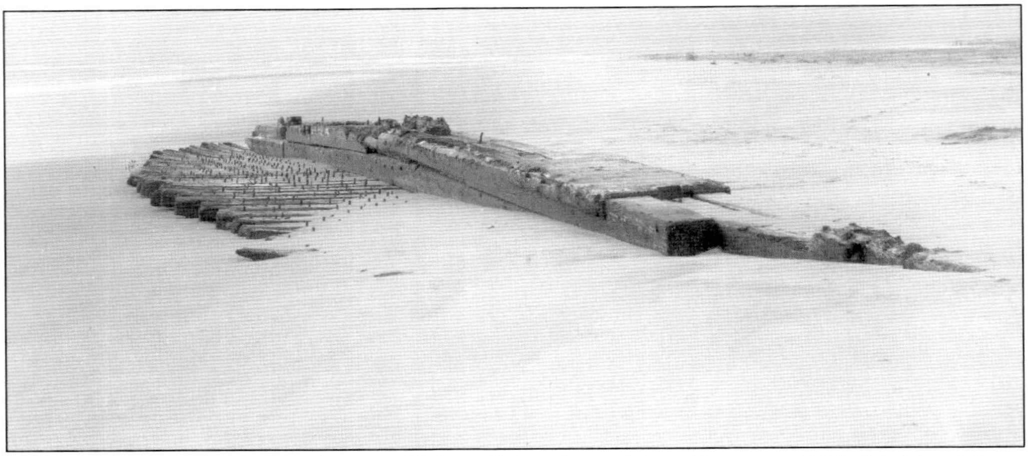

The three-masted, 600-ton schooner *William E. Lee*, bound from Boston to Philadelphia without cargo, came ashore near North Wildwood at Hereford Inlet in October 1891. Her seven crew members were saved, but the ship was a total loss. Only her sand-covered keel and ribs are seen in this October 1903 photograph. She was owned by Richard S. Leaming, proprietor of the Dennis Creek shipyard, where she was built in 1877. (CMCHGS.)

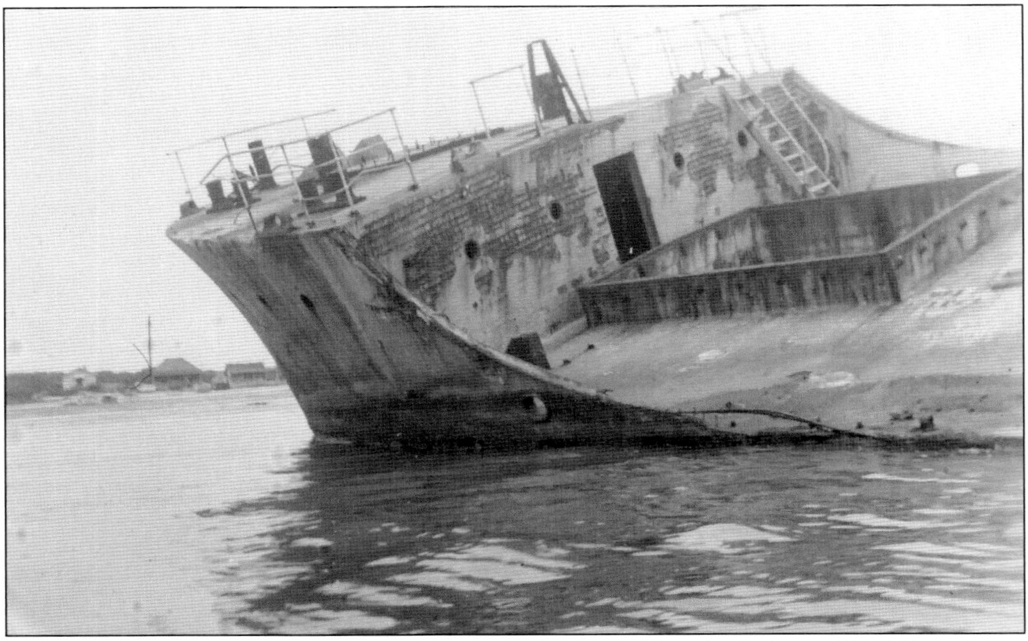

The *Atlantus*, seen here in 1936, was one of several concrete ships built during World War I. She was decommissioned after the war and was later towed to Steamboat Landing, where an investor planned to use her as part of a ferry terminal between Cape May and Lewes, Delaware. She broke her moorings in a 1926 storm and ran aground off Sunset Beach, where she still lies. (CMCHGS.)

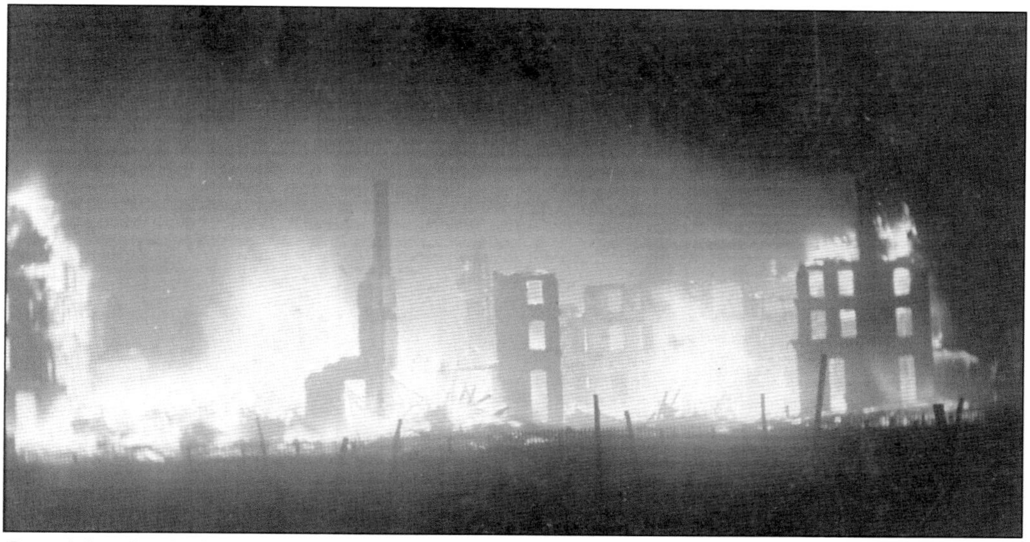

Cape May City's Great Fire of 1878 was set by arsonists in a vacant hotel on Perry Street in November. The city's fire apparatus was woefully inadequate, doing little to stop the flames from spreading. Seven hotels, more than 30 cottages and rooming houses, and about 2,000 bathhouses on 35 acres in the heart of the city burned to the ground. (CMCHGS.)

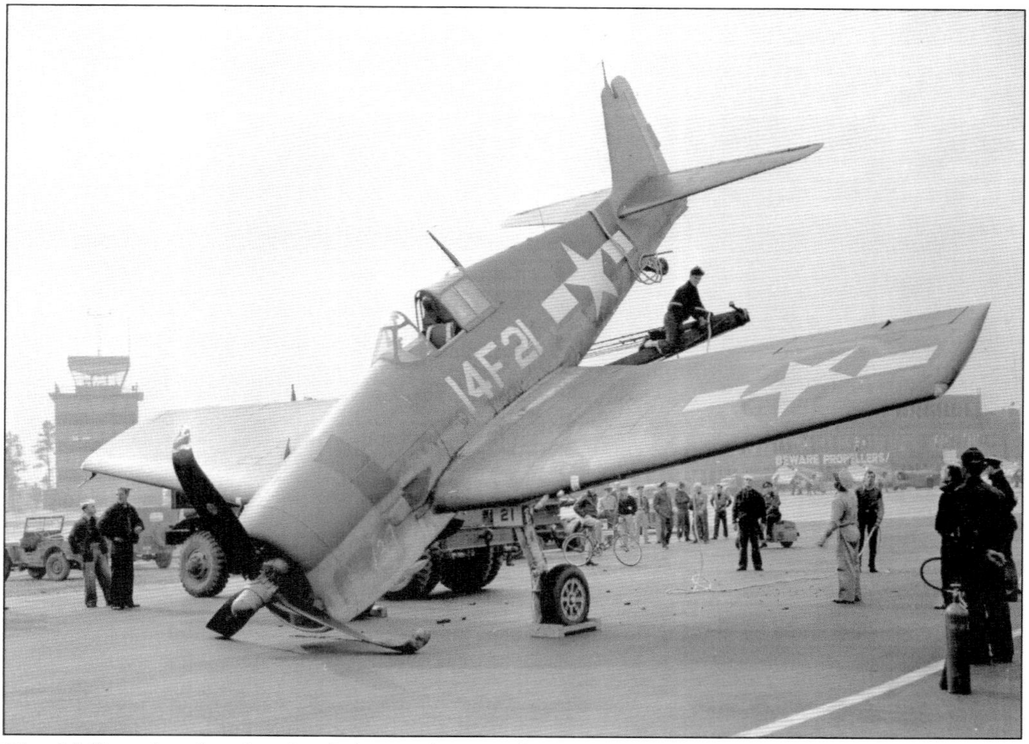

This Hellcat dive-bomber landed nose-first on the runway just north of the control tower and Hangar No. 1 at US Naval Air Station Wildwood during World War II. Aside from bent propellers, the fighter plane appears to be fairly intact. Forty-two US Navy airmen are known to have lost their lives while training at the air station. (NASW.)

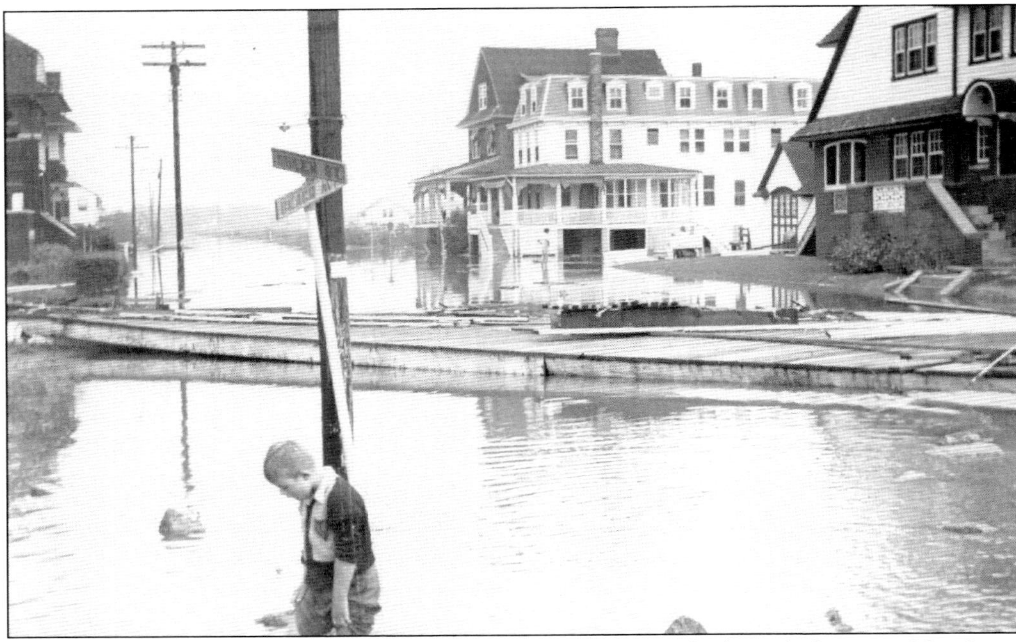

The Great Atlantic Hurricane of 1944 wreaked havoc from Florida through the entire New Jersey coastline. This view, looking west from Beach Avenue in Cape May City down Queen Street, shows pieces of the boardwalk washed into the streets. In fact, the entire two-mile-long boardwalk was destroyed by a 40-foot storm surge. The houses seen here still stand. (HGM.)

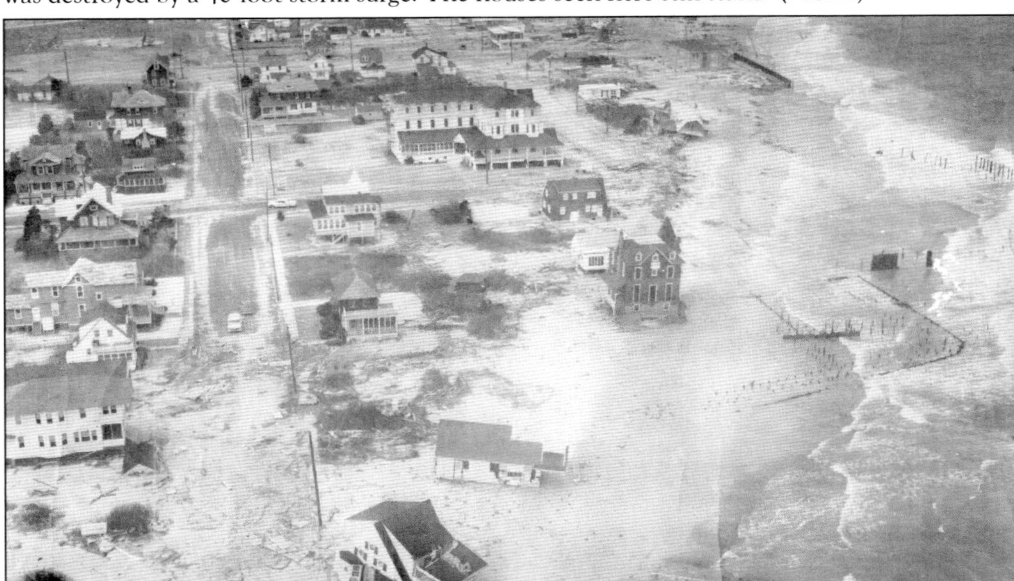

A three-day nor'easter in 1962 caused as much damage as a hurricane. With a view looking south, this aerial photograph of Avalon depicts the north end of the island. The wide street running vertically on the left side is Dune Drive. The first discernible cross street is Seventh Street; the L-shaped building between Seventh and Eighth Streets east of Dune Drive is the recently demolished Avalon Hotel. (AHC.)

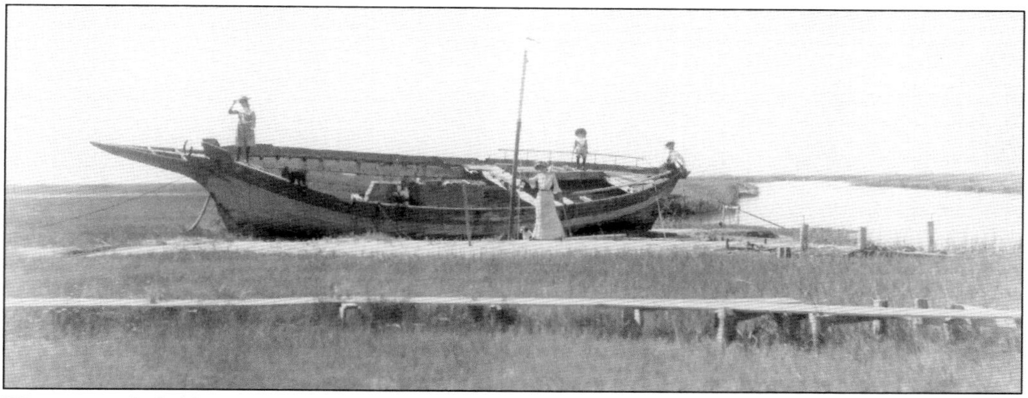

Women and children investigate the wreck of the *Sussex* that ran aground in the early 1900s along Wildwood's inland waterway. Nothing is known of the *Sussex*, but she appears to have been a fishing sloop. Visiting beached or stranded wrecks was a popular pastime at the Jersey Shore in the summer months, with some entrepreneurs charging a fee to board them. (CMCHGS.)

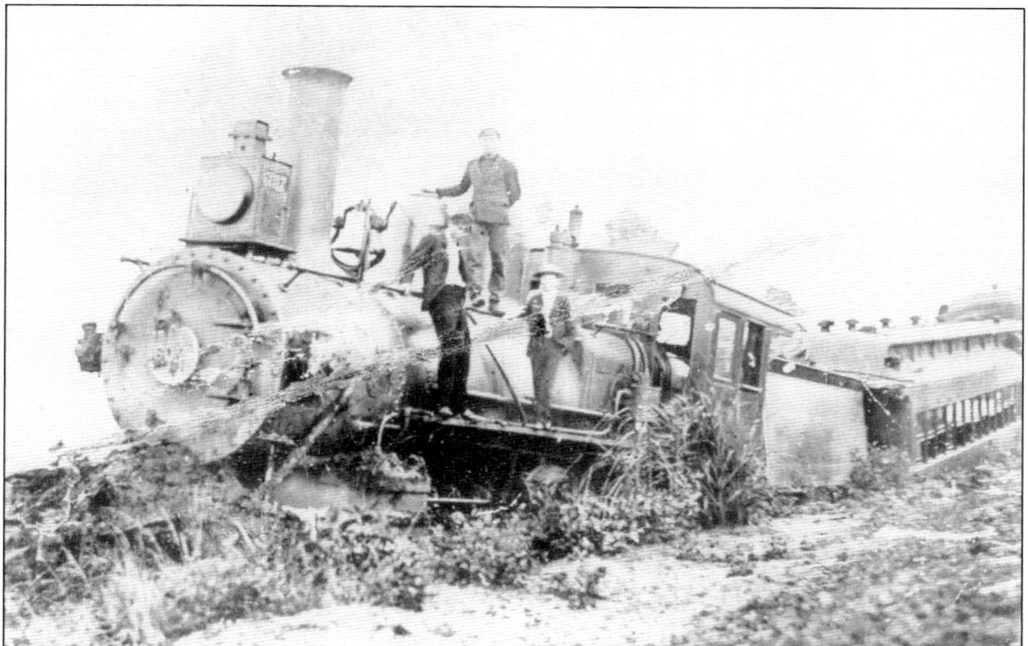

Construction of the railroad serving Anglesea, now North Wildwood, was completed in 1883. Crossing the salt marshes by rail was often problematic because of the unstable base, resulting in several trains like this one sinking into the muck. Old-timers often referred to the train seen here as the "Mud Hen." (HGM.)

INDEX

About the Organization

Naval Air Station (NAS) Wildwood Foundation is a not-for-profit organization whose mission is to restore Hangar No. 1 at the Cape May Airport, Cape May County, New Jersey, and to create an aviation museum honoring the 42 Navy airmen who died while training at the station during World War II.

In June 1997, NAS Wildwood Foundation purchased Hangar No.1 at the Cape May Airport. The 92,000-square-foot, all-wooden structure was in a state of disrepair and required extensive renovation. Under the stewardship of NAS Wildwood Foundation, the hangar was listed in the New Jersey and National Registers of Historic Places and is considered nationally significant for the role it played during World War II.

NAS Wildwood Aviation Museum now boasts over 26 aircraft displays as well as exhibits of military memorabilia, engines, photographs, and more. Additionally, the Franklin Institute of Philadelphia donated a wealth of interactive exhibits that allow visitors to discover the science of flight. The museum features a library, food vending area, and a recently expanded gift shop.

In its role as a community resource, NAS Wildwood Aviation Museum hosts activities including fly-ins, aviation festivals, big band concerts, swing dances, veterans' ceremonies, historical lectures, school field trips, and senior tours.

The museum is open daily during the spring, summer, and fall; call for winter hours. You are invited to become a member of NAS Wildwood Aviation Museum. Your membership supports the mission of the foundation, which is a tax-exempt 501(c)(3) organization.

Membership entitles you to:

- Free admission to NAS Wildwood Aviation Museum
- 10 percent discount in the Gift Shop
- Advance invitations to special events and museum functions
- Reduced admission to special events
- Issues of aviation museum quarterly newsletter the *Osprey*

Please help us give the past a future and become a NASW member. Visit our website, usnasw.org.

Naval Air Station Wildwood Aviation Museum
500 Forrestal Road
Cape May Airport, NJ 08242
(609) 886-8787
(609) 886-1942 (fax)

Discover Thousands of Local History Books Featuring Millions of Vintage Images

Arcadia Publishing, the leading local history publisher in the United States, is committed to making history accessible and meaningful through publishing books that celebrate and preserve the heritage of America's people and places.

Find more books like this at
www.arcadiapublishing.com

Search for your hometown history, your old stomping grounds, and even your favorite sports team.

Consistent with our mission to preserve history on a local level, this book was printed in South Carolina on American-made paper and manufactured entirely in the United States. Products carrying the accredited Forest Stewardship Council (FSC) label are printed on 100 percent FSC-certified paper.

MADE IN THE USA